GENDER, VIOLENCE, AND HUMAN SECURITY

Gender, Violence, and Human Security

Critical Feminist Perspectives

Edited by
Aili Mari Tripp,
Myra Marx Ferree,
and Christina Ewig

NEW YORK UNIVERSITY PRESS
New York and London

NEW YORK UNIVERSITY PRESS
New York and London
www.nyupress.org

References to Internet websites (URLs) were accurate at the time of writing.
Neither the author nor New York University Press is responsible for URLs that
may have expired or changed since the manuscript was prepared.

Library of Congress Cataloging-in-Publication Data

Gender, violence, and human security : critical feminist perspectives / edited by Aili Mari
Tripp, Myra Marx Ferree, Christina Ewig.
pages cm
Includes bibliographical references and index.
ISBN 978-0-8147-7020-7 (hardback) — ISBN 978-0-8147-6034-5 (paper)
1. Women —Violence against. 2. Feminist theory. 3. Human security. I. Tripp, Aili Mari.
II. Ferree, Myra Marx. III. Ewig, Christina.
HV6250.4.W65.G4722 2014
303.601 — dc23

2013019858

New York University Press books are printed on acid-free paper,
and their binding materials are chosen for strength and durability.
We strive to use environmentally responsible suppliers and materials
to the greatest extent possible in publishing our books.

Manufactured in the United States of America

10 9 8 7 6 5 4 3 2 1

Also available as an ebook.

CONTENTS

AI	Amnesty International
AIDS	acquired immunodeficiency syndrome
ANFASEP	Asociacion Nacional de Familiares de Secustrados, Detenidoes y Desaparecidoes del Perú [National Association of Relatives of the Kidnapped, Detained and Disappeared of Peru]
ARK	Anti-War Campaign (Croatia)
CEDAW	UN Convention on the Elimination of All Forms of Discrimination against Women
CHS	UN Commission on Human Security
CoE	Council of Europe
CONAVIP	Coordinadora Nacional de Poblaciones Afectadas por la Violencia Política [National Coordinating Committee of Populations Affected by Political Violence]
CSM	Centre for Peace, Non-violence and Human Rights (Osijek)
CVR	Final Report of the Truth and Reconciliation Commission (Peru)
DRC	Democratic Republic of the Congo
ECHR	European Court of Human Rights (ECHR)
EU	European Union (EU)
FYR	Former Yugoslav Republic
GMS	Greater Mekong Subregion (GMS)
GPE	Global Political Economy (GPE)
HDZ	Croatian Democratic Union
IAC	Inter-American Convention on Human Rights
IACHR	Inter-American Court of Human Rights
ICTJ	International Center for Transitional Justice
IDP	Internally Displaced Persons

IFOR	UN Implementation Force (in Bosnia-Herzegovina)
IIPE	Illicit International Political Economy
INGO	International Non-Governmental Organization
IPE	International Political Economy
IR	International Relations
JNA	Yugoslav National Army
NGO	Non-Governmental Organization
NOW	National Organization of Women
OSCE	Organization for Security and Co-operation in Europe
PCR	Postconflict Reconstruction
PRWORA	Personal Responsibility and Work Opportunity Reconciliation Act
PTSD	Post-Traumatic Stress Disorder
R2P	Responsibility to Protect
RSK	Republic of Serbian Krajina
SFOR	UN Stabilisation Force (in Bosnia-Herzegovina)
SIDA	Swedish International Development Cooperation
SMO	Social Movement Organization
TAN	Transnational advocacy network
TANF	Temporary Assistance for Needy Families
TRC	Truth and Reconciliation Commission (TRC) (Peru)
UN	United Nations
UNDP	United Nations Development Programme
UNHCR	UN High Commissioner for Refugees
UNPROFOR	UN Protection Force
UNTAC	UN Transitional Authority (in Cambodia)
UNTAES	Transitional Administration for Eastern Slavonia, Baranja and Western Sirmium
UPDF	Ugandan People's Defense Force
USA	United States
USAID	United States Agency for International Development
VAWA	Violence against Women Act
WHO	World Health Organization
WPS	Women, Peace and Security network

PART ONE

Retheorizing Human Security through a Gender Lens

1

Toward a Gender Perspective on Human Security

AILI MARI TRIPP

One of the major successes of international feminism in the mid-1990s was to transform the human rights discourse from a gender-neutral frame into one that acknowledged that "women's rights are human rights" (Agosin 2001; Cook 1994; Peters and Wolper 1994). Today, the United Nations and many other international actors and national governments around the globe, including Canada, Norway, Japan, and the United States, have adopted the concept of "human security" in their policymaking. In fact, human security has become the dominant frame for international regulation today. It allows diverse actors from the North and South, governmental and nongovernmental sectors, and conservatives as well as progressives to talk about security in ways that were not possible when the only frame available was that of the nation-state (Christie 2010, 170). Human security shifts the focus away from state security to threats to security that affect people, for example, threats emerging from famine, epidemics, economic decline, environmental degradation, migration, and other such crises. It focuses on human agency in confronting these challenges, rather than simply state agency.

From a feminist perspective, there are many limitations in the ways that the concept has been used and for some, it does not sufficiently differ from traditional state-centered notions of security. But like human rights, the concept has become important enough in international policymaking to call for feminist attention. Moreover, there are significant overlaps with feminist approaches that make it well worth recasting from a gender perspective to make it a more useful concept. Indeed, feminist perspectives have already had an influence in transforming the concept, particularly in the context of key UN resolutions involving women's involvement in peacemaking.

Some human rights activists fear human security will displace the focus on individual rights and human rights. Others are concerned that it makes development and human rights into security concerns, embedding human rights policy, for example, in a security discourse rather than a legal one. Human rights and human security, however, should be seen as complementary approaches that can mutually reinforce one another. Rather than displacing "human rights," human security is able to focus on threats to human life that are not adequately protected by the conventional notions of "human rights" and by narrowly legal solutions (Owen 2004, 382, cited in Howard-Hassman 2010, 27). But it can also enrich the human rights approach by pointing to connections between human rights abuses and other forms of insecurity and by adding a collective approach to security to the individual focus that is at the core of most human rights discourses.

Among many international practitioners and scholars, there has been a discursive shift from a state-centered to a human-centered approach to security, and from a focus on strategic national interests to the collective needs of humankind, although some argue that the changes have not been adequately reflected in institutional frameworks and power relations (Chandler 2008, 465). The shift to a human security perspective, not surprisingly, coincides with the end of the Cold War and the global decline in the amount and intensity of intrastate and interstate conflict that took place globally after 1990 (Goldstein 2011; Gurr 2000; Human Security Report 2005). These changes have forced practitioners and theorists alike to focus on the wide variety of insecurities that have persisted despite these changes in the nature of conflict, as well as new forms of human insecurity that have emerged.

In this book, we critically explore the relationship between human security and gender, with particular attention to violence at all levels of social organization. We are interested both in expanding the notion of human security to make clear how it can and should be attentive to gender relations as well as in using the human security framework to better understand how violence is related to people's daily lives and livelihoods in gendered ways. While some argue that human security has become a new orthodoxy (Christie 2010) and a guise for the continuation of traditional state-oriented foreign policy, we see it as an opening of discursive space that has already allowed for new policy interventions by feminists and has additional potential to be tapped.

We explore how a human security perspective helps us understand how gender and violence are related, but also how violence itself is both gendered and creates gender. This approach brings a stronger concern with gender justice to the human security perspective itself. While there are countless themes that touch on the relationship between human security and gender, we focus on violence as an entry point into understanding human security in contexts of civil conflict, economic vulnerability, trafficking, domestic violence, social marginalization, and other gendered phenomena. By examining the structure of gender relations and the construction of gender in violence, we show how insecurities may foment violence in gendered ways, and how an understanding of gender dynamics can and should be brought into defining solutions.

The volume takes a critical look at gender, violence, and human security from several angles: theoretical perspectives that engage the debates regarding human security and empirical examinations through case studies.

This introductory chapter examines the utility of the concept of human security from a feminist perspective by first outlining the history of the concept. It describes some of the feminist engagements with "security studies" and identifies some synergies between feminist approaches and human security approaches. The rest of the chapter looks critically at the continuing limitations of the human security approach and how a feminist perspective might enrich the concept. The chapter concludes with a brief overview of the book chapters.

This chapter argues for an approach to human security that is concerned with linkages between various forms of insecurity and gender-based violence and among the various levels of violence, from interstate wars and civil conflicts to interpersonal violence at a local level. Rather than treating the state as gender neutral, as the human security approach generally does, the state itself is seen as gendered. So too are the economic, political, and social relations that give rise to violence. Violence is perpetrated both against individuals and against women or men as a group. Agency similarly has both individual and collective dimensions. This perspective shifts the focus of the term human security from its defensive emphasis to a more proactive notion of peace that requires addressing the structural issues that give rise to violence. It critiques the ways in which global inequalities are often overlooked by human security theorists, as well as some of the disembodied notions of human security that overlook power relations. Finally, it takes up the idea of intersectionality to show how the "human" is only present in specific intersecting forms that reflect gender, race, ethnicity, religion, age, sexual orientation, and other structural positions.

Evolution of the Concept of Human Security

The concept of human security emerged from discussions among communities of policy makers, academics, and NGO activists in the mid-1990s (Truong, Wieringa, and Chhacchi 2006, x). Human security was first defined by the United Nations Development Programme (UNDP) in 1994 as encompassing generalized threats such as those derived from economic, food, health, or environmental insecurity, and threats to personal, community, and political security, or human rights violations (UNDP 1994). The focus from the start was on forms of insecurity that are not encompassed in frameworks of either human development or human rights nor in the traditional state security framework. The objective of human security is to "safeguard the vital core of all human lives from critical pervasive threats, in a way that is consistent with long-term human fulfillment" (Alkire 2003).

Security was no longer tied to orthodox neorealist notions of security nor to an external military threat to the state. Unlike the traditional realist focus on national self-interest, military and economic power, and the survival of the state, human security recognizes insecurity emerging from interstate and intrastate conflict, postconflict contexts, as well as insecurity related to phenomena like migration, poverty, health epidemics, and environmental disasters.

Some, like the Canadian government, have focused on the "freedom of fear" aspect of human security and the need to protect citizens from violent conflict, recognizing that violence is tied to poverty, inequality, and lack of state capacity. Others, like the Japanese government, have focused on a broader "freedom from want" approach that includes hunger, disease, and natural disasters, because more people are killed from these insecurities than from conflict or genocide. The Japanese include protection against poverty and provision of basic education, health care, and social protection in their definition of human security. A third approach to human security sees it as an umbrella concept for all nontraditional security issues, for example, HIV/AIDS, terrorism, small arms, land mines, and human trafficking (Newman 2010).

The focus of human security was to be on the impact of insecurities on *people*, not just their consequences for the state. Influential peace researcher Ramesh Thakur defined human security as "concerned with the protection of people from critical and life-threatening dangers, regardless of whether the threats are rooted in anthropogenic activities or natural events, whether they lie within or outside states, and whether they are direct or structural. It is 'human centred' in that its principal focus is on people both as individuals and as communal groups. It is 'security oriented' in that the focus is on freedom from fear, danger and threat" (Thakur 2004).

The concept of human security redefined security from state security to the security of ordinary citizens. Traditional security studies had citizens supporting the sovereignty of the state. The human security approach flipped this around so that the state and state sovereignty were to serve their citizens (Newman 2010, 79). Moreover, with the human security approach, states became responsible not only for their citizens, but also for people outside their own state. States thus had responsibilities to protect people when their own states could not provide that protection. This later morphed into the Responsibility to Protect (R2P) policy, approved by the UN General Assembly in 2005, which stipulates that the international community can militarily intervene when states fail to protect their citizens from massive loss of life. R2P encompassed key human security principles, including a focus on the protection of the individual citizen rather than state security; the focus on the political, economic, and social causes of humanitarian crisis; and prevention of crisis. The state still features prominently in many human security approaches because, it is argued, the state is the most important protector of people's human security (Christie 2010, 173). The centrality of the state in the practice of implementing human security objectives has led some to worry that human security will be used to justify greater state intervention by using protection as a pretext (Shani 2007, 7).

Human security is distinct from the idea of *human development*, which focuses on long-term human capabilities (Nussbaum and Sen 1993; Nussbaum 2000), and that of *human rights*, which focuses more on legal frameworks for individual rights and security. Women's human rights are codified in the 1979 United Nations Convention on the Elimination of All forms of Discrimination against Women (CEDAW), which requires states to take steps to end discrimination against women and ensure that women can enjoy human rights. This chapter takes the position that all three concepts—human security, human development, and human rights—are necessary. The human security framework, in fact, highlights the links between development and security and the ways in which lack of human security, conflict, inequality, and lack of choice negatively impact development. It also highlights the links between human rights and insecurity. People may have the legal rights and protections from discrimination and violence, but in reality structural constraints, including lack of income, education, and access to the legal system, as well as cultural constraints, may prevent them from exercising those rights. It also has the potential to address some of the concerns of feminist critics of the human rights approach, particularly anthropologists, who have challenged the ways in which universal assumptions about women's rights might be tempered by local understandings and definitions of justice and rights. (See the work of Dorothy Hodgson, Sally Merry, Lila Abu-Lughod, Pamela Scully, and many others.) By focusing on agency, the concept can help bridge the need to protect women's rights with local priorities and conceptions of gender justice.

The concept of human security has arisen at a time when the nature of insecurity is changing globally: interstate conflict and even intrastate conflict are diminishing. Yet threats to individuals and communities persist. Economic, food, health, and environmental crises produce human insecurities that can be regarded as forms of violence. Moreover, interpersonal violence, large-scale violence, and structural violence can mutually reinforce each another. Violence as an issue is universal: Whether states are economically developed or struggling to meet basic human needs, they face issues of violence internally, at their borders, and in their international engagements. Violence is also particular: individuals, communities, and nations experience it in gender-specific ways that intersect with class, race, age, sexuality, and nationality.

Human security is, in principle, an attractive normative frame for feminists because it looks at the impact of insecurities on people, not just the consequences of conflict for the state. It focuses on societal activities, not just on state action. It highlights the agency of those affected by insecurity, and focuses on positive action to expand human capabilities, not just defenses of rights.

Feminist Security Studies

Feminist security studies—which range in perspective from critical feminism, to feminist constructivism, liberal feminism, poststructuralism, and postcolonial feminism—have succeeded in problematizing the notion of security for over two decades (Sjoberg and Via 2010, 4). The early work by feminist international relations scholars questioned the conventional realist understandings of conflict and the frames that defined the study of war and militarism (e.g., Ann Tickner, Cynthia Enloe, V. Spike Peterson, Anne Sisson Runyan, Christine Sylvester). The critique was deepened with a new generation of international relations feminist scholars (e.g., Laura Sjoberg, Laura Shepherd, Sandra Via, Elisabeth Prügl, Charli Carpenter, Helen Kinsella). The questions of feminist security scholars parallel the questions asked by human security advocates in asking *whose security* policy makers are seeking: that of the state, of people, or of women, in particular. Feminist scholars have challenged the lack of women in international security policymaking, documenting the masculine nature of the state and security agencies nationally and globally. Like human security theorists, feminists have broadened our understanding of security to include not just war, but also interpersonal violence, rape, poverty, and environmental destruction. They have questioned how safe women are as a result of state protection.

But feminist security scholars have gone well beyond the human security framework to critique the gendered nature of concepts of state violence, war, peace, peacekeeping, militarization, and soldiering. They have interrogated the essentialist link that is so often drawn between women and peace, without fully appreciating women's roles in promoting and participating in war (Blanchard 2003). They have examined the relationship between masculinity and war, not just assumptions about men as fighters, but also men as civilians who are targeted because of gender stereotypes. These scholars have critiqued the way "gender" and "women" are used interchangeably in international security discourse, most prominently within UN documents. They have described the state as patriarchal and shown how the increase of women in military institutions does not necessarily change the patriarchal nature of the institutions and the extension of militarism into civilian life (Enloe 2000). The scholars have examined the ways in which gender defines and is defined by international actors, for example, when the military often relies on the unpaid labor of women to care for wounded soldiers. They have challenged the instrumental use of women as a rationale to go to war and examined how state foreign policies are influenced by masculinity, heterosexism, and the gendered nature of militarism (Peterson and Runyan 1999). They have also disagreed over the extent to which the incorporation of women into the military changes the nature of the military establishment and many other issues.

Bringing a feminist perspective to security studies challenges the focus on military solutions and shifts attention to addressing structural problems before they become violent crises. Greater significance would be given to prevention rather than intervention, and to civilian solutions rather than military ones. At the same time, women need to be part of the equation when conflicts break out. They need to be integrated into all peacemaking efforts at all levels and at all points in time: in addressing long-term structural inequalities, in being part of early warning initiatives, within conflict management, conflict resolution, peacekeeping, and in postconflict disarmament contexts. Women's involvement is critical to pursuing a broad range of peacemaking strategies that go beyond narrow military responses.

Bringing Feminist Perspectives to Human Security

Many feminist security scholars have critiqued the new concept of human security and its applications—and rightly so—for adopting too much of a traditional focus on state security and using the same logic of national security as more conventional notions of scurity have employed (Berman 2007). Some feminists have dismissed the concept outright because they fear that its applications, particularly the Responsibility to Protect norm (R2P), will differ little from traditional state-based strategies. Applications of a human security framework so far have all too often looked like conventional interventions (Muggah and Krause 2006; Wibben 2011, 84).

While recognizing that the idea of human security can be coopted by states and multinational organizations to serve more traditional security interests, Giles and Hyndman (2004, 308) find that "human security also offers a potentially radical new site of accountability to more feminist security studies." It has already provided an important conceptual space for activists to push states to adopt more feminist orientations in policymaking. For example, feminists in the Women, Peace and Security[1] network (WPS) have been successful in using the human security framework to make gender mainstreaming relevant in the area of international security (Hudson 2010). Their work influenced the writing of key UN Security Council resolutions (1325 and 1820) that insist on women's incorporation in all aspects of peacemaking and peace building.

Natalie Hudson (2010) sees the human security frame as having been informed by gender mainstreaming in human development and human rights frames. Earlier gains had been made in mainstreaming gender and women into development through a Gender and Development framework (especially after the 1995 UN Beijing Conference on Women) and into human rights discourse after the Vienna Conference on Human Rights (1993). These ideas influenced the work of WPS activists around UN Security Resolution 1325 and other resolutions pertaining to women and peace negotiations, peacemaking, and peacebuilding. The WPS network used the human security framework to create a space to prioritize women's rights and adopt a gender-sensitive perspective. Hudson argues that while useful, the human rights frame was insufficient in creating a commitment to showing how the security needs of women are a key component of advancing peace and security globally (Hudson 2010, 9). Indeed, it was the contribution of feminist theory to a notion of human security that allowed UNIFEM/ UN Women, working in postconflict situations, to bring gender into discussions of policing and many other arenas. It has also helped bring together those in the UN working in humanitarian affairs, development, and security who previously had not collaborated on gender-related issues (Hudson 2010, 146).

However, others have been more critical of the approach. Women's rights activists became especially critical of the concept of human security when the Commission on Human Security intentionally left out women as a special concern, instead claiming the concept encompassed all inequalities, in its report *Human Security Now* (2003). As cochair of the Commission, Sadako Ogata explained: "In its deliberations, the Commission examined how gender-based inequality and gender-based violence affect the security of people within the household, community, and society, in general. Taking the view that gender-based inequality and violence cut across all matters related to human security, the Commission decided not to isolate women as a special area of concern or as a category of victims of conflict or as 'instruments of development.'"

Human Security Now failed to articulate what human security means for women and what constitutes gender-based violence. Where women were mentioned in the report, they were lumped together with children in an infantilizing way as people in need of special protection in times of conflict, famine, and economic crisis. This type of reference to "special protection" has historically disempowered women, Chenoy (2009) argues, and underscores their lack of agency. It also fails to incorporate a gender analysis that would appreciate the need for protection of civilian men as well.

Women's rights activist Charlotte Bunch (2004) was critical of the fact that while the report referred to women in different contexts, by using the term "people" to encompass women, the centrality of women was obscured. As a consequence, she argued that there are key areas where women are left at the margins of the report, particularly those having to do with bodily integrity: reproductive rights and violence against women in the family. By not paying particular attention to women as a subject, women are easily sidelined, especially since they are not generally in the forefront of mainstream analyses to begin with. Yet, as Bunch cogently argues, violence perpetrated against women globally is at the core of so much of the human experience. According to the World Health Organization, one third of all girls globally experience their first sexual encounter through force or coercion. This violence, coupled with lack of control over reproduction, creates enormous bodily insecurity. Violence against women in the home is normalized, creating a culture that accepts war, militarism, and other forms of domination in addition to a culture of impunity for such violence (Bunch 2004, 32). Popular culture—from the media, movies, music, and novels—contributes to a perception that violence against women is something that can be expected, and that violence in general can be entertainment.

Another concern raised by feminists is how human security as an approach focuses on securitization of sectors as a means of giving salience to contexts that have been previously ignored. The Copenhagen School, starting in the early 1980s, argued that by placing gender in the human security framework, gender would be elevated in policy importance because of the power-laden nature of the term "security." Attaching the label "security" to gender may allow for greater state resources to be allocated to this concern (Hudson 2010, 31). This approach contributes to a bigger problem of valorizing the notion of security, but there is still the dilemma of getting women recognized as a security concern in the first place (Hansen 2000). While it is true that the language of security commands greater attention than the language of "peace," and linking women to security gives them potentially more gravitas and resources in a world of competing agendas, securitizing gender even with a human security approach can have potentially disastrous consequences, increasing fear and anxiety, expanding conflict, and moving the world away from cooperation, reconciliation, and peace.

Some regard the use of the human security frame as too broad and an exercise in relabeling that serves little if any analytical purpose (Mack 2004). Feminists have also critiqued the concept of human security for being too vague a concept, thus making everything into a security threat so that security problems lose their salience (Paris

2004). Specific human security threats are often treated in isolation from one another in practice, and policymakers often have no basis for prioritizing these competing insecurities because the concept is so all-encompassing.

In 2012, a disagreement emerged between human security scholars and some feminist international relations scholars over the prevalence of sexual violence in conflict, with the 2012 Human Security Report arguing that there has been a tendency to treat the worst affected countries as the norm. Feminist critics take issue with the Human Security Report's claim that conflicts in Congo, Rwanda, Sudan, Sierra Leone, Liberia, and Bosnia are exceptional cases (see, for example, MacKenzie 2012). This particular debate can only be resolved with further empirical research.

Finally, feminists emphasize that it is not enough to incorporate women into discussions of security and peace. How they are incorporated matters, particularly if they are "securitized" and used in instrumental ways to advance a national security agenda. Women were used, for example, as a pretext for military intervention in Afghanistan after 9/11. Greg Mortenson, in his now discredited work, *Three Cups of Tea: One Man's Mission to Promote Peace . . . One School at a Time*, captured the popular imagination with the idea that educating girls in Afghanistan and Pakistan would help end the conflict in the region. As he wrote: "If we try to resolve terrorism with military might and nothing else, then we will be no safer than we were before 9/11. If we truly want a legacy of peace for our children, we need to understand that this is a war that will ultimately be won with books, not with bombs." Mortenson influenced the Joint Chiefs of Staff and other U.S. policymakers, who have now framed women in instrumental ways, arguing that educating women and girls will help prevent terrorism and conflict.[2]

Essentialist arguments of this kind suggesting that women, especially educated ones, are natural peacemakers often devolve into utilitarianism. The needs of women are displaced—although they may benefit from being educated—in favor of absorbing women into a national security and military strategy that is fundamentally state-based. Human agency is not of or for women, but directed to what the military can get women to do to meet their objectives of pacifying a population. Giving a human face to the military is not what human security is about.

Toward a New Feminist Perspective on Human Security

The concerns raised above are ones we cannot ignore. We are not naïve about the potential of any one framework to address all the problems relating to gender violence. Moreover, many applications of human security thinking have been far from ideal. Nevertheless, a human security approach has opened up conceptual ground for feminists to advance their concerns both in theory and in practice. This book now moves the discussion forward in a number of constructive ways that take advantage of the synergies between the concepts of human security and gender. Critical engagements of the idea of human security from a feminist perspective offer some contributions.

Linkages between Different Forms of Insecurity

First, a gendered approach to human security focuses on the *linkages between the various forms of insecurity.* The linkages are along many different lines: It is not unusual for violent conflict to leave in its wake famine, disease, and even ecological devastation. Violence in one context can spill over into violence at another level. Domestic violence, for example, has been shown to increase in contexts of armed conflict. Moreover, violence against women often continues after wars have officially ended (Baines 2005). The gender constructions that give rise to violence against women generally result in violence against gays and lesbians as well (Shepherd 2008, 43).

If one takes seriously the linkages between various forms of insecurity, then one needs a way to talk about those connections. To do so, we build on the work of Ann Tickner, who shows how an understanding of security can see the interrelationships of violence at all levels of society. We therefore choose cases to inform theory in ways that illuminate both the interrelationships between various forms of violence, the *connections between macro and microforms of violence,* the power relations that undergird violence at both the largest and smallest scale, and how both the origins and responses to violence relate to inequality.

Power and Insecurity

Second, applications of human security—like conventional discourses on security more generally—often regard the state as neutral rather than gendered in ways that privilege power over certain groups. Without articulating how gender relates to power, one might assume that women can always access power like men or that there are no differences between women in accessing power. By contrast, feminists have drawn attention to the structural relationships between state power and masculinity (Chenoy 2009).

We similarly stress the power dimensions of human security, not only by exposing the inequalities that create and are created by various insecurities, but also by seeing solutions to human security problems in relational and intersectional terms. Patriarchy—or culturally condoned and institutionalized masculinized hierarchical power relations that express themselves through the state, in rebel movements, in the home, and in society—lies at the root of much insecurity in the world. It is nurtured by unequal but nevertheless mutually dependent masculinities and femininities (Enloe 2005, 282; Walby 1990). Cynthia Enloe has critiqued the ideological linkages between masculinity and militarization, showing how gender hierarchies exacerbate women's insecurity.

Power and violence are central to our understanding of gender. Changing and dynamic understandings of gender are reproduced and reconstituted through violence and insecurity. Violence is both gendered and gendering: it is one of the sites where culturally and historically specific understandings of gender as a power relationship are reproduced (Shepherd 2008, 50). Following Butler and Shepherd, gender itself—and all its power dimensions—is then constituted and reconstituted in a dynamic fashion through human insecurity; and conversely human security is gendered because it is imbued with gendered power relations.

Some interpretations of human security treat all insecurities in the same way without privileging one over another. The insecurities are said to be context specific. For women and other social groups that are marginalized, context matters, but by placing them on a flat plain, one can't distinguish how women around the world may face particular constraints that men do not in a drought or economic crisis because of systematic structural inequalities that are more similar than different.

Recognizing these gendered power imbalances requires a response that redefines power itself in more positive relational terms, as Hudson puts it, "where the survival of one depends on the well-being of the other" (2005, 156). As the prominent feminist international relations scholar Anne Tickner (1992) has argued, security means nothing if it is built upon the insecurity of others. This book applies this principle to thinking within countries about civilian security as well as to considering how nation-states or intrastate groups create insecurities in war. Thus, not only is women's security enhanced by focusing on human security, but so also is the security of men, who are harmed by social constructions of masculinity that force them into conflict.

However, while there are links between masculinity and conflict, one should not draw them too tightly. Women are active participants, like men, in creating patriarchal norms that dictate what women and men can do. The consequences may be gendered, but women participate in the same social constructions of violence. Women, thus, are not only victims of violence, they are also peacemakers, and they can also be passive or even active perpetrators of violence.

Global Inequalities and Human Security

Third, we stress that power relations operate along many different dimensions, including global structural relationships. Feminist scholars have been critical of those who have ignored the political and economic structures beneath expressions of inequality, in particular, the global inequalities that contribute to human security problems. Thus, we look at the global dimensions of human security and how deep *global inequalities* contribute to human security problems.

Some human security approaches locate problems such as terrorism, migration, drugs, and sexual abuse within poor countries; this way of seeing security is often used to justify the interventions of more powerful states. McCormack (2008, 114) argues that the human security approach has inverted "existing international power inequalities, presenting the weakest and most powerless states as existential threats to the most powerful ones. This serves to entrench existing power inequalities rather than challenge them." Whether through the World Bank, military incursions, donor aid, or international judicial institutions, these interventions typically disguise the ways in which wealthier countries contribute to these problems through trade regimes, intellectual property rights laws, climate-changing pollution, drug purchases and arms sales, and other actions by those individuals and states in more privileged global positions (Berman 2007; Shani 2007).

These cautions are well taken and for this reason we suggest a conception of human security that considers sources of insecurity rooted in globalization, global interdependence, as well as political and economic inequalities on a global scale.

Agency and Human Security

Fourth, one corollary to the people-centered emphasis of the human security approach is its emphasis on the *agency* of people. However, there are many aspects of the human security approach relating to agency that need to be sharpened in order to make the concept workable from a gender studies perspective. Some analysts of human security reify women and children as perpetually "vulnerable," and in so doing depict a fairly essentialist and instrumentalist view of women.

Not enough attention is paid to the ways in which women contribute to their families, communities, and nations in such circumstances, mainly because of the focus on the high politics of men, statist solutions to crises, and international interventions. Many women in Liberia, for example, were involved in community peacemaking initiatives and strategies throughout the periods of war (1989–1996, 1999–2003) and these efforts, by all accounts, became indispensable to the final conclusion of the conflict, especially when they took them to the 2003 national peace talks in Accra, Ghana, and pressured the negotiators to speed up the negotiations while their compatriots held peace demonstrations in Monrovia to put pressure back home. It is very likely that had women's roles been supported and recognized all along, the war would have ended even sooner.

But for those who do see women as actors in their own right, agency is often depicted in fairly positive terms and indeed there are plenty of such examples to point to—of women protesting for peace in times of conflict, making extraordinary sacrifices to protect their households in times of economic strain, and contributing to their communities under duress. However, the realities of conflict or famine or a natural catastrophe also may make agency a more ambiguous concept.

Wars and other threats to existence make people act in ways they would never dream of doing under normal circumstances in order to stay alive. Agency itself is not neutral and can serve multiple and competing purposes, both for ill and for good. Even peace activists—more often than is acknowledged—cut unholy deals and collaborate with "the enemy" in order to survive. Some women in Liberia accepted top positions within government ministries of the corrupt and autocratic Charles Taylor government in order to advance their careers personally, but also because they felt that this put them in a better position to negotiate for peace and advance gender-related goals. Theft, corruption, and deceit are rampant during conflict.

The more severe the circumstances, the more agency becomes problematic. How, for example, should one understand agency when the actions of one victimized group result in the suffering and misery of others? What is the meaning of agency when women use what little agency they have simply to survive through whatever brutal means are available to them? Kidnapped girl child soldiers in Sierra Leone found that the more violent and ruthless they were in their attacks on civilian populations, the more privileges they attained in the context where they themselves were victims of physical and other insecurities. Some girl soldiers used their fighting skills to defend themselves by killing combatants who tried to rape them (Denov and Gervais 2007). What is the meaning of agency when it is directed at solutions that are almost as bad as the problem? These give rise to their own set of dilemmas, for example, women, girls, and combatants sometimes use marriage and exchange sexual relations with fighters for survival and protection (Denov and Gervais 2007; Maclure and Denov 2006). Women's agency, like that of others, is largely defined or constrained by the broader gendered social structures within which women operate. Gender-based discrimination sets parameters on women's action, while conflict and other forms of crisis can distort agency in ways not as evident in less extreme contexts.

A related dilemma is how to understand individual versus collective insecurity and action. Human security approaches, like human rights approaches, often tend to focus on the individual as both the means and the end of human security (Buzan 2004, 37; Tadjbakhsh and Chenoy 2007). In practice, the way problems are framed has often resulted in statist liberal solutions that focus on individual agency and the rights of the individual (Ambrosetti 2008; Christie 2010; Krause and Williams 1997, 46; Richmond 2007). The state-individual dichotomy is premised on a liberal notion of rights as being located primarily with the individual, and the theoretical disregard of group identities and collective actors. Yet as both targets of violence and as responders to violence and insecurity, women act both individually and as collectives. Both individual and collective actors need to be accounted for, and both individual as well as structural solutions need to be addressed.

Women may be targets of violence not only as individuals, but because they are part of a collective group—namely, women. They may be targeted because they are regarded as transgressing gender norms (in the case of honor killing), or because they are the bearers of the children of a particular ethnic or racial group (in the case of wartime rape), or because of a cultural norm legitimating physical harm (in the case of female genital cutting). Not all women are always targeted, but specific women are targeted because they are part of a gendered collective (Hansen 2000, 293). Similarly, agency is not only enacted by individuals; it often takes collective forms because insecurity itself is experienced at every level of interaction from the interpersonal to the international (Giles and Hyndman 2004).

In terms of responding to insecurity, women's demands to participate in peace negotiations from Burundi to the Democratic Republic of Congo, Liberia, and Somalia, have almost always been made as a collective and have been made in order to advance a women's rights agenda to benefit women as a collectivity (Tripp et al. 2009). In fact, conflict exacerbated the consequences of women's exclusions, making it all the more imperative to make demands as a social group. Thus, the concept of human security needs to embrace both the individual as well as the collective dimensions of women's security.

From a Security to a Peace Agenda

Fifth, security dominates the lexicon of violence rather than peace. There are no ministries or departments of peace within governments.

The notion of human security adopts a defensive posture rather than one of actively and proactively pursuing peacemaking and peacebuilding or of addressing structural problems before they have violent consequences. When people or states feel threatened, they talk of the need for security and the need to defend themselves. They do so sometimes in violent and irrational ways, often lashing out first with aggression, and engaging in peace talks only later. Efforts to ensure security often have unintended consequences. Being able to defend oneself is generally seen as a righteous response, but it can be violent nevertheless, often creating new insecurities for the many citizens who had no part in creating the sense of threat.

Here, too, feminism can contribute to the notion of human security by placing peace as a goal above others; a peace that is not just an absence of conflict, but one that is based on eliminating inequality and addressing environmental concerns (Tickner 1992, 128). Human security should promote equality at all levels, at the societal level (gender, race, class-based) as well as global equality as a means of creating the structural conditions for peace (Feminist Institute of the Heinrich Böll Foundation 2006, 26).

Addressing Long-Term and Structural Insecurities

Sixth, complementing the short-term focus of most human security approaches, feminists stress the *long-term continuous threats* that create human insecurity. An immediate crisis of violence exposes gender-based inequalities, but the causes of the crisis and the ways in which people respond to them are premised on structural inequalities based on capabilities, rights, and access to resources that have evolved over decades and even centuries. These problems are not exclusively based on gender relations, but arise from intersectionalities of gender, race, class, sexual orientation, and other identities.

We highlight the *structural bases of problems*, which we see as *dynamic*. In some human security approaches, structural inequalities are ignored even when addressing ethnic tensions, the rise of fundamentalisms, and other manifestations of insecurity (McCormack 2008; Thomas 2004; Uvin 2004). Thus, the policy issues considered at the end of this book go beyond interventions such as a microcredit, health, or literacy program to discussions of how to address the underlying unequal economic, political, and social structures and their gendered, class, raced, and intersectional dimensions that necessitate such interventions in the first place.

Deconstructing the "Human" in "Human Security" and Intersectionality

Finally, but perhaps most importantly, feminist international relations scholars have been justifiably critical of the collapsing of masculinities and femininities into the term "human," thus erasing the gendered nature of security (Hudson 2010, 37). We seek to *complicate notions of "people-centeredness"* as used in human security discourses. We attempt to clarify what is meant by "people," especially where there are multiple and competing interests of different "people" embedded in power relations, including gender relations. For example, men and women do not always have the same motivations and objectives in peacemaking processes, nor are men and women themselves unitary groups with distinct and coherent objectives.

Attention to issues of intersectionality is critical to understanding the broader implications of problem solving, whether it is individuals, communities, or states that are acting. Intersectionality incorporates both a recognition as well as redress of inequality along intersectional lines, showing how different axes of power and difference are "socially situated and politically defined" (Truong, Wieringa, and Chhacchi 2006, xi, xiv).

Outline of the Book

The chapters in the first section of the book seek to critique and retheorize human security from a gender perspective. Fionnuala Ní Aoláin in her chapter, "What Does Postconflict Security Mean for Women?" continues the argument of this chapter, showing how postconflict security conversations continue to exclude women's experiences with violence and focus primarily on state actors. She argues for a view of security that "encompasses physical, social, economic, and sexual security" as a way of addressing gendered security. Such a view includes democratic transformation, and incorporates equality principles of multiple legal spheres along with a redistributive economic dimension. Meaningful security, for Ní Aoláin, targets not only state violence, but also transforms the underlying causes in the private sphere, thus revealing the linkages between causes of violence.

V. Spike Peterson focuses on sources of insecurity rooted in globalization, global interdependence, as well as political and economic inequalities on a global scale. For example, she shows how neoliberal globalization has resulted in the expansion of informalization, particularly in conflict zones. These processes of informalization are gendered and are linked to processes of economic exploitation and political militarization that divide the globe. She also draws out the connections between criminal and conflict economies at the local and macrolevel, highlighting the many ways in which the global trade in drugs, arms, and commodities such as gold, diamonds, and copper supports and is supported by violence. Peterson analyzes the complicity in crime and warfare that survival may strategically demand of individuals.

The second section of the book involves case studies of gendered violence within the context of broader insecurities. Edith Kinney interrogates the implications of "securitizing" social problems like trafficking in the Thai context. She shows how activists sometimes end up unintentionally promoting questionable security frames by adopting a human security approach in order to underscore the urgency of a particular situation, without being adequately attentive to the fact that a human security frame does not necessarily guarantee accountability or legal obligations. In Thailand this meant that trafficking was framed in a way that made it seem that trafficked migrants undermined the security of local communities and the Thai nation. NGO advocates became involved in rehabilitation and repatriation processes in ways that created tensions between victims' rights and immigration control in trafficking interventions.

Lisa Brush vividly describes the lives of poor women in the United States in her chapter in this volume, "Work and Love in the Gendered U.S. Insecurity State." As she shows, the state is hardly gender neutral or an impartial arbiter. For Brush, "the definition of 'family violence,' the instrumental and structural masculinization of law enforcement and the judicial system, and other features of the law-and-order state

institutionalize differences between women and men and naturalize expectations about men's aggression and women's subordination,
dependence, and domesticity." The penal security state and the social
security state are two sides of the U.S. state that complement one
another in addressing poverty and battering. They draw on similar
understandings of what causes poverty and battering and they both
advocate gendered personal responsibility and women's employment as
the keys to success in addressing these issues. Brush shows how futile
the state solutions of empowerment, individual initiative, and personal
responsibility are without other social supports in dealing with problems that are structural in nature.

Elizabeth Stites explores the importance of masculinities within
Karimojong society in eastern Uganda. In her chapter, "A Struggle for
Rites: Masculinity, Violence, and Livelihoods in Karamoja, Uganda,"
she identifies three interlinking processes that have led to extreme
insecurity in Karimojong, whose people are subject to constant cattle
raids by neighboring groups. These insecurities include the erosion of
the livelihoods of males and their generation-specific rites; the stagnation of a customary authority system that was supposed to allow men
to claim power but that no longer functioned as it was intended; and
finally, the increase of violence as men sought alternative forms of status and recognition. Stites reminds us of the importance of culture in
creating insecurities through the ways in which society is gendered, but
also points to how change—in this case environmental and economic—
impact the gendered cultures that structure men's as well as women's
lives.

Katherine Pratt Ewing also addresses culturally based insecurities,
but her case study of concerns about honor killing in Germany focuses
instead on how culture is actively mobilized to create gender-specific
anxieties about immigration. Presenting culture not as static but as a
process of meaning creation, Ewing distinguishes the real murder of a
woman who violated gender norms from the "apparently good copy"
of it constructed by the media. Her account also shows how women
as well as men take part in the scare-mongering about immigrants as
threatening in the discourse about honor killing in Europe today.

The third part of the book explores the policy considerations
involved in efforts to gender human security and reduce violence.

Kristin Bumiller in "Feminist Collaboration with the State in Response to Sexual Violence: Lessons from the American Experience," shows some of the pitfalls of overreliance on the state in addressing human security issues. Like Ewing's, her chapter highlights the intersectional impacts of feminist attention to violence against women. She provides a historical analysis of policy responses to sexual violence in the United States to show how state-based strategies initiated by feminists unwittingly contributed to criminalizing a large section of American men who disproportionately represent ethnic minorities and immigrant groups. She reveals the limits of state-based responses in lieu of broader reforms that would address the multiple social dimensions of the problem and criticizes the portrayal of sensational episodes of sexual violence in the media.

Laura Heideman, in "The Vulnerable Protecting the Vulnerable: NGOs and Human Security in the Aftermath of War," argues in the context of postwar Croatia that human security issues are of central concern and should not be treated as secondary to state security. Moreover, the causes of state insecurity and human insecurity are similar, necessitating solutions that are intertwined. This forces issues of gender, ethnicity, and vulnerability into the center of security debates. From the Greek civil war in the 1940s to the more recent conflict in the Democratic Republic of Congo, research has shown that local cleavages were more important than national ones (Autessere 2010; Kalyvas 2006). Thus, addressing human security concerns is not just a dividend of peace, Heideman argues. It is indispensable to postconflict reconstruction and preventing the recurrence of conflict. It puts people's welfare at the center of the agenda, along with their priorities and needs.

Ruth Rubio-Marín and Dorothy Estrada-Tanck in their chapter, "Violence against Women, Human Security, and Human Rights of Women and Girls: Reinforced Obligations in the Context of Structural Vulnerability," particularly focus on the courts and the emergence of an international legal framework that considers human security not as an alternative to human rights but as a way of strengthening and expanding that concept. They see such a view potentially doing more to hold states themselves accountable and as enhancing the human rights approach with a stronger, more complex, and less individualized gender component. They see considerable signs of hope for human rights law appreciating better the contexts of structural vulnerability within which abuses occur.

Narda Henríquez and Christina Ewig in their chapter take up the challenge of connecting human rights mechanisms with those of attending to human security needs that Rubio-Marín and Estrada-Tanck posed and show that such an integrative approach can be productive in addressing a specific postconflict peace-building project. "Integrating Gender into Human Security: Peru's Truth and Reconciliation Commission" shows the deep linkages between everyday insecurities and the violence of war in Peru's internal conflict between the military and Shining Path guerrillas in the 1980s and 1990s. Peru's Truth and Reconciliation Commission, they argue, was a model of integrating gender into a human security framework in that the Commission gave marginalized Peruvians voice, visibility, and legitimacy. This was especially true for indigenous Peruvian women at the bottom of Peru's social hierarchy, who were especially able to name the injustices of the *status quo ante*.

Finally, the book concludes with a chapter by Myra Marx Ferree. Ferree summarizes some of the major contributions of the book and connects them both to the challenges described in this chapter and to the unfinished agenda of creating a feminist view of human security. She stresses the distinction between just talking about gender and intersectional discourses that integrate gender with other forms of social injustice and address them more holistically. Insofar as gender can be and is being "mainstreamed" into human security discourses, it is opening up opportunities for feminists to do more than name women's special needs, protect them from victimization, or invite them into a male-controlled peace process. The feminist view of human security offered in these chapters points to bringing gender into the core of the concept, changing what it can offer both women and men in both richer and poorer countries.

Conclusion

There are enough problems with the framing and practice of human security from a gender studies perspective to handily reject the concept. However, like "human development" and "human rights," "human security" is now part of the vocabulary of international and national policy and it is not going to disappear. As with the other two concepts, there are many dimensions of human security that are compatible with a feminist approach, but that require elaboration and reformulation from a gender perspective. It is not so much that human security should be applied to a gender perspective as gender perspectives need to be integrated into the concept of human security, as Hoogensen and Stuvøy (2006) suggest. Human security approaches already incorporate important agency-oriented, people-centered, and bottom-up perspectives that are in many ways attractive to those adopting a gendered approach to security and peace. Moreover, feminists have already been able to make advances in UN and national policy regarding women's rights by drawing on this framework.

It is for this reason that the authors in this volume argue for a human security approach that looks at linkages between various forms of insecurity. Feminist scholarship has long argued for connecting various levels of violence, showing the connections between civil conflict and violence in the home; or the ways in which poverty makes women more vulnerable in natural disasters; or understanding why conflict results in more women as refugees.

While the human security approach tends to regard the state as gender neutral, the authors in this volume show how it is thoroughly gendered and patriarchal, with serious consequences for both men and women and for their security. As a result, violence itself, as Laura Shepherd and Judith Butler have argued, has gendered outcomes and is a site where gender itself is created and re-created. The human security approach focuses on the individual as the target of violence. However, from a gender perspective, women are often targeted with violence not only as individuals but also because they are part of the collectivity of women. Agency, likewise, has both individual and collective dimensions, particularly when women respond to attacks on women as a group.

The focus on "security" rather than "peace" leaves us in a defensive mode that can lead to the securitization of gender and to continued violence and retribution. It does not necessarily point to proactive solutions that address some of the structural dilemmas that led to the violence in the first place. These structural dilemmas operate both at the national and international level, in the form of global inequalities that need to be addressed in a human security approach. Too many of the applications of the human security framework have targeted poor countries as the cause of insecurity in the form of migration, drugs, terrorism, and sex trafficking, rather than seeing these as outcomes of globalization and the inequalities it creates.

While one should be cautious about the applications of human security to advance a statist agenda, one can embrace the aspirations of the human security approach to adopt a people-centered approach. At the same time, feminists are deeply suspicious of a disembodied notion of "human." Humans are always embedded in power relations and one such relationship is gender. We draw on understandings of intersectionality, not only to clarify the difference gender makes to our understanding of human security, but also other overlaps of class, race, sexual orientation, ethnicity, and other manifestations of difference.

Finally, we would argue for a more complex understanding of agency than that associated with the human security framework. Agency is often upheld as something positive and there certainly is a great need to acknowledge to a greater extent the positive efforts of women to cope with the strain of poverty, war, and natural disasters. Nevertheless, it is part of the toll of those same phenomena that also force women and men to act in opportunistic ways and take actions that may create suffering for others. These, then, are a few of the ways in which this volume engages the concept of "human security" to give it more analytic purchase from a gender perspective.

NOTES

1. WPS includes representatives from Amnesty International, Women's Commission for Refugee Women and Children, International Alert, Women's Caucus for Gender Justice, The Hague Appeal for Peace, and Women s International League for Peace and Freedom. UNIFEM.

2. Joint Chiefs of Staff, "Mullen Helps Celebrate New Opportunity for Afghans," n.d. http://www.jcs.mil/newsarticle.aspx?ID=125, retrieved 2.29.12.

REFERENCES

Abass, Ademola. 2010. *Protecting Human Security in Africa*. Oxford; New York: Oxford University Press.

Agosin, Marjorie. 2001. *Women, Gender, and Human Rights: A Global Perspective*. New Brunswick, N.J.: Rutgers University Press.

Alkire, Sabina. 2003. "A Conceptual Framework for Human Security." In *CRISE Working Paper*. Queen Elizabeth House, University of Oxford: Centre for Research on Inequality, Human Security and Ethnicity.

Ambrosetti, David. 2008. "Human Security as Political Resource." *Security Dialogue* 39 (4):439–445.

Anthony, Mely Caballero, Ralf Emmers, and Amitav Acharya. 2006. *Non-Traditional Security in Asia: Dilemmas in Securitization, Global Security in a Changing World*. Aldershot, U.K.; Burlington, Vt.: Ashgate.

Autessere, Séverine. 2010. *The Trouble with the Congo. Local Violence and the Failure of International Peacebuilding*. New York: Cambridge University Press.

Baines, Erin. 2005. "Is Canada's Freedom from Fear Agenda Feminist? A Critique of Policy and the Literature." In *Conflict and Development Programme Working Paper Series, Liu Institute for Global Issues, University of British Columbia*. Vancouver: University of British Columbia.

Berman, Jacqueline. 2007. "The 'Vital Core': From Bare Life to the Biopolitics of Human Security." In *Protecting Human Security in a Post 9/11 World: Critical and Global Insights*, edited by Giorgio Shani, Makoto Sato, and Mustapha Kamal Pasha. Basingstoke and New York: Palgrave Macmillan.

Blanchard, Erik. 2003. "Gender, International Relations, and the Development of Feminist Security Theory." *Signs: Journal of Women in Culture and Society* 28 (4):1289–1312.

Bunch, Charlotte. 2004. "A Feminist Human Rights Lens on Human Security." *Peace Review: A Journal of Social Justice* 16 (1): 29–34.

Buzan, Barry. 2004. "A Reductionist, Idealistic Notion That Adds Little Analytical Value." *Security Dialogue* 35 (3):369–370.

Caprioli, Mary. 2005. "Primed for Violence: The Role of Gender Inequality in Predicting Internal Conflict." *International Studies Quarterly* 49 (2):161–178.

Chandler, David. 2008. "Human Security II: Waiting for the Tail to Wag the Dog—A Rejoinder to Ambrosetti, Owen and Wibben." *Security Dialogue* 39 (4):463–469.

Chenoy, Anuradha M. 2005. "A Plea for Engendering Human Security." *International Studies* 42 (2):167–179.

———. 2009. "The Gender and Human Security Debate." *IDS Bulletin* 40 (2):44–49.

Christie, Ryerson. 2010. "Critical Voices and Human Security: To Endure, to Engage or to Critique?" *Security Dialogue* 41(2):169–190.

Commission on Human Security. 2003. *Human Security Now*. New York: Commission on Human Security. http://reliefweb.int/sites/reliefweb.int/files/resources/91BAEED BA50C6907C1256D19006A9353-chs-security-may03.pdf

Cook, Rebecca, ed. 1994. *Human Rights of Women*. Philadelphia: University of Pennsylvania Press.

Denov, Myriam, and Christine Gervais. 2007. "Negotiating (In)Security: Agency, Resistance, and Resourcefulness among Girls Formerly Associated with Sierra Leone's Revolutionary United Front." *Signs: Journal of Women in Culture and Society* 32 (4):885–910.

Denov, Myriam, and Richard Maclure. 2009. "Girls and Small Arms in Sierra Leone: Experience, Implications, and Strategies for Demobilization and Reintegration." In *Sexed Pistols: The Gendered Impacts of Small Arms and Light Weapons*, edited by A. Schnabel and V. Farr. Tokyo: United Nations University Press.

Enloe, Cynthia H. 2000. *Bananas, Beaches and Bases: Making Feminist Sense of International Politics*. Updated ed. Berkeley: University of California Press.

———. 2005. "What If Patriarchy Is 'the Big Picture'? An Afterword." In *Gender, Conflict, and Peacekeeping*, edited by Dyan E. Mazurana, Angela Raven-Roberts, and Jane L. Parpart, 280–283. Lanham, Md.: Rowman & Littlefield.

Feminist Institute of the Heinrich Böll Foundation. 2006. "Peace and Security for All: A Feminist Critique of the Current Peace and Security Policy." In *Working Group "Gender in Peace and Security Policy and Civil Conflict Prevention."* http://www. glow-boell.de/media/en/txt rubrik 2/security for all englisch2006.pdf

Giles, Wenona Mary, and Jennifer Hyndman. 2004. *Sites of Violence: Gender and Conflict Zones*. Berkeley: University of California Press.

Goldstein, Joshua. 2011. *Winning the War on War: The Decline of Armed Conflict Worldwide*. New York: Dutton/Penguin.

Gurr, Ted Robert. 2000. "Ethnic Warfare on the Wane." *Foreign Affairs* 79 (3):52–64.

Hampson, Fen Olser, Jean Daudelin, John B. Hay, Holly Reid, and Todd Martin. 2001. *Madness in the Multitude: Human Security and World Disorder*. Oxford: Oxford University Press.

Hansen, Lene. 2000. "The Little Mermaid's Silent Security Agenda and the Absence of Gender in the Copenhagen School." *Millenium: Journal of International Studies* 29 (2):285–306.

Hoogensen, G., and K. Stuvøy. 2006. "Gender, Resistance and Human Security." *Security Dialogue* 37 (2):207–228.

Howard-Hassmann, Rhoda E. 2010. "Human Security: Undermining Human Rights?" Canada Research Chair in International Human Rights, Wilfrid Laurier University, Waterloo, Ontario.

Hudson, Heidi. 2005. "'Doing' Security as though Humans Matter: A Feminist Perspective on Gender and the Politics of Human Security." *Security Dialogue* 36 (2):155–174.

Hudson, Natalie Florea. 2010. *Gender, Human Security and the United Nations: Security Language as a Political Framework for Women*. Routledge Critical Security Studies Series. New York: Routledge.

Human Security Centre. 2005. "Human Security Report." Vancouver: Simon Fraser University.

Human Security Report Project. 2006. *Human Security Report*. Vancouver: Human Security Report Project, Simon Fraser University.

———. 2012. *Human Security Report*. Vancouver: Human Security Report Project, Simon Fraser University.

Kalyvas, Stathis. 2006. *The Logic of Violence in Civil War*. Cambridge: Cambridge University Press.

Kinsella, Helen. 2011. *The Image before the Weapon: A Critical History of the Distinction between Combatant and Civilian*. Ithaca: Cornell University Press.

Krause, Keith, and Micahel Charles Williams. 1997. *Critical Security Studies: Concepts and Cases*. Minneapolis: University of Minnesota Press.

Mack, Andrew. 2004. "A Signifier of Shared Values." *Security Dialogue* 35 (3):366–367.

MacKenzie, Megan. 2012. "War Rape Is Not Declining." In *Duck of Minerva*. accessed December 11, 2012. http://www.whiteoliphaunt.com/duckofminerva/2012/10/war-rape-is-not-declining.html

Maclure, Richard, and Myriam Denoy. 2006. "'I Didn't Want to Die so I Joined Them': Structuration and the Process of Becoming Boy Soldiers in Sierra Leone." *Terrorism and Political Violence* 18 (1):119–135.

McCormack, Tara. 2008. "Power and Agency in the Human Security Framework." *Cambridge Review of International Affairs* 21 (1):113–128.

Melander, Erik. 2005. "Gender Equality and Intrastate Armed Conflict." *International Studies Quarterly* 49 (4):695–714.

Muggah, Robert, and Keith Krause. 2006. "Putting Human Security to the Test: Reflections on Two Peacekeeping Missions in Haiti." *Whitehead Journal of Diplomacy and International Relations* Autumn/Winter, 129-141.

Newman, Edward. 2010. "Critical Human Security Studies." *Review of International Studies* 36:77–94.

Nussbaum, Martha C. 2000. *Women and Human Development: The Capabilities Approach* Cambridge: Cambridge University Press.

Nussbaum, Martha C. , and Amartya Sen. 1993. *The Quality of Life*. Oxford: Clarendon Press.

Owen, Taylor. 2004. "Human Security—Conflict, Critique and Consensus: Colloquium Remarks and a Proposal for a Threshold-Based Definition." *Security Dialogue* 35:373–387.

Paris, Roland. 2004. "Still an Inscrutable Concept." *Security Dialogue* 35 (3):370–371.

Peters, Julie Stone, and Andrea Wolper, eds. 1994. *Women's Rights, Human Rights: International Feminist Perspectives*. New York: Routledge.

Peterson, V. Spike, and Anne Sisson Runyan. 1999. *Global Gender Issues*. 2nd ed., *Dilemmas in World Politics*. Boulder, Colo.: Westview Press.

Richmond, Oliver P. 2007. "Emancipatory Forms of Peacebuilding." *International Journal* 62 (3):458–477.

Shani, Giorgio. 2007. "Introduction." In *Protecting Human Security in a Post 9/11 World: Critical and Global Insights*, edited by Giorgio Shani, Makoto Sato, and Mustapha Kamal Pasha, xv, 226 pp. Basingstoke, U.K.; New York: Palgrave Macmillan.

Shani, Giorgio, Makoto Sato, and Mustapha Kamal Pasha, eds. 2007. *Protecting Human Security in a Post 9/11 World: Critical and Global Insights*. Basingstoke, U.K.; New York: Palgrave Macmillan.

Shepherd, Laura J. 2008. *Gender, Violence and Security: Discourse as Practice*. London; New York: Zed Books.

Sjoberg, Laura, and Sandra E. Via, eds. 2010. *Gender, War, and Militarism: Feminist Perspectives*. Santa Barbara: Praeger, ABC-CLIO.

Tadjbakhsh, Shahrbanou, and Anuradha M. Chenoy. 2007. *Human Security, Concepts and Implications*. London: Routledge.

Thakur, Ramesh. 2004. "A Political Worldview." *Security Dialogue* no. 35 (3):347–348.

Thomas, Caroline. 2004. "A Bridge between the Interconnected Challenges Confronting the World." *Security Dialogue* 35 (3):353–354.

Tickner, J. Ann. 1992. *Gender in International Relations: Feminist Perspectives on Achieving Global Security*. New York: Columbia University Press.

Tripp, Aili Mari, et al. 2009. *African Women's Movements: Transforming Political Landscapes*. Cambridge; New York: Cambridge University Press.

Truong, Thanh-am, Saskia Wieringa, and Amrita Chhachhi. 2006. *Engendering Human Security: A Feminist Perspective*. London: Zed Books.

United Nations Development Programme. 1994. *New Dimensions of Human Security, Human Development Report*. http://hdr.undp.org/en/reports/global/hdr1994/

Uvin, Peter. 2004. "A Field of Overlaps and Interactions." *Security Dialogue* 35 (3):352–353.

Walby, Sylvia. 1990. *Theorizing Patriarchy*. Oxford: Basil Blackwell.

Wibben, Annick T. R. 2011. *Feminist Security Studies: A Narrative Approach, PRIO New Security Studies*. London; New York: Routledge.

2

What Does Postconflict Security Mean for Women?

FIONNUALA NÍ AOLÁIN

When women are afraid to go out in the street, they can't take advantage of the theoretical freedoms that are now available to them.[1]

Security is a concept with significant impact on and a practical relationship with the postconflict environment.[2] Security or its absence in postconflict societies deeply and unrelentingly affects women's daily lives. As this essay will explore, women are consistently excluded from decision making related to the security of their environment, their bodies, and their lives in postconflict societies. Gender-based exclusions from security discourses and practices are not unusual or unique. The absence of a gender dimension in the establishment, revision, and operation of new legal and political institutions in postconflict societies has been generally acknowledged (Bell et al. 2004). What is less well understood perhaps is the extent to which exclusions from "security" conversations affect and influence other exclusions, and operate to compound or extend women's postconflict vulnerabilities.

This essay starts with an assessment of the genesis of postconflict exclusions for women. It addresses contexts and realities in which security-focused conversations take place, outlining how such structural realities affect women's inclusion in these spaces. I assert that understanding where and how such barriers start is an important first step to addressing them. I then turn to examine the relationship between the international presence that becomes part of many postconflict settings, and address the relationship that follows between local and international patriarchies. I argue that women's exclusions in the security realm are not only related to cultural and social norms in the national setting, but also are compounded by the importation of a set of patriarchal values that arrive with international interveners. The final section addresses the relationship broadly mapped between security and transition from conflict. I offer some general views on the importance of deeply and intrinsically integrating gender perspectives into these conversations, to achieve better security outcomes for both men and women.

The Genealogy of Omissions

In many conflicted states, women's experiences of conflict and a lack of security are located in a broad set of socioeconomic and political externalities that mark the status of women as lower than that of men as a matter of normal political and social practice. On top of such regularized prohibitions are additional exclusionary layers for women that can be traced directly to omissions from peacemaking and transitionary "deal making." Understanding the way in which peace processes in conflict settings operate to leave women out allows us to understand how critical microarenas evidence a dearth of attention to the specific needs of women. I underscore that these early structural exclusions compound the normative legal gaps facilitating further exclusions down the line once "normality" is restored to the postconflict setting. However, additional exploration is required to assess why women remain structurally excluded and, in particular, why they remain excluded as the processes of transition become increasingly internationalized.[3] I believe it is important to explore why internationalization, which at least in theory leads us to presuppose that the security outcomes will be better for women (thus perhaps leading to greater institutional involvement and gain), does not deliver that dividend.

Understanding how women experience layered exclusions requires us to examine the structure of peacemaking and transitions from conflict. Self-evidently, given the variety of conflicts and their causes, no one peace process looks exactly like another. Yet, not unexpectedly, commonalities exist. Christine Bell has identified three key stages to conflict transition which are a useful way to frame an analysis of gender exclusion (Bell 2008). By marking out three key stages by which parties to a conflict (whether state, nonstate, or both) typically come to political agreements to end or transition from communal conflict, we can identify pivotal points in the process of conflict endings where women may be structurally excluded. In the context of this analysis, pinpointing where important security conversations occur also allows us to probe the gender security interface more robustly.

First, prenegotiation agreements: Prenegotiation agreements are concluded prior to any formal peace settlement and invariably revolve around ensuring the presence of those perceived as key political actors at the negotiation table. This phase can be both formal and informal, sometimes evolving organically within a state, but more typically advanced by external cajoling from other states or international institutions. The prenegotiation phase is critical to security conversations as it generally involves having armed actors (both state and nonstate) agree to ceasefires, ending of hostilities, and the outline perimeters of amnesty, demobilization, and demilitarization. The absence of security and the proliferation of violence is the causal reason why prenegotiations are often dominated by security considerations. Prenegotiations can include broad context-setting initiatives as well as setting statements of principle. The prenegotiation stage is likely to exclude women for a number of structural reasons. It is rarely a civil society-dominated phase, but typically includes only state and nonstate military actors at the highest echelons.[4] It is often secret in its operation and, given the high value placed on the ending of public violence, the prenegotiation phase tends to place disproportionate emphasis on the military and security outcomes perceived as essential to facilitate broader political engagement.

The second phase that Bell identifies involves the "Substantive/ Framework" agreements that "aim to sustain ceasefires and provide a framework for governance that will address the root causes of the conflict" (Bell 2008, 60–62). These are, in some sense, the classic peace agreements. These documents are generally ambitious and far-reaching, not only tackling matters such as demilitarization, prisoner release, amnesty, and the military's status, but also addressing legal and political reform, social and economic reparation, and institutional reform. An important point, however, is that framework agreements draw directly from the "deals" made in the prenegotiation phase, as commitments made there are honored formally to maintain the presence and buy-in of central military figures and organizations. Security figures prominently, as such agreements memorialize security sector reform, amnesty, demilitarization, and demobilization. Framework agreement phases are more likely to include women at least in some minimal and public way. This is often the most high profile phase of conflict negotiations and frequently involves international actors and agencies as they support a peace process. The extent to which women's presence in such fora substantially affects the outcomes of negotiations remains an open question, with little concrete evidence to illustrate a sustained effect from symbolic female participation (Bell and O'Rourke 2010). The extent to which women, even when present, can shift and reframe commitments being sustained from earlier informal negotiations is limited. More often than not, women may find themselves at negotiating tables where the actual space for negotiation is limited in ways that may not be evident from external view. Security considerations are likely to be part of the terrain that is not available for renegotiation.

The third phase of agreements identified by Bell's paradigm is "implementation agreements," which "take forward and develop aspects of the framework, fleshing out their detail" (Bell 2008, 62–65). Because framework agreements are broadly worded treaty agreements, they frequently avoid detailed outlining of specific implementation measures necessary to transform principle to practice. This means that much of the difficult work of real compromise can be left to the implementation phase, where both genuine opportunity and pitfalls exist for women.

The purpose of implementation agreements is often technical—they can be seen as simply moving forward the work (with greater detail and clarity) to which the parties have previously committed. In practice, their negotiation and content is far more contested. Often the opportunity to renegotiate offered by this kind of agreement means that parties view them as sites to revisit and regain losses (perceived or actual) in other parts of the negotiation process (Ní Aoláin 2011). Women face significant barriers to involvement in the implementation phase. The first is a barrier of time. Specifically, women often do not have the ability or support to divert their attention from the burden of caregiving and other home-based responsibilities to be free to engage in the politics of the moment. Second is the barrier of capacity; women are often not provided with the security and support necessary to become political actors. Both elements are organically linked. After all, the end of violent public conflict does not usually mean an end to violence for women, and thus the postconflict environment is not inevitably a secure space for them. This lack of security has a profound practical effect on women's capacity to continue to engage in ongoing political negotiations when hostilities have formally ended: they may not have the physical security necessary to participate or the political security to be included.

The Patriarchies at Play in Postconflict Societies

A key element in the perceived success of many postconflict accountability mechanisms and the willingness to establish new legal and political institutions lies in engaging the support of international organizations and other states in their establishment.[5] The transition from conflict to peace is usually only one point on the continuum of a protracted legal and political engagement between the transitional state and the international community. The conflicted state is captured between the multiple interests of other states, their willingness to articulate views about a conflict, and the moments of their formal or informal interaction with key actors at pivotal change moments. While much could be said about this complex interaction in general, this analysis will focus on two particular aspects: first, the relationship between the international communities' previously articulated views on human rights compliance during a conflict; and second, the complex role that the international community can play in compounding gender inequality and unaccountability once entangled with a transitional society (Ní Aoláin 2009). Both these elements influence the conversations and policies about security in postconflict societies.

Recall that international entanglement with and oversight of transitional societies rarely happens just at the crucial transitional moment. Rather, there has usually been a long interplay between the multiple interests of other states, their willingness to articulate views about a conflict, and the moments of their formal or informal interaction with key actors at significant change moments. This analysis suggests that there is a definable connection between the international community's previously articulated views on human rights compliance during a conflict and the extent to which this view has ignored and/or sidelined women's experiences of harm. There is an organic link between the naming of harms, accountability for them, and the security that is perceived as necessary in both conflicted and postconflict societies. By calling out particular harms one sets the context in which prevention and hierarchies of action are established. When one ignores gendered harms, one is not solely excluding the possibility of accountability, but also broadly affecting what national and international security discourses understand themselves to be responding to. Harm naming is central to calling out what makes men and women feel insecure. The failure to name, identify, and hold individuals accountable for some harms and not for others has a direct relationship with what creates or undermines individual and group security in societal settings.

We know that highly violent societies have often been the subject of substantial international scrutiny prior to any settlement. Conflicted societies have been deeply violent and international oversight may have "named and shamed" systematic and significant human rights violations in the pretransition phase. As a result, the kinds of human rights violations that have been identified externally as particularly egregious during the conflict will have a clear ascendency in the hierarchy of harms that are perceived to merit review and redress in the postconflict period. Gender-based harms struggle to gain place in this hierarchy, thereby compounding the broader set of social and political reasons why gender harms may be on the sidelines of importance in conflicted societies generally. For example, international nongovernmental organizations (NGOs) such as Amnesty International, Human Rights First, and Human Rights Watch may have been active, sending investigative missions, producing numerous reports, and providing a large range of supports for their domestic NGO counterparts. When it comes time in the settlement phase of a conflict or a regime handover, these prior interventions are critical to framing the way in which accountability is sought, articulated, and constructed. This construction comes from intact Western conceptions of human rights hierarchies imbued with their inability to consider their own patriarchy and unwilling to recognize it at work in an export form (Rees 2002). It is important to recognize that the narrative constructed about the nature and form of violations in transitional societies has as much to do with the demands for accountability at the transitional moment as it has with the prior narrative of violence and causality. The watchful and deeply involved international community actively constructs this narrative, which has a distinctly gendered dimension. What I seek to underscore is that a lack of accountability for certain kinds of gendered harms is not simply measured in terms of accountability gaps for women, but it has a direct interplay with women's sense of security (as individuals and as a social group) in postconflict societies. Feminists have generally recognized the gendered effects of the accountability gap, but not its organic link to a security gap.

How are we to understand these international patriarchies and to appraise the nature of their effects? While patriarchy is broadly understood to capture the idea of male power over the female, its etymology is traced to the Roman law construct of familial social organization affirming the superiority of the father in the family or clan, the dependence of women and children upon him, and the reckoning of descent and inheritance in the male line. In contemporary times, theorists have identified organic linkages between patriarchy and its contemporary workings and various forms of masculinity as they arise within societies and institutions. A preponderance of literatures across disciplines has deepened our understanding of how masculinities are constructed and differentiated (Chodorow 1994; Connell 1987). In parallel, the role of masculinity norms "in giving rise to violence against women is being theoretically scrutinized" (Anderson 2008), and as a result some international organizations have recognized (albeit on an ad hoc basis) that there is a pressing need to deconstruct and reduce the negative aspects of masculinity and to integrate men and boys into programs aimed at reducing violence against women.[6] In general, much less scrutiny has been given to dissecting the patriarchy inherent in international institutions, and even less to revealing the masculinity bias of the same bodies and the actors who represent them. This essay asserts that this bias illuminates why transitional processes in the broadest sense fail women and also why the enforcement of the cornerstone of transition in conflicted societies (specifically security) fails to meet the basic test of gender neutrality.

In this context, we should note that international interface and influence in postconflict societies is compounded by the role of such key international actors as the United Nations. Where the UN has paid particular attention to a conflicted society in the form of resolutions, mandated Special Rapporteurs,[7] Special Representatives, and inclusion in thematic oversight in addition to review by treaty bodies, a substantive narrative already exists in the international/national context about the form and nature of violations that have taken place. This narrative reveals a fundamental structural problem, namely, that certain kinds of bodily harm are elevated over others in terms of their perceived seriousness. Thus, violence toward women often fails to fit the narrow legal categories that dominate the general understanding of serious human rights violations,[8] and normal pervasive sexual and physical violence against women is simply not counted in the overall narrative of conflict. From the point of view of this analysis, such harms and violence will also be obscured in the conversation about security. If gender-based violence does not figure in the context setting of the "harms to be addressed" and the hierarchy of accountability, it will likely not figure in the priority setting around security, but will remain largely invisible or be seen as irrelevant.

Zarkov and Cockburn (2002) have argued that the postconflict environment, like conflict, is "vividly about male power systems, struggles and identity formation, illustrated through their examination of the impact of peacekeeping on postwar Bosnia-Herzegovina." (id. at 9–21). Moreover, there may be an enormous flux in that male postconflict fraternity, both on an individual and communal level. Men who were in power are losing power, other men are taking their place, and as is often the case when a conflict stalemate arises, internationals (generally culturally and politically differentiated other males) are coming into a society to fill a vacuum. As Handrahan has noted, this "international fraternity—the community of decision makers and experts who arrive after a conflict on a mission of good will—holds the upper hand, morally, economically and politically."[9] However, while the international presence is lauded for rescuing such societies from the worst of their own excesses, what is little appreciated is that such men also bring with them varying aspects of gender norms and patriarchal behavior that are transposed into the vacuum they fill.[10] Moreover, despite an array of cultural differences between locals and internationals, it is frequently overlooked that the internal and external elites share fundamentally similar patriarchal views which operate in tandem to exclude, silence, or nullify women's needs from the transitional space. As Zarkov and Cockburn's edited collection explores, the loosening of rigid gender roles from the social flux that conflict inevitably creates is not necessarily sealed off at a conflict's end or transition by national male leadership, but rather this role is taken up by the male international development community, "whose own sense of patriarchy-as-normal is quite intact." (See also Bennett et al. 1995.)

Security and Transitions from Conflict

When one starts by challenging the assumption that women's and men's security are identical in postconflict settings, a variety of standard postconflict approaches become more complex (Caprioli 2004). As research on women's security highlights, there are numerous obstacles in the postconflict and transitional political environment to meaningful security for women. Such obstacles include the lack of a secure physical environment, making it dangerous for women to function in any meaningful sense in the public sphere for fear of harm or a particular vulnerability to sex-based violence unchecked by the formal end of hostilities or the changeover in regime, allied with a lack of political acknowledgment giving credence to a wider and more embracing notion of security beyond a narrow militaristic and state-oriented approach. In parallel, a broader approach to security could function to prevent or ameliorate the systematic emergence in many transitional societies of organized crime and racist or minority-targeted violence in the transitional phase (Center for the Study of Violence and Reconciliation 1998; Ukeje 2001; Xaba 2001). So while the primary purpose of addressing gender security remains to redress the imbalance and distortion produced by dominant security discourses and the policies that accompany them, its broader effects may transform the postconflict environment in unexpected ways.

Strong theoretical challenges have been mounted to the dominance of state-based approaches to security studies by asserting that individual and societal approaches to security can give greater insight into the structural causes of violence and conflict, thereby realigning how the approach to conflict resolution and transition is constructed (Bilgin 2002). From these studies, some central insights are highly relevant to the ideas explored here. Johan Galtung (1969) and Kenneth Boulding (1978) were amongst the first to assert the need to acknowledge both individual and social elements of security. Galtung, in particular, emphasized that peace did not simply mean the absence of war—it was also related to the establishment of the conditions for social justice. His views on violence are particularly convincing here, noting that violence is all those "unavoidable insults to basic human needs, and more generally to *life*, lowering the real level of needs satisfaction below what is potentially possible" (Galtung 1996, 197, emphasis in original). From this he constructs a key distinction between negative and positive peace. He argues that the absence of armed conflict can be defined as negative peace and positive peace means the absence of both direct physical violence and indirect structural and cultural violence.[11]

This position has a strong resonance with the argument advanced here, namely, that in projecting a narrow focus on particular forms of physical violence to the person, the transitional context (and specifically its accountability mechanisms) ignore a much wider range of institutional and structural elements that may cause greater harm to society as a whole and to women in particular. A key element of this critique of the dominant language of security is that emphasis on direct physical violence (generally specific to defined periods of conflict), whether through truth processes or political rhetoric, tends to exclude the broader relevance of the language of security for women (Ní Aoláin 2006, 829). For many women, the relationship between the physical violence experienced during conflict (noting that the term will be broadly understood) and the security of the postconflict environment are not discontinuous realities, but rather part of one singular experience that is not compartmentalized. Furthermore, recent work suggests that violence against women not only persists, but "even increases beyond pre-war levels and sometimes even beyond wartime levels" (Pankhurst 2007). Thus, accountability for violence may not have the same end point for women in the postconflict/transitional environment as it may have for male combatants or male political actors. This central insight ought to profoundly redefine how we come to determine what constitutes security in the postconflict environment and whose securities are being advanced by narrow as opposed to a broad definition.

Some inroads are being made on the traditionally narrow and state-oriented view that security discourse belongs to and is only really about the state. For example, the Commission on Human Security (2003) has started to move the discourse to a more inclusive basis, beginning with the premise that achieving human security requires not only protection, but also a strategy to empower people to support themselves.[12] A real and pressing question is whether we consider massive economic deprivation as a security threat, particularly when those made most vulnerable in most societies as a result of such deprivations are women and children. Notably, the former Secretary-General of the UN has stated in his report, *The Rule of Law and Transitional Justice in Conflict and Post-Conflict Societies*, that the relationship between massive economic deprivation and violence needs to be more carefully considered in transitional processes.[13]

The starting point is to understand the centrality of security as a concept for individual and community well-being. Significant debates are ongoing concerning the definition of security.[14] Two divergent starting points offer themselves. First, there is a broad concept of security that encompasses physical, social, economic, and sexual security. This essay asserts that when all these securities are combined in a manner that elevates and affirms the experience and relevance of gender, then gendered security is achievable. This method is identified as a process of "regendering" security. In this view, gendered security can be seen as an umbrella that brings together a wide set of institutions and structures that guarantee security within the state. In this approach, reform would be linked to democratic transformation, a broader transformation that is based on equality principles of multiple legal spheres and contains a redistributive economic dimension. While these goals may seem wider than the narrow set of imperatives that have traditionally dominated transitional justice discourse, there is increasing recognition that a failure to address the broader demand for economic and political transformation can have profoundly disabling and limiting effects on the capacity for accountability in the traditional transitional justice mode.

Some scholars have identified cultural elements as the most substantive barrier to security, but the analysis contained in this essay has suggested the cultural evaluation ought to include reflection on the ingrained patriarchies that international interface and oversight brings to transitional societies, and should not be presumed to apply to "native" culture only (Dirlik 1987; Mayer 1985; and Wall 1995).[15] Research has also identified the organic link between a lack of gender security and entrenched structures of inequality and discrimination (Tickner 2005). Others have focused on the prevalence of violence that women in transitional societies experience, both in the public and private spheres. Such research confirms that meaningful security and equality for women will not be achieved by simply placing barriers to state (or public) violence directed against them; rather, fundamentally transformative action against violence and its underlying causes in the private sphere must be part of the transformative project.

Conclusion—A New Paradigm of Gendered Security

The dominant theme in much policy work addressing postconflict security reform evidences a dominant narrative of masculinity pervading security sector reform analysis. This metanarrative is also linked to a pervasive emphasis on what is deemed to constitute the core elements of the security sector in such societies. Typically the emphasis on certain providers of security (military, police, intelligence agencies, state security, paramilitary organizations, and border guards) continues to emphasize the public providers of security and fails to engage with the broader sites and causes of harms, including private violence experienced by women. Moreover, what is seen as progress in security parlance may actually simply not respond in any way to the need for mainstreaming, integrating, or cross-cutting gender into security reform. Thus, for example, some contributions speak positively to the advances made by integrating defense reform, police reform, and judicial sector reform under an integrated umbrella—instigating "a holistic approach to the provision of security, integrating all the relevant institutions and their connections"—but gender or other marginal voices are not integrated in any way (Brzoska 2003, 5). From a feminist perspective, security reform in this holistic model could actually serve to perpetuate and extend structural patriarchies rather then unpick and replace them.

This blind spot or imperviousness is, in part, created by the nexus of complementary patriarchies as they present between local and international actors. As one pays attention to the import of patriarchy derived from international oversight and/or intervention and its social, political, and legal interaction with local patriarchies, it becomes apparent that the lack of attention to gender is a common ground on which male elites feel comfortable. The international community occupies a complex role in postconflict societies, evidenced by the interplay between Western and local masculinities. Its role is particularly heightened as the perceived guarantor of security and stability, though as the analysis explores, such presence or support may not be synonymous with gender security.

In conclusion, and taking a lead from the International Center for Transitional Justice's analytical approach to truth commissions, it is valuable to ask why we need to specifically pay attention to gender when engaging in security reform. As the ICTJ's Report noted, this attention is required because "dominant hierarchies will marginalize women's priorities, interests and participation"; they will "render invisible the gendered patterns and structures" that accompany (in this case) security reform. Identifying the pervasiveness of this invisibility for women highlights the likelihood of substantial resistance to a transformative vision of security and security reform. As Farr notes, "those who wield power within violent and exclusionary structures will [not] easily give it up" (Farr 2004). It is also evident that strategies to rectify such exclusion require broad and transformative approaches addressing the social reality of women's inequality and the violence that pervades normality for many. Only when such broader contextualization becomes part of the "fix," in step with micro schemes and strategies to transform the security context, will gender security be effectively realized for women.

NOTES

1. Gender expert in Kabul, quoted in "Human Rights Watch, Killing You Is a Very Easy Thing for Us: Human Rights Abuses in Southern Afghanistan," *Afghanistan* 15: 5 (July 2003):73.

2. Some of the ideas in it are drawn from Fionnuala Ní Aoláin, "Women, Security, and the Patriarchy of Internationalized Transitional Justice," *Human Rights Quarterly* 31: 4 (2009):1055–1085.

3. These exclusions remain despite UN Security Council Resolutions 1325 (2000) and 1820 (2008).

4. An example from the Palestinian/Israeli context was the Oslo, Cairo, Wye River, and the U.S.-backed "Roadmap" negotiations, which did not include women. Two Israeli women participated in the nonstate sanctioned Geneva Accord of 2003.

5. High Commissioner's Office in Bosnia; Implementation Force (IFOR) and the Stabilisation Force (SFOR) in Bosnia; Interim Authority in Kosovo; United Nations Transitional Authority in Cambodia (UNTAC) in Cambodia.

6. For a review of the effects of such integration in a variety of postconflict and health-related programs, see Barker and Ricardo 2005.

7. See, for example, the United Nations interface with Guatemala, where between 1982 and 1986 the Commission on Human Rights mandated a Special Rapporteur to study the human rights situation in the country. This was followed in 1987 by a replacement mandate—a Special Representative of the Commission to receive and evaluate information from the government on the implementation of human rights protection measures included in the new Constitution of 1985.

8. For example, it is relatively recently that the European Court of Human Rights has interpreted the ECHR prohibition on torture to include the experience of rape. See Aydin v. Turkey—Application No. 23178/94, Judgment of 15 Apr. 1997 (see Radacic 2008).

9. Id. at 433.

10. See Lesley Abdela Kosova, "Missed Opportunities, Lessons for the Future" (2000), Report on file with author (Report of the former Deputy-Director, NGO, Civil Society Building for the OSCE Mission–Kosova [1999]). Details the consistent lack of integration of women and gender-related issues into the planning of the Interim Arrangements for Kosova. See also Human Rights Watch, *Not on the Agenda: The Continuing Failure to Address Accountability in Kosovo Post-March 2004*—available at http://www.hrw.org/en/node/11308/

11. Id. at 32.

12. Commission on Human Security, *Human Security Now* (2003), available at http://www.humansecurity-chs.org/finalreport/English/FinalReport.pdf.

13. Report of the Secretary-General on the rule of law and transitional justice in conflict and postconflict societies, S/2004/616, at page x.

14. These divergent views have a very specific effect on the articulations of policy and practice in the area of security sector reform outlined in Part IV infra.

15. See also Galtung (1990), who defined cultural violence as those mechanisms which render both direct violence and structural violence acceptable.

REFERENCES

Abdela Kosova, Lesley. "Missed Opportunities, Lessons for the Future" (2000), Report on file with author (Report of the former Deputy-Director, NGO, Civil Society Building for the OSCE Mission–Kosova [1999]).

Anderson, Kirsten 2008. "Violence against Women: State Responsibilities in International Human Rights Law to Address Harmful 'Masculinities.'" *Netherlands Quarterly of Human Rights* 26(2):173–197.

Barker, Gary, and Christine Ricardo. 2005. "Young Men and the Construction of Masculinity in Sub-Saharan Africa: Implications for HIV/AIDS, Conflict, and Violence." World Bank, 26 *Social Development Papers*.

Bell, Christine. 2008. *On the Law of Peace: Peace Agreements and the Lex Pacificatoria*. Oxford: Oxford University Press.

Bell, Christine, Colin Colm Campbell, and Fionnuala Ni Aoláin. 2004. "Justice Discourses in Transition." *Social and Legal Studies* 13(3):305–328.

Bell, Christine, and Catherine O'Rourke. 2010. "Peace Agreements or Pieces of Paper? The Impact of UNSC Resolution 1325 on Peace Processes and Their Agreements." *International and Comparative Law Quarterly* 59(4):941–980.

Bennett, Olivia, Jo Bexle, and Kitty Warnock. 1995. *Arms to Fight, Arms to Protect: Women Speak Out about Conflict*. London: Panos Publications.

Bilgin, Pinar. 2002. "Individual and Societal Dimensions of Security." *International Studies Review* 5:203–222.

Boulding, Kenneth. 1978. *Stable Peace*. Austin, Tex.: University of Texas Press.

Brzoska, Michael. 2003. "Development Donors and the Concept of Security Sector Reform." Geneva Ctr. for the Democratic Control of Armed Forces, Occasional Paper No. 4.

Caprioli, Caprioli. 2004. "Democracy and Human Rights versus Women's Security: A Contradiction." *Security Dialogue* 35(4):411–428.

Center for the Study of Violence and Reconciliation. 1988. *Into the Heart of Darkness: Journeys of the Amagents in Crime, Violence and Death* (Johannesburg: Council for Scientific and Industrial Research, 1998).

Chodorow, Nancy. 1994. *Femininities, Masculinities, Sexualities: Freud and Beyond, The Blazer Lectures*. Lexington, Ky.: University Press of Kentucky.

Commission on Human Security, *Human Security Now* (2003), available at http://www.humansecurity-chs.org/finalreport/English/FinalReport.pdf.

Connell, Raewyn. 1987. *Gender and Power: Society, the Person, and Sexual Politics*. Cambridge, U.K.: Polity Press in association with B. Blackwell.

Dirlik, Arif. 1987. "Culturalism as Hegemonic Ideology and Liberating Practice." *Cultural Critique* 6:13–50.

Farr, Vanessa. 2004. "Voices from the Margins." In *Security Sector Reform: Potentials and Challenges for Conflict Transformation*, edited by Clem McCartney, Martina Fischer, and Oliver Wils. Berghof Handbook Dialogue Series No. 2.

Galtung, Johan. 1969. "Violence, Peace and Peace Research." *Journal of Peace Research* 6 (167): 291–305.

———. 1996. *Peace by Peaceful Means: Peace and Conflict, Development and Civilization.* New York: Sage.

Handrahan, Lori. 2004. "Conflict, Gender, Ethnicity and Post-Conflict Reconstruction." *Security Dialogue* 35:433.

Human Rights Watch. *Not on the Agenda: The Continuing Failure to Address Accountability in Kosovo Post-March 2004*, available at http://www.hrw.org/en/node/11308/

International Center for Transitional Justice, Truth Commissions and Gender: Principles, Policies and Procedures. 2009, found at http://ictj.org/publication/truth-commissions-and-gender-principles-policies-and-procedures

Kendall-Tackett, Kathleen A., Sarah M. Giacomoni, and Civic Research Institute. 2007. *Intimate Partner Violence.* Kingston, N.J.: Civic Research Institute.

Mayer, Ann Elizabeth. 1995. "Cultural Particularism as a Bar to Women's Rights: Reflections on the Middle Eastern Experience." In *Women's Rights, Human Rights: International Feminist Perspectives*, edited by Julie Peters and Andrea Wolper, 176–188. New York: Routledge.

Ní Aoláin, Fionnuala. 2006. "Political Violence and Gender in Times of Transition." *Columbia J. Gender & Law* 15:829–849.

———. 2009. "Women, Security, and the Patriarchy of Internationalized Transitional Justice." *Human Rights Quarterly* 31(4):1055–1085.

Ní Aoláin, Fionnuala, Dina Haynes, and Naomi Cahn. 2011. *On the Frontlines: Gender, War and the Post-Conflict Process.* Oxford: Oxford University Press.

Pankhurst, Donna. 2007. "Post-War Backlash Violence against Women: What Can Masculinity Explain?" In *Gendered Peace: Women's Struggles for Post-War Justice and Reconciliation*, edited by Donna Pankhurst. New York: Routledge.

Radacic, Ivana. 2008. "Rape Cases in the Jurisprudence of the European Court of Human Rights: Defining Rape and Determining the Scope of the State's Obligations." *European Human Rights Law Review* 357–375.

Rees, Madeline. 2002. "International Intervention in Bosnia-Herzegovina: The Cost of Ignoring Gender." In *The Post-War Moment: Militaries, Masculinities and International Peacekeeping*, edited by Dubravka Zarkov and Cynthia Cockburn, 51–57. London: Lawrence and Wishart.

Tickner, J. Ann. 1992. *Gender in International Relations: Feminist Perspectives on Achieving Global Security.* Series *New Directions in World Politics.* New York: Columbia University Press.

———. 2005. *The Rule of Law and Transitional Justice in Conflict and Post-Conflict Societies: Report of the Secretary-General to the Security Council* (S/2011/634) (Aug. 23, 2004).

Ukeje, Charles. 1001. "Youths, Violence and the Collapse of Public Order in the Niger Delta of Nigeria." *African Development* 26(1–2):337–366.

Wali, Sima. 1995. "Human Rights for Refugee and Displaced Women." In *Women's Rights, Human Rights: International Feminist Perspectives*, edited by Julie Peters and Andrea Wolper, 335–344. New York: Routledge.

Xaba, Thokozani. 2001. "Masculinity and Its Malcontents: Confrontation between 'Struggle Masculinity' and 'Post-Struggle Masculinity' (1990–1997)." In *Changing Men in Southern Africa*, edited by Robert Morrell. London: University of Natal Press/Zed Books.

Zarkov, Dubravka, and Cynthia Cockburn. 2002. *The Post-War Moment: Militaries, Masculinities and International Peacekeeping*. London: Lawrence and Wishart.

3

Gendering Insecurities, Informalization, and "War Economies"

V. SPIKE PETERSON

Essentially, the fragmentation and informalization of war is paralleled by the informalization of the economy. (Kaldor 1999/2001, 104)

The phenomenon of the informal economy is both deceivingly simple and extraordinarily complex, trivial in its everyday manifestations and capable of subverting the economic and political order of nations. (Portes and Haller 2005, 403)

David Roberts (2008) observes that defining human security is more contentious than defining human *in*security (also Burke 2007). Like many others, Roberts draws on diverse literatures referencing institutional, indirect, or structural violence to generate a definition of *in*security as "avoidable civilian deaths, occurring globally, caused by social, political and economic institutions and structures, built and operated by humans and which could feasibly be changed" (2008, 28). Indirect or structural violence refers to the presumably unintended but recurring patterns of suffering or harm that result from the way social institutions or structures "order" expectations, norms, and practices.[1] "War" is arguably a display of structural violence at its extremity. Feminists have produced incisive accounts of how in/security, violence, conflicts, and wars are pervasively gendered.[2] But existing analyses tend to focus on masculinist identities and ideologies in the context of embodied and "political" forms of violence, leaving aside how these are inextricably linked to economic phenomena.

This tendency to conceptualize politics and economics as "separable" has a long history, and is exacerbated by disciplinary divisions institutionalized in higher education. Nonetheless, it serves us poorly, and is especially problematic for making sense of contemporary global conditions.[3] In the late twentieth century, structural changes in the capacity of state governments to "manage" national economies compelled International Relations (IR) scholars to rethink the relationship between states and markets, politics, and economics. One effect was the consolidation in the 1970s of a subfield characterized as International Political Economy (IPE).[4]

While IPE scholars go some way toward integrating the study of political and economic dimensions of global dynamics, their inquiries remain limited. On the one hand, a divide between IR focused on "security" and IPE focused on "global economics" continues to forestall holistic, systemic analyses. On the other hand, feminist contributions continue to be marginalized in both fields of inquiry. IR and IPE scholars occasionally include sex as a variable, in effect, "adding women" (treating gender as an *empirical* category) to existing frameworks. But they rarely acknowledge gender as an *analytical* category, in effect, ignoring the *theoretical* implications of gender as a governing code. Indeed, addressing this feminist insight would challenge the foundational assumptions and existing frameworks of IR and IPE.[5]

The importance of such conceptual reframing is forcefully articulated by feminist IR scholars Marianne Marchand and Anne Sisson Runyan in their Introduction to the second edition of *Gender and Global Restructuring* (2011b). They note that since the events of September 11, 2001, feminists increasingly draw connections between the economics of neoliberal globalization and the heightened militarism and imperialism of President Bush's "war on terror" (2011b, 2). Reflecting on terminological choices, Marchand and Runyan sideline the more familiar "globalization" in favor of "global restructuring," which better addresses the "fraternal twins" of neoliberal economic globalization and neoimperial political/military domination (2011b, 6). In their words, "the concept of global restructuring takes us beyond a narrow economistic view of (neoliberal) globalization and instead emphasizes a multidimensional, interconnected and profound set of transformations" that include "new security dimensions" (2011b, 2). In addition to urging a merger of economic and political analyses, Marchand and Runyan observe the "deep recognition in transnational feminist thinking of the close and complex relations between 'the intimate' and 'the global'" (2011b, 6).

With these points as background, I attempt in this chapter to pursue the following questions: How are economic practices—especially, informal activities—and forms of political violence *interconnected*? How are both neoliberal globalization and militarized conflicts *gendered*, and hence, how might feminist analyses of Global Political Economy (GPE) advance feminist (IR) analyses of war and global *in*securities? In particular, I am interested in exploring how global restructuring in recent decades—characterized here as the ideology and practices of neoliberalism imposed worldwide—shapes conditions of direct *and* indirect (structural) violence, manifested in relatively "new" patterns of militarized conflict and war (Kaldor 1999/2001, 2006).

The most visible insecurities in this context are widening economic gaps between the rich minority global North and the poor majority global South.[6] Some of these inequalities play a role in initiating and/or exacerbating violent "political" conflicts. At the same time, neoliberal globalization erodes the autonomy of states. It thus alters their ability to regulate internal activities, advance public welfare, and/or ensure public order through conventional modes of centralized, legitimate, governmental authority. In these senses, deteriorating economic conditions and the inequalities they generate are inextricably linked to political practices and the insecurities they entail.

Hence, what I attempt in this chapter is to illuminate connections among the following: the structural violence constituted by neoliberal economic restructuring; the scale and significance of *economic* informalization, especially in relation to inequalities and attendant insecurities; the implications of *political* informalization, especially in relation to violent conflicts constituting "new wars"; and gender-sensitive research on economic *and* political informalization as processes that together shape the resolution or continuation of conflict conditions. This feminist lens permits additional angles of vision: it illuminates not only economic conditions within and outside of households, but also how power relations operate from "the intimate" to "the global" level by shaping who does what work and how all work is gendered and differentially valorized. Given the vast terrain of these topics, my attempt can only be preliminary and partial. I explore an arguably novel blend of particular literatures with the hope of generating insights of potentially wider significance.

I first discuss informalization, the expansion of informal—unregulated, unofficial—economic activities, and why this development is significant economically (due to expanding inequalities), politically (due to expanding insecurities) and analytically (due to posing gendered quandaries). My focus then turns to the literature on "new wars" and ways in which these reconfigure security issues, especially in relation to informal and especially underground or black market activities. The next section provides a brief review of the implications of such illicit activities in conflicts and "war economies." I then distinguish among "coping, combat, and criminal" types of informal activities variously operating in conflict zones. This framework affords me a way to systematically compare the agents, motivations, and activities of each, their gendering, and their potential positive or negative implications for resolving militarized conflicts.

Informalization and Insecurities in Today's Global Economy

Growth in the number of informal-sector and women workers is the centerpiece of global restructuring. (Ward 1990, 2)

Contemporary neoliberalism gives particular meanings to human activity through the choices it provides, the regulatory ideals it imposes and the identities it prescribes as most suitable. (Griffin 2009, 8)

Understanding the current expansion of informal activities requires familiarity with neoliberal ideology and practices that have shaped global restructuring since the 1970s.[7] In brief, neoliberalism combines the tenets of neoclassical economics, which champion individual market rationality and the efficiency of private enterprise, with those of classical political liberalism, which champion the separation of politics from economics and the minimum of public/governmental power. Late twentieth-century neoliberalism takes this to the global level, promoting "unfettered global markets and a consumer-based individualistic ethic which transcends national communities" (Tooze 1997, 227).

The market reforms promoted by neoliberalism were initially characterized as supply-side economics or "the Washington consensus." Some favor the label "market fundamentalism," which draws attention to what critics deem inappropriate reliance on "free market" principles to address not only economic but also social and political issues. While recurring and escalating financial crises spur extensive critiques, neoliberal principles continue to dominate economic thinking and practice. As Penny Griffin observes, the recent post-Washington consensus "Second Generation Reform" is hardly less market-centered than its predecessor, "the difference being that it is simply more concerned to acknowledge and remedy 'market imperfections'" (2009, 10). Despite devastating crises and global economic turbulence, neoliberal policies are at best being mildly reformed, but are not being fundamentally challenged or transformed today.

The concept of "liberalization" that pervades neoliberal discourse is understood as minimizing government interventions in business activities and hence enabling the "free" circulation of ideas, capital, and goods worldwide. Policy reforms are variously aimed at relaxing or eliminating state-based restrictions: deregulation (to remove existing regulatory constraints); privatization (to replace public ownership and control); and greater free trade (to ensure more open borders). Complementing these supply-side reforms are fiscal and monetary "stabilization policies" claimed to reduce government spending and deficits. Finally, national specialization in economic activities is promoted, assuming that countries as units enjoy comparative advantages, and export-oriented policies are favored for economic development and growth.

Historical, sociocultural, and geopolitical differences shape the implementation and implications of neoliberal policies. While the effects are therefore not uniform, some patterns are widely acknowledged. In a snapshot: deregulation, liberalization, and privatization have reduced most states' capacity for and/or commitment to social welfare provisioning. At the same time, these policies have fueled "flexibilized" production processes, undercut the power of organized labor, exacerbated un- and underemployment (especially of men), and deepened economic inequalities within and between nations.[8] With flexibilization, we observe a global "*feminization* of work": simultaneously an embodied transformation of work practices (more women working), a deterioration of labor conditions (more insecure, precarious jobs, as had been always true of women's work), and a reconfiguration of worker identities (more female breadwinners).[9]

Flexibilization and feminization also relate to informalization, since downsizing, outsourcing, and subcontracting processes shift production toward less formal (secure, regulated) work conditions. This increases the insecurity of the global majority, who face limited options in their pursuit of income generation and survival resources. As economic restructuring and financial crises reduce the availability of "decent jobs"—formal, secure, safe work—more and more people are working wherever and however they can; hence, the global expansion of informal activities. The "feminization" of these activities is registered by their devalued status and the structural vulnerability of those who do this poorly paid work: women, migrants, the urban "underclass," youth, and the poorest populations worldwide.

Informality refers to work that occurs outside of formal (official, recorded) market operations and hence eludes government regulation and taxation.[10] Until recently, accounting for this work was of little interest to economists, who tend to focus on official, recorded market transactions. They also expected informality to wane with state development and modern industrialization. Today, however, most observers agree that informality is a central dynamic of the world economy: it shapes the resource-pooling and survival strategies of households worldwide, constitutes the primary source of income generation and new job growth in the global South, and has expanded dramatically in the global North.[11]

Mainstream analyses of informality are constrained by reliance on the dominant positivist and masculinist conceptual premises of neoclassical economics.[12] In particular, orthodox accounts assume that formal and informal activities are non-overlapping categories; treat clandestine or criminal types of informal activities as a separate area of inquiry; and exclude the unpaid domestic labor of social reproduction. These assumptions are too restrictive to adequately analyze the global politics of informalization. To acknowledge a wider range of activities and take women's work seriously, I consider informal activities as existing along a *continuum* of distinctions (unpaid reproductive labor; nonstandard, "irregular" work; illicit revenue generation) without presuming discrete categories. This captures how deteriorating conditions of work and changing regulatory frameworks increasingly expose the pretense of clear boundaries.[13] It also builds on feminist arguments regarding the *economic* significance of the unpaid but socially necessary labor of social reproduction.

Social reproduction refers to activities in support of ensuring the daily and generational continuity of individuals and collectivities. Access to market, community, and public resources shapes the conditions of social reproduction, but most of the *work* involved is unpaid, assigned to women, and situated in or near households. Feminists argue that economic theory is impoverished by its failure to account for this labor and its structural importance. This "domestic" work sustains reproductive processes (upon which society depends), produces intangible social assets (upon which market activities depend), and significantly shapes the quality and quantity of labor, goods, services, and financial assets available (e.g., through production, consumption, savings, intergenerational transmission of assets). In effect, (unpaid) household labor underpins and articulates with (paid) work—both formal and informal—so that counting the former is necessary for generating adequate accounts of the latter.

I refer to "households" (rather than families) as basic economic units to emphasize the *pooling* of material and nonmaterial resources from multiple activities to ensure well-being and reproduction of social groups (which may or may not be kinship based) over time.[14] As an effect of neoliberal restructuring, public resources devoted to welfare provisioning decline just when the need for such support grows. Loss of cash income increases pressure on nonmonetized (unpaid) work to ensure household survival. These entwined developments reveal tensions between state capacities, patterns of capital accumulation, and the viability of households as basic socioeconomic units.

Feminists identify a *crisis of social reproduction* as pressure increases to ensure the survival of households in deteriorating economic conditions.[15] It is primarily women who are expected to make up the difference between human needs—emotional, physical, economic—and decreasing resources from monetized income, public welfare, or community transfers. But as the limits to human capacity are reached, social reproduction is threatened. The current downturn compounds these dynamics.

If we assume an extensive, inclusive continuum of informal work, the majority will involve domestic, subsistence activities in support of household reproduction and "irregular," small-scale entrepreneurial activities, such as scavenging, street vending, home-based production, and petty trade. These forms of work are rarely considered illegal, though in practice the distinction between licit and illicit is increasingly difficult to establish. By definition, income generated through underground, illegal, or black market activities avoids being recorded, taxed, or regulated, and so falls within the continuum of informality. Illicit economic activities have a long history and today constitute big business on a global scale; they are an underrecognized aspect of militarized conflicts.

A key insight is that economic informalization and *political* informalization (weak or eroded state capacity) are often interconnected. Political informalization appears most frequently in the IR literature on "fragile" or "failed states," where it is typically assumed that these pose a variety of risks: as potential sites of political violence, criminal organizations, or even terrorist activities (Di John 2010, 10–11). Any state weakened by economic restructuring, unstable regimes, or militarized conflict is less able to control informal and even criminal activities. These activities may become war-profiteering opportunities and sources of combat funding that fuel conflicts and complicate their resolution. Moreover, recent scholarship suggests that states have an ambivalent attitude toward informal activities, and do not always wish to eliminate even those that are clearly criminal. There are various reasons why states may be selective in how they enforce prohibitions, manipulate crime statistics or report "terrorist" activities (Friman 2009; Andreas and Greenhill 2010).

In sum, informalization is *economically* important because of its global scale, its implications for working conditions, wages, profits, and tax revenues, and its effects on resource distribution within and among nation-states. Informal and formal work together to produce patterns of monetized income, household strategies of resource-pooling, and people's capacity for social reproduction. Informalization typically places downward pressure on formal wages, increasing the *in*security of jobs, income, and household survival.

Informalization is *politically* important because it complicates public policymaking and alters power relations. In all states, effective policies depend on accurate estimates of various economic activities, and informalization thwarts reliable recording and measurement. Unregulated work practices pose safety, health, and environmental risks; criminal activities thwart public interests in law and order; and diminished state ability to sustain legitimate forms of order threatens the security of all, though not homogeneously. The insecurities that informalization increases in turn shape whether and how political and even militarized conflicts occur.

Informalization is *analytically* important because it exposes prevailing accounts as inadequate and challenges foundational gendered dichotomies about work and value. It defies theorists' expectations that informal activities would fade as industrial capitalism matured. Informalization remains key to analyzing the intersectionality of structural inequalities. In effect, it constitutes devalued (feminized) work and hierarchies of gender, ethnicity/race, class, and nation which then shape which devalued (feminized) workers are most likely to be doing it: the poor, ethnic minorities, women, youth, migrants, the urban underclass, and the global South. Informalization thus offers a productive lens for "seeing" how power operates to reproduce structural inequalities. These are all gendered processes, frequently entail insecurities, and variously shape conflicts. In the next section I consider those particular insecurities fueled by the diminishing ability of states to regulate economic and political activities more generally, and the conduct of war more specifically.

Rethinking "War" and Human In/Securities

Political violence at the beginning of the twenty-first century is more omnipresent, more directed at civilians, involves a blurring of the distinctions between war and crime, and is based on and serves to foment divisive identity politics—these are the characteristics of "new wars." (Kaldor 2006, ix)

Criminality is a major characteristic of new wars. (Mittelman 2009, 170)

How to understand and potentially transform "war" is the central question of International Relations (IR) inquiry, and it points to how war changes over time. A proliferation of violent "civil conflicts" in the late twentieth century prompted many to reconsider what "war" is. Mary Kaldor (1999/2001, 2006) coined the term "new wars," arguing that the dominant modality of warfare has changed and demands fundamental rethinking.[16]

For Kaldor, a key difference is that "new wars involve a blurring of distinctions between war . . . , organized crime . . . and large-scale violations of human rights" (2). Kaldor distinguishes earlier from new wars in terms of goals, methods, and financing (6–12). First, the goals of warfare now feature "identity politics"—claims to power based on an identity that is relatively delinked from statecentric interests and tends to be exclusivist and nostalgic, rather than cosmopolitan and aspirational. Such identity politics displaces earlier territorially based geopolitical objectives. Significantly, the "new wave of identity politics is both local and global, national as well as transnational." It is facilitated by new technologies, which enhance the speed and spatial dispersion of political mobilizations (7).

Second, the methods of warfare have shifted from earlier vertically organized, centralized state-based units that were appropriate for gaining and securing physical territories to ones that are horizontally organized, involve strategies of guerrilla warfare, and feature decentralized actors who attempt to control populations by sowing fear and hatred, as well as by the literal expulsion of "Others." A prominent effect is dramatic increases in human rights violations and civilian casualties.

Third, the war economy has shifted from statecentric to decentralized and external resources. This relates to the structural changes due to neoliberal globalization discussed above: increasing unemployment, expanding the informal economy, decreasing tax revenues, and facilitating transnational flows of licit and illicit resources. These processes erode the autonomy of the state and its ability to control violence. Neoliberal policies "provided an environment for growing criminalization and the creation of networks of corruption" (Kaldor 1999/2001, 83). The effects are devastating for democratic processes and the pursuit of a global cosmopolitan project.[17]

Militarized conflicts today *vary* in how, and to what extent, they exhibit these dynamics. War conditions keep changing, and in her 2006 preface Kaldor acknowledges a decline in wars and war-related deaths since 1999.[18] She contends, however, that insecurity has increased since 9/11 and that key claims regarding "new wars" are even more pertinent in the twenty-first century. In her words:

What the international community has succeeded in doing is freezing conflicts, in stabilizing the level of war-related violence. However, in most conflict-affected regions, there are still high levels of human rights violations and crime; a variety of armed actors remain at large; there is high unemployment and a large informal or illegal economy; and very little has been done to confront identity politics. (2006, x)

However much actual wars vary, all conflicts today *do* take place in a global context profoundly shaped by neoliberal policies that exacerbate inequalities, insecurities, and the decline of centralized state governance and control. Here I turn to consider the gendered linkages between licit and illicit informal activities and how these relate to the conduct and conclusion of militarized conflicts.

Illicit Informality and Conditions of War

As crime and security come to govern ever-wider policy domains, including migration, finance, and health, there has arguably never been a more pressing time to consider the international political economy (IPE) of crime. (De Goede 2009, 104)

We know that patterns of resource distribution are key to both "causes" of conflict (e.g., fueling resentments and militarizing demands for redistribution) and capacities for sustaining conflict (e.g., supplying and financing militarized activities). The new wars literature argues that in intra- rather than international wars, funding is not simply a matter of formal military budgets. In civil conflicts, self-financing is an issue for combatants and is secured through formal as well as informal work (licit and illicit), and through partnerships with armed groups, arms suppliers, organized crime, and corrupt governments. Increasingly, security analysts need to track *licit and illicit* economic activities and resource flows to better understand the causes, conduct, and consequences of conflicts, and to identify effective crime- and conflict-reducing policies.

Informal activities, by definition, pose tremendous challenges for reliable assessment and yet militarized globalization has, ironically, generated interest in better accounting of what violence costs. One reason is increasing awareness of illicit practices as routine features of low-intensity conflicts, civil wars, and terrorist activities.[19] Indeed, since 9/11 illicit activities have assumed a key role in the study of "war economies." These studies suggest new questions about informalization and its effects on human security (e.g., linking illicit trade in drugs or arms with military strategies and outcomes). In addition, they provide crucial empirical data on the key players in, motivations for, and profits generated by informal activities in times of conflict. Finally, they may begin to explain how national and transnational policies enable or constrain informalization and illicit activities. This growing literature explores the interaction of what Zartman (2005) calls "need, creed, and greed" in contemporary conflicts.[20] The shared starting point of these studies is that modalities of warfare are profoundly altered by globalization processes, especially in their economic dimensions.

This literature foregrounds what Andreas (2004, 641) calls the "illicit international political economy" (IIPE; also Friman and Andreas 1999; Naim 2005). In addition to clandestine provision of war-making *materials* (equipment), illicit activities such as trafficking in drugs, sex workers, migrants, dirty money, and black market goods provide the *financing* necessary for war. These markets defy territorial boundaries and state-based legal regimes; they are increasingly regional and even global. Deregulation amplifies opportunities for criminal networking activities and money laundering. This burgeoning research suggests patterns of gendered insecurity change as informal, "shadow," or underground economies are expanding, and provide supplies and financing for conflict activities (Le Billon et al. 2002; Ballentine and Sherman 2003; Jung 2003). Boundaries distinguishing licit from illicit activities blur as criminal, corporate, and corrupt governmental interests converge (Ruggiero 2000; Duffield 2001; Naylor 2002). International regulatory regimes raise legal issues as national security interests connect war-fighting and crime-fighting (Andreas 2003; Andreas and Price 2001). Regional, systemic conditions gain prominence as key determinants of local conflicts and longer-term prospects for social stability (Le Billon et al. 2002; Pugh and Cooper 2004).

On the whole, this research supports Kaldor's claim that neoliberal policies guiding *economic* globalization are having deleterious, indeed disastrous, *political* effects by exacerbating corruption, criminality, and militarized conflict. Informalization and illicit activities increase as the centralized power, regulatory capacity, and public accountability of states is eroded in favor of unaccountable decentralized markets, private interest networks, and international agencies. Where conflict emerges, there are powerful incentives for seeking, and many opportunities for securing, resources and profits through both licit and illicit informal activities. Centralized governments weakened by economic restructuring and/or protracted conflict are less able, and sometimes also insufficiently motivated, to prioritize law and order. In militarized conflicts where effective public control and authority are limited, post-conflict reconstruction may be continually undermined by established networks of private, often illicit, resource provision. In short, a disturbing trend is emerging in which new forms of violence are becoming endemic when the processes of economic and political informalization converge.[21]

Coping, Combat, and Criminal Informal Economies

From this literature I draw more specific insights regarding the gender dynamics of war economies and the insecurities they generate. Relying on Pugh and Cooper (2004), I posit three subgroupings of informalization found in conflict zones. These "coping, combat, and criminal economies" are overlapping and interdependent; they interact with each other and are structurally linked to "regular," formal economies.[22] Each has distinctive tendencies in what motivates the agents, who these agents are, and what the primary activities of each economy are. I provide only an abbreviated sketch of the three economies here, where my objective is to suggest how they are gendered and what this might mean for feminist analyses of human security and insecurities.[23]

Informal coping economy. Processes of social reproduction and strategies of family/household survival are central here. Agents are primarily motivated by the need to secure basic (life-sustaining) resources as conflict conditions undermine social stability, erode the formal economy, and disrupt traditional livelihoods. Agents may include individuals, families, households, kin networks, neighborhood communities, or social solidarity groups. As conflicts worsen and/or economic conditions deteriorate, coping strategies may increasingly involve informal and even illicit activities. Possibilities include dealing in black market goods; engaging in sex work and debt bondage; selling organs for transplant; and participating in potentially lucrative but high-risk criminal activities. Agents in this economy have more stakes in ending conflicts than perpetuating them, because they are structurally the most vulnerable and rarely command sufficient resources to prosper much from societal disruption. To what extent these agents are committed to ending conflicts will depend, however, on how they imagine postconflict conditions: What forms of security will be put into place? Will they be sustainable? How will their social reproduction and economic provisioning be affected? What if anything will the formal economy offer them?

This coping economy is obviously feminized, as social reproduction and caring labor are quintessentially women's work. As in nonconflict conditions, more women than men are responsible for sustaining families, households, kinship networks, and even neighborhoods. A global increase in female-headed households exacerbates the pressures on women to generate coping strategies that enable social reproduction, and these pressures increase when war destroys basic infrastructure and traditional labor patterns, still further worsening unemployment and the decline in public welfare and state services. Due to daily risks of conflict conditions as well as masculinized state priorities, women may experience decreasing access to or agency in public spaces. Militarized conditions tend to privilege male desires, entertainment, consumption, education, and employment at women's cost. The heightened masculinization of war zones may also deepen heteropatriarchal attitudes, with effects that vary by culture and context.

For these and other reasons, women may have a particular stake in seeing conflicts concluded. Yet only exceptionally are they recognized as key players or included in political negotiations. Postconflict plans also pay minimal attention to meeting the economic losses and heightened emotional problems of families and households in the aftermath of war and its violence.

Informal combat economy. Activities that involve directly engaging in combat, as well as supplying, supporting, and funding fighters, are central to this economy. Agents are primarily motivated by desire for achieving military objectives. These include armed groups and their political supporters, as well as conflict entrepreneurs who facilitate acquisition of war resources. Activities typically blur licit-illicit boundaries, as combatants turn to a variety of sources. Because of the erosion of central authority and weaker regulatory mechanisms, transborder movement of supplies and financial arrangements are common. Some involve informal, far-flung diasporic connections, while others may even involve transnational organized crime networks. Depending on context, financing a conflict may include looting, theft, smuggling, piracy, kidnapping, trafficking, and other black market activities, aid manipulation, and expropriation of natural resources. In support of military objectives, particular areas or natural resources controlled by opponents may be targeted to undercut their economic power. On the one hand, such agents may resist peace if they anticipate a loss of status or power through negotiations, by losing land or access to other valued resources, or by being shamed, punished, or held accountable for crimes. On the other hand, agents may seek peace if they anticipate postconflict benefits, such as life being less traumatizing, less violent, and more sustainable and jobs and livelihoods being more available and secure. This combat economy is the most obviously masculinized, since defending and fighting "for" families and political identity groups are quintessentially manly pursuits.

This generalization, however, erases the history of female participation in conflicts and obscures the complexity of wartime conditions. The disruptions of war often challenge conventional gendered identities and divisions of labor. Still, in most conflicts the majority of combatants are men, especially young men, for whom battle may mark a transition to fully adult status.[24] The combat economy combines such direct combat activities with funding, supplying, and otherwise facilitating military objectives, where women and older men may be more prominent.

Moreover, feminist studies of nationalism emphasize that idealized constructions of womanhood symbolize the cultural values of a group. In this sense, as identity politics assume greater importance, pressure increases on women to conform to masculinist group expectations with respect to their appearance, demeanor, and social behavior. Not doing so can place women at considerable risk, for example, subjecting them to violent forms of discipline by their identity group. Conforming to their socialization—and especially in militarized contexts—men are more likely to participate in, rather than protest, harsh treatment of these women.

Devaluation of the feminine translates here into silencing, objectifying, violating, assaulting, and even killing women and (feminized, Othered) civilians; discriminating against and often punishing "insufficiently masculine" men; using women as sexual decoys (Eisenstein 2007); abducting women and girls for ransom; trafficking in women and children; and prioritizing masculinized identities, practices, and objectives in the name of military needs. Whether or not combatants have a stake in ending conflict depends critically on their estimated probability of victory, or at least their share of postconflict resources and power. In new wars, the interaction of identity politics and militarized masculinities appears to deepen combatants' resistance to negotiations that promise less than complete victory. Insofar as this is the case, it obviously exacerbates the already significant difficulty of achieving a sustainable peace.

Informal criminal economy. Activities that directly and indirectly supply, finance, and profit from conflict are central to this economy. Agents are primarily motivated by desire for profits. Conflict zones present unique opportunities for this insofar as regulatory mechanisms break down or are suspended, and centralized authority is weakened by war, fractured by political divisions, or disabled by corruption. Agents include petty criminals, conflict entrepreneurs, traffickers, war profiteers, money launderers, and those who produce and/or transport trafficked goods. In most cases, the agents of the criminal and the combat economy interact and even overlap. This is especially likely as conflict continues, when profit making can displace military objectives. Criminal agents may also interact and overlap with the coping economy as individuals and households pursue, or feel forced to engage in, illicit activities as a survival strategy.

Activities in this economy fall outside of state regulation and documentation. They include smuggling, trafficking, predatory lending, aid manipulation, natural resource expropriation, fraud, tax evasion, and money laundering. While understood as a criminal economy, some of these activities straddle the licit-illicit distinction, for example, predatory lending. This economy also tends to be transnational and to involve larger regional activities such as smuggling, trafficking, and supplying arms. Financial arrangements for these purposes may involve money laundering and banking activities outside the country. Agents in this economy resist peace if they expect to lose income, have fewer profit-seeking opportunities, be apprehended, and be held accountable. They may seek peace when they anticipate prosperous postconflict conditions, including long-term investment opportunities, or turning to more profitable legitimate businesses. In the absence of strong central authority and reliable law enforcement, however, Goodhand notes that "there are few incentives for entrepreneurs to make the shift toward longer-term productive activities" (2004, 65).

The criminal economy is more obviously extensive and complex, especially in terms of its financing. Its agents may be variously gendered, depending on cultural context, the activities involved, and where individuals are positioned in criminal networks. The profit-making motive driving this economy reveals how inseparable all three economies are, since coping economies require access to cash or credit as part of survival strategies and combat economies must secure various resources in formal and informal markets powerfully shaped by flows of capital and finance within and beyond the conflict zone. These globally restructured cash flows and markets are not directly under the control of the agents of the three informal economies. These points reinforce Kaldor's key claim that new wars must be understood in the context of globalization: "the intensification of global interconnectedness—political, economic, military and cultural" (Kaldor 1999/2001, 3).

Moreover, the depersonalized, competitive, objectifying, and commodifying dynamics of profit making are arguably no less masculinist than are formal relations of production, political activities, military institutions, and organized crime. At the same time, this informalization disrupts any rigid boundaries between production and reproduction, public and private, licit and illicit, which might exist. In light of this complexity, specifying the gender of any informal economy is complicated and the gendered effects never wholly predictable. To use gender analysis productively, the specifics of context are crucial. Similarly, how and to what extent agents in the criminal economy are invested in prolonging, rather than concluding, new wars will depend on multiple factors and can only be determined through empirical investigation of particular cases.

Conclusion

Feminists have produced telling accounts of gender in relation to security and war. This chapter explored how *economic* phenomena are relevant for analyzing conflicts that are typically addressed solely as *political* phenomena. Across the world, decades of neoliberal ideology and practice have had uneven and contradictory effects. While a small elite benefits in the short run, the long-term pattern is one of increasing inequalities within and between nations. These inequalities constitute *in*securities at all levels from the intimate and local to the national and global. This chapter offered a schematic mapping of informalization as a prominent feature of neoliberal globalization, suggested how global expansion of informality articulates with changing modalities of warfare, and drew linkages between economic and political informalization in conflict zones. Deploying the analytical framework of identifying coping, combat, and criminal informal economies, and specifying how these are gendered, highlights how pervasively and significantly gender shapes the conduct and consequences of war. It also suggests the challenges feminists must confront to analyze and respond effectively to *in*securities shaped by these entwined processes of economic exploitation and political militarization.

NOTES

1. Johan Galtung (1969, 1971) early on articulated "structural violence" as a security issue; recently, the insecurities of human life under contemporary conditions include Agamben's "bare life" (1998) and Butler's "precarity" (2009).

2. The research is now extensive, and well represented in this edited volume. See also Jacobs et al. 2000; Goldstein 2001; Giles and Hyndman 2004; Mazurana, Raven-Roberts, and Parpart 2005; Hunt and Rygiel 2006; Sjoberg 2006; Enloe 2007; Eisenstein 2007; Anderlini 2007; Shepherd 2008; Kaufman and Williams 2010; Sjoberg and Via 2010; and special issues of *International Feminist Journal of Politics* 2001; *Security Dialogue* 2004; *Security Studies* 2009; *Journal of Peacebuilding & Development* 2010.

3. Michael Mann, a prominent scholar of states, war, and capitalism, argues that the lamentable failure of "social scientists . . . to address some of the most fundamental problems of modern society" is in part due to "divid[ing] up reality between different academic disciplines" that have "encouraged each other's worst vices" (1988, vii).

4. To foreground transnational dynamics, I favor referring to the Global Political Economy (GPE). For recent accounts of the field and its varying approaches, see

Abbot and Worth 2002; Peterson 2003; O'Brien and Williams 2007; Miller 2008; Oatley 2010.

5. For feminist critiques of masculinist IR and IPE, see, for example, Tickner 2005; Peterson 2005; Waylen 2006; Griffin 2009.

6. "Global South" and "global North" reference social (not narrowly geographical) locations of vulnerability and privilege respectively. On increasing inequalities within and between nations, see, for example, Cornia 2004; Wade 2004; APSA 2008.

7. The literature here is vast, but accessible overviews and insightful analyses include Stiglitz 2002; Ong 2006; Klein 2007; Peck 2010.

8. From a critical perspective: deregulation has permitted the hypermobility of capital, spurred phenomenal growth in crisis-prone financial markets, and expanded the power of private and corporate capital interests (at the expense of public, collective interests); liberalization is selectively implemented (powerful states choose when to engage in protectionism, while less powerful states lose control over protecting domestic industries, goods produced, and the jobs provided); and privatization has meant a loss of nationalized industries and their potential public benefits, as well as a decrease in public sector employment and welfare service provision. See, for example, Scholte 2005; van Staveren et al. 2007; Peterson and Runyan 2010; Marchand and Runyan 2011a.

9. The "feminization" of economic restructuring has been widely noted and researched, e.g., Standing 1999; Beneria 2003; Peterson 2003; Hoskyns and Rai 2007; Berik et al. 2009. I deploy "feminization" in my work to emphasize the *de*valuation—ideationally *and* materially—of ideas, identities, bodies, practices, skills, etc.—when associated with "the feminine"/femininity. For theoretical elaboration of this claim and its wider application, see Peterson 2007, 2009b.

10. To avoid clumsy phrasing, I use informal activities, informality, and informalization interchangeably in this essay. Controversies regarding how to define, hence measure, and/or interpret the relationship between formal-informal activities pervade the literature. For recent overviews, see Portes and Haller 2005; Fernandez-Kelly and Shefner 2006; Guha-Khasnobis, Kanbur, and Ostrom 2006a. I cannot address definitional debates here, but attempt to do so in Peterson 2010, and through a critical lens on GPE I situate informality in the context of interdependent reproductive, productive, and virtual economies in Peterson 2003; see both for detailed references.

11. On increases in the scale of informal work, see Guha-Khasnobis, Kanbur, and Ostrom 2006b; Chant and Pedwell 2008; ILO 2008; Barta 2009. Gender-sensitive discussions of the financial crisis include Young and Schuberth 2010; *Gender & Development* 2010; Runyan and Marchand 2011.

12. For feminist critiques of orthodox economics, see Hewitson 1999; Barker and Kuiper 2003; Ferber and Nelson 2003; Barker and Feiner 2004; Zein-Elabdin and Charusheela 2004; Kaul 2008; Griffin 2009. See Peterson 2010 for a detailed discussion and literature review of three prevailing approaches to theorizing informality: mainstream, structuralist, and feminist.

13. Guha-Khasnobis, Kanbur, and Ostrom also propose a "continuum," acknowledging how formal-informal are contested but "cannot be suppressed—they are now too well ingrained in the academic and policy discourse" (2006b, 7); see also Fernandez-Kelly and Shefner 2006.

14. My account combines points in Smith and Wallerstein 1992; Dunaway 2001; Douglass 2006. Douglass (2006, 423) deploys the term *"householding"* to underscore how "creating and sustaining a household is a continuous process of social reproduction that covers all life-cycle stages and extends beyond the family." *Global* householding references the many ways in which these processes increasingly occur across national boundaries, for example, through transborder marriages, overseas education, labor migration, and war displacements. On global householding, see the Critical Perspectives section of *Politics & Gender* (2010); Safri and Graham 2010.

15. Bakker and Gill 2003; Hoskyns and Rai 2007; Bakker and Silvey 2008.

16. Security scholars use a variety of terms to capture changing conditions of war: "low intensity conflict," civil war, unconventional warfare, and postmodern war. In this essay I do not engage with debates about defining war, nor do I contend that "new wars" displace all other forms; indeed, they exhibit many parallels with earlier colonial and imperialist wars. My objective is rather to explore ways in which conditions of war—that are typically analyzed as political, militarized phenomena—are altered by the economic phenomena of neoliberal globalization, including its erosion of centralized state power and autonomy. In effect, the "new wars" literature affords a stark illustration of informalization as economically and politically significant. Kaldor's *New and Old Wars* was initially published in 1999; cited pages here refer to the 2001 version that includes a new Afterword. In the Preface to the 2nd edition (2006), Kaldor acknowledges a decline in the number of wars and of people killed in wars since the first edition; I return to this below.

17. "Cosmopolitanism" for Kaldor refers "both to a positive political vision, embracing tolerance, multiculturalism, civility and democracy, and to a more legalistic respect for certain overriding universal principles which should guide political communities at various levels, including the global level" (2001, 115–116). In the second edition, Kaldor places greater emphasis on "the construction of legitimate political authority" (2006, x).

18. The decline is especially marked in the African context, and accompanied by important gender gains; see especially Tripp 2010. Critics of oversimplified claims associated with "new wars" research include Cramer 2006; Duffield 2007; Keen 2007.

19. See, for example, Biersteker and Eckert 2008; Andreas and Greenhill 2010; and the burgeoning IPE research on "risk."

20. Paraphrasing Arnson's description (2005, 11): "need" refers to grievances ranging from political repression to economic deprivation; "creed" to generalized belief and identity feelings; "greed" to personal or factional ambitions of private gain. Which of these factors warrants priority in explaining wars is continually debated.

21. This point is made from a variety of perspectives. See, for example, Kaldor 2001; Pugh and Cooper 2004; Naim 2005; Jung 2003.

22. The Pugh and Cooper volume refers to "combat, shadow and coping economies" (2004, 8), and I have modified these terms somewhat. I prefer "criminal"
rather than "shadow" to more explicitly distinguish the illicit character of that
economy, and I include aspects of social reproduction when referencing the "coping"
economy. The mainstream IIPE literature is virtually silent on both the significance
of social reproduction and the gendered dimensions of war and reconstruction. For
feminist treatments, see references in note 2 above.

23. Material presented here overlaps with Peterson 2008, 15–17; see Peterson
2009a for a preliminary case study of how these informal economies "appear" and
operate in the context of the war in Iraq; on gender in the latter, see also Sjoberg
2006; and on gender and war in Middle East wars, see Al-Ali and Pratt 2009.

24. Recruiting—or using various means of compelling—especially male but also
female *children* to participate in combat activities is relatively recent.

REFERENCES

Abbot, Jason P., and Owen Worth, eds. 2002. *Critical Perspectives on International
Political Economy*. New York: Palgrave.

Agamben, Giorgio. 1998. *Homo Sacer: Sovereign Power and Bare Life*. Translated by
Daniel Heller-Roazen. Stanford, Calif.: Stanford University Press.

Al-Ali, Nadje, and Nicole Prattt, eds. 2009. *Women and War in the Middle East: Transnational Perspectives*. London: Zed Books.

Anderlini, Sanam Naraghi. 2007. *Women Building Peace: What They Do, Why It Matters*. Boulder, Colo.: Lynne Rienner.

Andreas, Peter. 2003. "Redrawing the Line: Borders and Security in the Twenty-First
Century." *International Security* 28, 2 (Fall):78–111.

———. 2004. "Illicit International Political Economy: The Clandestine Side of Globalization." *Review of International Political Economy* 11, 3 (Aug.):631–652.

Andreas, Peter, and Kelly M. Greenhill, eds. 2010. *Sex, Drugs, and Body Counts:
The Politics of Numbers in Global Crime and Conflict*. Ithaca: Cornell University
Press.

Andreas, Peter, and Richard Price. 2001. "From War Fighting to Crime Fighting:
Transforming the American National Security State." *International Studies Review* 3,
3 (Fall):31–52.

APSA (American Political Science Association). 2008. *The Persistent Problem: Inequality, Difference, and the Challenge of Development. Report of the Task Force on Difference, Inequality, and Developing Societies*. July.

Arnson, Cynthia J. 2005. "The Political Economy of War: Situating the Debate." In
Rethinking the Economics of War, edited by Cynthia Arnson and I. William Zartman, 1–22. Baltimore: Johns Hopkins University Press.

Bakker, Isabella, and Stephen Gill, eds. 2003. *Power, Production and Social Reproduction: Human In/security in the Global Political Economy*. Houndsmill, Hampshire:
Palgrave Macmillan.

Bakker, Isabella, and Rachel Silvey, eds. 2008. *Beyond States and Markets: The Challenges of Social Reproduction.* London: Routledge.

Ballentine, Karen, and Jake Sherman, eds. 2003. *The Political Economy of Armed Conflict: Beyond Greed and Grievance.* Boulder: Lynne Rienner.

Barker, Drucilla K., and Susan F. Feiner. 2004. *Liberating Economics: Feminist Perspectives on Families, Work, and Globalization.* Ann Arbor: University of Michigan Press.

Barker, Drucilla K., and Edith Kuiper, eds. 2003. *Toward a Feminist Philosophy of Economics.* London and New York: Routledge.

Barta, Patrick. 2009. "The Rise of the Underground." *Wall Street Journal* 14 March: Global Economics, W1.

Beneria, Lourdes. 2003. *Gender, Development and Globalization: Economics as If All People Mattered.* New York: Routledge.

Berik, Günseli, Yana van der Meulen Rodgers, and Stephanie Seguino. 2009. "Feminist Economics of Inequality, Development, and Growth." *Feminist Economics* 15, 3 (July):1–33.

Biersteker, Thomas J., and Sue E. Eckert, eds. 2008. *Countering the Financing of Terrorism.* London: Routledge.

Burke, Anthony. 2007. *Beyond Security, Ethics and Violence: War against the Other.* New York: Routledge.

Butler, Judith. 2009. "Performativity, Precarity and Sexual Politics." *AIBR* 4, 3:i–xiii. Www.aibr.org

Chant, Sylvia, and Carolyn Pedwell. 2008. *Women, Gender and the Informal Economy: An Assessment of ILO Research and Suggested Ways Forward.* Geneva: ILO.

Cockburn, Cynthia. 2007. *From Where We Stand: War, Women's Activism and Feminist Analysis.* London: Zed Books.

———. 2010. "Gender Relations as Causal in Militarization and War." *International Feminist Journal of Politics* 12, 2:139–157.

Cornia, Giovanni Andrea, ed. 2004. *Inequality, Growth, and Poverty in an Era of Liberalization and Globalization.* Oxford: Oxford University Press.

Cramer, Christopher. 2006. *Civil War Is Not a Stupid Thing: Accounting for Violence in Developing Countries.* London: C. Hurst & Co.

De Goede. 2009. "Governing Finance in the War on Terror." In *Crime and the Global Political Economy,* edited by H. Richard Friman. Boulder, Colo.: Rienner.

Di John, Jonathan. 2010. "The Concept, Causes and Consequences of Failed States: A Critical Review of the Literature and Agenda for Research with Specific Reference to Sub-Saharan Africa." *European Journal of Development Research* 22, 1:10–30.

Douglass, Mike. 2006. "Global Householding in Pacific Asia." *International Development Planning Review* 28, 4:421–445.

Duffield, Mark. 2001. *Global Governance and the New Wars: The Merging of Development and Security.* New York: Zed Books.

———. 2007. *Development, Security and Unending War.* Cambridge: Polity.

Dunaway, Wilma A. 2001. "The Double Register of History: Situating the Forgotten Woman and Her Household in Capitalist Commodity Chains." *Journal of World-Systems Research* VII, 1 (Spring):2–29.

Eisenstein, Zillah R. 2007. *Sexual Decoys: Gender, Race and War in Imperial Democracy.* London: Zed Press, New York: Palgrave.

Enloe, Cynthia. 2007. *Globalization and Militarism: Feminists Make the Link.* Lanham, Md.: Rowman & Littlefield.

Ferber, Marianne A., and Julie A. Nelson, eds. 2003. *Feminist Economics Today: Beyond Economic Man.* Chicago: University of Chicago Press.

Fernandez-Kelly, Patricia, and Jon Shefner, eds. 2006. *Out of the Shadows: Political Action and the Informal Economy in Latin America.* University Park, Pa.: Pennsylvania University Press.

Friman, H. Richard, ed. 2009. *Crime and the Global Political Economy.* Boulder, Colo.: Rienner.

Friman, Richard, and Peter Andreas, eds. 1999. *The Illicit Global Economy and State Power.* Lanham, Md.: Rowman and Littlefield.

Galtung, Johan. 1969. "Violence, Peace and Peace Research." *Journal of Peace Research* 6, 3:167–191.

———. 1971. "A Structural Theory of Imperialism." *Journal of Peace Research* 8, 2:81–117.

Gender & Development. 2010. Special Issue: Economic Crisis. *Gender & Development* 18, 2 (July).

Giles, Winona, and Jennifer Hyndman, eds. 2004. *Sites of Violence: Gender and Conflict Zones.* Berkeley, Calif.: University of California Press.

Goldstein, Joshua S. 2001. *War and Gender.* Cambridge: Cambridge University Press.

Goodhand, Jonathan. 2004. "Afghanistan in Central Asia." In *War Economies in a Regional Context: Challenges of Transformation,* edited by Michael Pugh and Neil Cooper, 45–89. Boulder and London: Lynne Rienner.

Griffin, Penny. 2009. *Gendering the World Bank: Neoliberalism and the Gendered Foundations of the World Bank.* Basingstroke: Palgrave Macmillan.

Guha-Khasnobis, Basudeb, Ravi Kanbur, and Elinor Ostrom, eds. 2006a. *Linking the Formal and Informal Economy: Concepts and Policies.* Oxford: Oxford University Press.

———. 2006b. "Beyond Formality and Informality." In *Linking the Formal and Informal Economy: Concepts and Policies,* edited by Basudeb Guha-Khasnobis, Ravi Kanbur, and Elinor Ostrom, 1–18. Oxford: Oxford University Press.

Hansen, Lene, and Louise Olsson. 2004. Guest editors' "Introduction." *Security Dialogue* 35:405–409.

Hewitson, Gillian J. 1999. *Feminist Economics: Interrogating the Masculinity of Rational Economic Man.* Cheltenham: Edward Elgar.

Hoskyns, Catherine, and Shirin M. Rai. 2007. "Recasting the Global Political Economy: Counting Women's Unpaid Work." *New Political Economy* 12, 3:297–317.

Hunt, Krista, and Kim Rygiel, eds.. 2006. *(En)gendering the War on Terror: War Stories and Camouflaged Politics.* Burlington, Vt.: Ashgate.

International Feminist Journal of Politics. 2001. Themed Issue: "Gender in Conflict and Post-Conflict Societies." 3, 1.

Jacobs, Susie, Ruth Jacobson, and Jen Marchband, eds. 2000. *States of Conflict: Gender, Violence and Resistance.* London: Zed Books.

Journal of International Development. 2003. "Special Issue: Explaining Violent Conflict: Going beyond Greed versus Grievance." 15, 4.

Journal of Peacebuilding & Development. 2010. "Special Issue: Gender Violence and Gender Justice in Peacebuilding and Development." 5, 3.

Jung, Dietrich, ed. 2003. *Shadow Globalization, Ethnic Conflicts and New Wars: A Political Economy of Intra-State War.* London: Routledge.

Kaldor, Mary. 1999/2001. *New and Old Wars: Organized Violence in a Global Era.* Stanford: Stanford University Press.

———. 2006. *New and Old Wars.* 2nd ed. Cambridge: Polity Press.

Kaufman, Joyce P., and Kristen P. Williams. 2010. *Women and War: Gender Identity and Activism in Times of Conflict.* Sterling, Va.: Kumarian Press.

Kaul, Nitasha. 2008. *Imagining Economics Otherwise: Encounters with Identity/Difference.* London: Routledge.

Keen, David. 2007. *Complex Emergencies.* Cambridge: Polity Press.

Klein, Naomi. 2007. *The Shock Doctrine: The Rise of Disaster Capitalism.* New York: Metropolitan.

Le Billon, Philippe, Jake Sherman, and Marcia Hartwell. 2002. "Controlling Resource Flows to Civil Wars: A Review and Analysis of Current Policies and Legal Instruments." Rockefeller Foundation Conference Report. Bellagio, Italy.

Mann, Michael. 1988. *States, War and Capitalism.* New York: Basil Blackwell.

Marchand, Marianne H., and Anne Sisson Runyan, eds. 2011a. 2nd ed. *Gender and Global Restructuring: Sightings, Sites and Resistances.* London: Routledge.

———. 2011b. "Introduction." In *Gender and Global Restructuring: Sightings, Sites and Resistances,* edited by Marianne H. Marchand and Anne Sisson Runyan, 1–23. 2nd ed. London: Routledge.

Mazurana, Dyan, Susan McKay, Khristopher Carlson, and Janel Kasper. 2002. "Girls in Fighting Forces and Groups: Their Recruitment, Participation, Demobilization and Reintegration." *Peace and Conflict: Journal of Peace Psychology* 8:97–123.

Mazurana, Dyan, Angela Raven-Roberts, and Jane Parpart, eds. 2005. *Gender, Conflict, and Peacekeeping.* New York: Rowman & Littlefield.

Miller, Raymond C. 2008 *International Political Economy: Contrasting World Views.* London: Routledge.

Mittelman, James H. 2009. "Social Research, Knowledge, and Criminal Power." In *Crime and the Global Political Economy,* edited by H. Richard Friman, 1–23. Boulder, Colo.: Lynne Rienner.

Naim, Moises. 2005. *Illicit: How Smugglers, Traffickers, and Copycats Are Hijacking the Global Economy.* New York : Doubleday.

Naylor, R. T. 2002. *Wages of Crime: Black Markets, Illegal Finance, and the Underground Economy.* Ithaca: Cornell University Press.

Oatley, Thomas. 2010. *International Political Economy: Interests and Institutions in the Global Economy*. 4th ed. New York: Longman.

O'Brien, Robert, and Marc Williams. 2007. *Global Political Economy: Evolution and Dynamics*. 2nd ed. London: Palgrave.

Ong, Aihwa. 2006. *Neoliberalism as Exception*. Durham: Duke University Press.

Peck, Jamie. 2010. *Constructions of Neoliberal Reason*. Oxford: Oxford University Press.

Peterson, V. Spike. 2003. *A Critical Rewriting of Global Political Economy: Integrating Reproductive, Productive, and Virtual Economies*. London: Routledge.

———. 2005. "How (the Meaning of) Gender Matters in Political Economy." *New Political Economy* 10, 4 (December):499–521.

———. 2007. "Thinking through Intersectionality and War." *Race, Gender & Class* 14, 3–4:10–27.

———. 2008. "'New Wars' and Gendered Economies." *Feminist Review* 88, 1:7–20.

———. 2009a. "Gendering Informal Economies in Iraq." In *Women and War in the Middle East: Transnational Perspectives*, edited by N. Al-Ali and N. Pratt, 35–64. London: Zed Books.

———. 2009b. "Interactive and Intersectional Analytics of Globalization." *Frontiers* 30, 1:31–40.

———. 2010. "Informalization, Inequalities and Global Insecurities." *International Studies Review*

Peterson, V. Spike, and Anne Sisson Runyan. 2010. *Global Gender Issues in the New Millennium*. 3rd edition. Boulder, Colo.: Westview Press.

Politics & Gender. 2010. "Critical Perspectives: Global Householding." 6:271–304.

Portes, Alejandro, and William Haller. 2005. "The Informal Economy." In *The Handbook of Economic Sociology*, edited by Neil Smelser and Richard Swedberg, 403–425. Princeton and Oxford: Princeton University Press.

Pugh, Michael, and Neil Cooper, with Jonathan Goodhand. 2004. *War Economies in a Regional Context: Challenges of Transformation*. Boulder and London: Lynne Rienner.

Roberts, David. 2008. *Human Insecurity: Global Structures of Violence*. London: Zed Books.

Ruggiero, Vincenzo. 2000. *Crime and Markets: Essays in Anti-Criminology*. Oxford and New York: Oxford University Press.

Runyan, Anne Sisson, and Marianne H. Marchand. 2011. "Postscript: Gender and (Post?) Financial Crisis." In *Gender and Global Restructuring: Sightings, Sites, and Resistances*, edited by Marianne H. Marchand and Anne Sisson Runyan, 245–249. 2nd ed. London: Routledge.

Safri, Maliha, and Julie Graham. 2010. "The Global Household: Toward a Feminist Postcapitalist International Political Economy." *Signs* 36, 1:99–125.

Scholte, Jan Aart. 2005. *Globalization: A Critical Introduction*. 2nd ed. Hampshire: Palgrave Macmillan.

Security Dialogue. 2004. Special Issue: "Gender and Security." 35 (Dec).

Security Studies. 2009. Special Issue: "Feminist Contributions." 18, 2.

Shepherd, Laura. 2008. *Gender, Violence and Security*. London: Zed Books.

Sjoberg, Laura. 2006. *Gender, Justice, and the Wars in Iraq: A Feminist Reformulation of Just War Theory*. Lanham: Rowman & Littlefield.

Sjoberg, Laura, and Caron E. Gentry. 2007. *Mothers, Monsters and Whores: Women's Violence in Global Politics*. London: Zed Books.

Sjoberg, Laura, and Sandra Via, eds. 2010. *Gender, War and Militarism: Feminist Perspectives*. Santa Barbara, Calif.: ABC-CLIO.

Smith, Joan, and Immanuel Wallerstein, eds. 1992. *Creating and Transforming Households: The Constraints of the World-Economy*. Cambridge: Cambridge University Press.

Standing, Guy. 1999. "Global Feminization through Flexible Labor: A Theme Revisited." *World Development* 27, 3:583–602.

Stiglitz, Joseph E. 2002. *Globalization and Its Discontents*. New York: W. W. Norton.

Tickner, J. Ann. 2005. "Gendering a Discipline: Some Feminist Methodological Contributions to International Relations." *Signs* 30, 4 (Summer):2173–2188.

Tooze, Roger. 1997. "International Political Economy in an Age of Globalization." In *The Globalization of World Politics: An Introduction to International Relations*, edited by John Baylis and Steve Smith, 213–230. Oxford: Oxford University Press.

Tripp, Aili Mari. 2010. "Legislating Gender-Based Violence in Post-Conflict Africa." *Journal of Peacebuilding & Development* 5, 3:7–17.

Van Staveren, Irene, Diane Elson, Caren Grown, and Nilufer Cagatay, eds. 2007. *Feminist Economics of Trade*. London: Routledge.

Wade, Robert H. 2004. "Is Globalization Reducing Poverty and Inequality?" *World Development* 32, 4 (Apr):567–589.

Ward, Kathryn B. 1990. "Introduction and Overview." In *Women Workers and Global Restructuring*, edited by Kathryn B. Ward, 1–24. Ithaca: ILR Press of Cornell University.

Waylen, Georgina. 2006. "You Still Don't Understand: Why Troubled Engagements Continue between Feminists and (Critical) IPE." *Review of International Studies* 32:145–164.

Young, Brigitte, and Helene Schuberth. 2010. *The Global Financial Meltdown and the Impact of Financial Governance on Gender*, 1–12. GARNET Policy Brief Number 10. Paris: Science Politique.

Zartman, I. William. 2005. "Need, Creed, and Greed in Intrastate Conflict." In *Rethinking the Economics of War*, edited by Cynthia Arnson and I. William Zartman, 256–284. Baltimore: Johns Hopkins University Press.

Zein-Elabdin, Eiman O., and S. Charusheela, eds. 2004. *Postcolonialism Meets Economics*. London and New York: Routledge.

PART TWO

Case Studies of Gendered Violence in a
Context of Broader Insecurities

4

Securitizing Sex, Bodies, and Borders

The Resonance of Human Security Frames in
Thailand's "War against Human Trafficking"

EDITH KINNEY

Since the late 1990s human trafficking has moved from the margins to the mainstream of international politics. Driven by prominent—and graphic—stories of exploitation, sexual suffering, and violence against women, a wide range of actors have taken steps to combat the trafficking of persons. These actors include transnational and domestic women's advocacy groups, migrants' rights organizations, international organizations, and state institutions such as police, courts, and immigration and social welfare agencies. Although ostensibly designed to protect innocent victims, their efforts to combat human trafficking are implemented within political spaces that include other dominant institutions that can radically alter the course of reform. In fact, efforts to promote the interests of trafficked persons often end up revictimizing those same persons.

The focus on and securitization of human trafficking has been especially clear in Thailand. When Thailand's former Prime Minister Thaksin Shinawatra announced the "war on human trafficking" in August 2004, the head of Thailand's antitrafficking bureau pledged that the government's resolve to tackle the problem of human trafficking was "as serious as it [was] in its declaration of war against drug trafficking," a controversial crackdown resulting in over 2,800 extrajudicial killings and the arbitrary arrest, detention, and abuse of thousands more (AFP 2004; Human Rights Watch 2004). Echoing the earlier call to arms in the war on drugs, Thaksin's declaration announcing the new antitrafficking campaign was "widely interpreted as providing criminal justice officials with implicit authority to use any means possible to secure arrests and convictions" (Gallagher and Holmes 2008, 327).

Although Thaksin also pledged to reform laws, root out corruption among enforcement agencies, and boost prevention and protection efforts for victims, activists for women, migrants, and ethnic minorities received Thaksin's law-and-order antitrafficking agenda with a mixture of hope and cynicism. One shelter operator for victims of trafficking mused, "even if it's just a way for the Thai government to 'save face' [in light of international criticism], it's better that Thaksin made trafficking a national priority because the police pay more attention now."[1] Legal advocates reported that after Thaksin's announcement, police and front-line officials were now familiar with the concept of human trafficking and more willing to cooperate with nongovernmental organizations (NGOs). However, activists at a migrants' rights clinic were more apprehensive, arguing that the new "war on trafficking" would simply serve as a convenient excuse to "raid more places to round up and deport more migrants, whether they're 'trafficked' or not."[2] The securitization of Thailand's response to trafficking raised the prospect both of successful efforts to rescue vulnerable persons and dangerous, if unintended, consequences.

This chapter analyzes the securitization of sex, bodies, and borders in Thailand's "war against human trafficking," and the gendered nature of the collateral damage suffered by migrants and sex workers caught in the crossfire of this war. More specifically, this chapter explores how activists navigate the tension between traditional security prerogatives and the array of human security and human rights issues that shape Thailand's response to human trafficking. Though Thailand's antitrafficking laws and policies officially promote gender-sensitive, rights-based reforms, these efforts are implemented within an institutional context that is not always well-suited to the complicated nature of the issue.

The analysis draws on a year of field research in Thailand involving interviews with key governmental and nongovernmental actors, as well as an extensive review of literature on human trafficking in Thailand

and participant observation of the 2007 Friends of the Helsinki Process Workshop on Human Trafficking held in Chiang Mai, Thailand.[3] Quotations are drawn from fifty one- to two-hour semi-structured interviews with activists from NGOs, legal advocates, UN program coordinators, local police, regional and international law enforcement officials, prosecutors, social workers, and public welfare bureaucrats. I employed the snowball method of sampling to identify additional interviewees and contacts in antitrafficking and migrants' rights advocacy networks. By highlighting some of the benefits and risks of "securitizing" sexual exploitation in Thailand's antitrafficking campaigns, this research reveals how the (securitized) institutional contexts in which antitrafficking interventions are implemented can cause those interventions to undermine, rather than promote, the rights and security of people vulnerable to trafficking and exploitation.

After providing a brief overview of the concept of human security and the "securitization" of social problems, I describe how threats to political, economic, and human security in the Greater Mekong Subregion (GMS) incentivize risky migration into Thailand and exploitative working conditions, particularly for women. Antitrafficking activists strategically securitized the bodies of Thai women and children prostituted to foreign men to galvanize a movement against forced prostitution and sex trafficking. The responses of NGOs and state actors to this framing reflect the tension between security-centric and rights-based approaches to the problem. Ultimately, this process reveals how efforts to promote human security can legitimate enforcement practices that adversely impact the rights and security of voluntary migrants, trafficked persons, and women working in the commercial sex industry. This chapter examines the gendered nature of insecurity and the unintended consequences resulting from the securitization of sexualized violence against women, even as interventions are designed to protect women and promote their human security.

Reframing Security: The Strategic Securitization of Social Problems

The transnational phenomenon of human trafficking exposes the challenges states face in governing a range of security threats in an increasingly borderless world. Human trafficking combines traditional national security concerns regarding external threats (transnational organized crime, illegal migration, and the alleged funding of terrorist groups), internal security threats (corruption, money laundering, and marginalized "insurgent" or migrant communities), and threats to human security (trafficking as a consequence of economic and social insecurity, particularly affecting women, children, refugees, and ethnic minorities lacking citizenship).

Expanding traditional conceptions of security centering on external and military threats to state sovereignty, the concept of "human security" makes the protection of individuals its primary referent. In 2003, the Commission on Human Security defined human security as "encompassing human rights, good governance, access to education and health care," recognizing a range of environmental, social, and economic threats to the security of people in their homes, jobs, and communities.[4] Thus, human security offers a framework not only to assess the complex and intersecting vulnerabilities that place individuals at risk of violence, exploitation, or deprivation; human security also provides a vehicle for different actors to challenge the meaning and practice of security and a frame for activists to use in characterizing reform.

The capacity of "security" to bear multiple meanings makes it a rhetorically powerful symbol with strong emotional appeal. Security discourses provide a "prioritizing imperative" that conveys "a sense of urgency and consequence that attracts public attention and governmental resources" (Buzan, Waever, and de Wilde 1998, 29; Zedner 2009, 42). As such, security frames can be an attractive and potent tool for political campaigning for both state and nonstate actors. Because "security" carries a normative meaning as a public good that must be defended by the state, "human security" provides an accommodating frame for political actors seeking to widen the security agenda. Actors can implicitly reframe social problems as threatening not only the security of individuals, but also communities and the state.

The turn toward human security and the expectation that states should develop programs to achieve it represents the "securitization" of social problems. Securitization is a speech act, a "process of social construction involving those who . . . articulate an existential threat to a referent object . . . calling for emergency or extraordinary measures to deal with it" (Buzan, Waever, and de Wilde 1998, 23–24). Thus, the process of "securitization" not only constructs humans requiring security, but also "[calls] forth the state/non-state networks of aid, subjectivity, and political practice necessary for that undertaking" (Duffield and Waddell 2006, 2). Consequently, the shift to human security requires the enrollment of an extended range of actors responsible for the governance of security and risk, including NGOs and community activists.

Social movement organizations (SMOs) can therefore strategically frame social problems as security problems to identify referent objects in need of security, articulate a policy response, and mobilize resources. Activists may deploy security frames to underscore the urgency of a social problem and target certain populations as in need of or threatening security. Like all framing processes, this securitizing move—what I call "strategic securitization"—is context-dependent and socially constructed, as understanding of what poses a "threat" and how best to protect against it is "inextricably linked with the prevailing political culture" (Zedner 2009, 65). Strategic securitization can serve as a potent tactic for social movements where "institutional and public efforts to provide safeguards against criminality are perceived as being unable to meet the social demand for security" in a given political field (Pavarini 1997, 79). Exemplifying Jonathan Simon's concept of "governing through crime," antitrafficking campaigns highlight the risks posed by the crime of trafficking and posit an idealized victim subject—"womenandchildren" trafficked into sexual slavery—thereby legitimizing an aggressive criminal justice response to a variety of governance projects including immigration, illicit market behavior, and social order campaigns (Simon 2007).

Securitization also provides a discursive opportunity where alternative frames (such as rights, equality, or antidiscrimination claims) lack cultural resonance. In political fields that are authoritarian or highly militarized, security frames may resonate with political elites and legitimize movement demands more effectively than rights frames grounded in a liberal political tradition. In such contexts, for example where rights-based claims have historically been derided as against traditional "Asian values," security frames may be more likely to foster partnership with the state to address social problems.[5]

"Human security" thus provides a powerful and integrated analytic framework for women's advocates to draw attention to the gendered nature of insecurity at a variety of levels. It can expand vertically to connect the situation of individual women to their communities, their states, and the global processes of which they are a part, such as gendered international labor markets. The security frame can also expand horizontally, allowing social movement activists to construct rationales for state intervention in cases that would otherwise be seen as politically radical. Strategic securitization may work to create a space to introduce new interventions, practices, and institutions with the potential to transform deeply entrenched gender inequality, discrimination, and cultural traditions that make women vulnerable to violence and exploitation.

Strategic securitization also has the power to mobilize substantial political and economic resources. The "imagining" of what security looks like, the identification of situations that threaten security, and the institutions to which one looks to address perceived threat(s) are all politicized and socially constructed. By attracting the attention of diverse, often well-funded institutions such as the police and foreign ministry, identification of "human security" concerns can encourage coalition building between state and nonstate actors to address sources of insecurity at the local level. Importantly, new forms of collaboration between social movement organizations and the security sector—through state/NGO antitrafficking task forces, or law enforcement agencies' enrollment of NGOs to provide shelter and rehabilitation services to prepare victims to testify in court—work to reconstruct and renegotiate both the meaning and practice of security. This allows social movement actors both discursive and political opportunities to reshape the trajectory of security interventions in certain arenas, particularly where traditional security institutions such as the police or military rely on the expertise and resources of NGOs to assist in implementing policy.

Framing social issues through the lens of security, however, poses several significant risks for social movement activists promoting reform. As the language of security "provokes a threat-defense logic," it can invite state mobilization and intervention in ways that may be unhelpful, such as the legitimization of emergency powers, imposition of martial law, sacrifice of civil liberties, or increased surveillance and discipline of targeted communities (those "at risk" as well as those harboring criminal threats) (Waever 1995). Further, securitizing social problems has potentially "distorting effect[s]," as the prioritizing imperative of security can demote intersecting concerns related to gender and/or economic exploitation, forestalling political debate regarding those deeper, systemic issues (Zedner 2009, 65; Krause and Williams 1997; Buzan, Waever, and de Wilde 1998). And unlike the discourse of human rights, with its attendant international proclamations, conventions, and case law, human security does not provide a framework for accountability or entail specific legal obligations. These contradictory dynamics are particularly problematic when "wars" waged against sociolegal problems such as drugs, irregular migration, and human trafficking target victims and villains from the same communities.

Intersecting Insecurities: Militarism, Migration, and the Sex Trade

Human trafficking clearly violates personal security and safety, as it is accomplished by means of violence, force, fraud, coercion, or the "abuse or threatened abuse of the legal process."[6] However, trafficking cannot be isolated from structural violence and other threats to human security, exemplified by the grim circumstances facing women, men, and children who migrate or are trafficked from, through, or into Thailand.[7]

Security is a scarce commodity in the Global Mekong Subregion, motivating risky migration to the relatively prosperous and peaceful country of Thailand. Politically, civil war and political repression threaten ethnic minorities living along the borderlands between Thailand, Myanmar, and Laos. This political insecurity has gendered dimensions; for example, Shan and other ethnic minority women and girls in Burma are subjected to systematic use of rape as a weapon of war by the Burmese military in its offensives against ethnic minority separatist groups (Shan Human Rights Foundation, Shan Women's Action Network 2002). Poverty, ill-planned development projects, poor health care, and limited education exacerbate economic insecurity, particularly for "non-Thai" ethnic minorities born in Thailand but denied nationality or citizenship rights. The low status of women, sex discrimination, and violence against women contribute to the social and personal insecurity of women and their families. Environmental degradation—and efforts to ameliorate it by prohibiting traditional slash-and-burn agricultural practices—further undermine socioeconomic security in many indigenous highland communities in Thailand and the GMS.

Indeed, previous iterations of the "war on drugs" in Thailand aimed to suppress poppy cultivation, the traditional cash crop crucial to the survival of "hill tribe" communities, resulting in economic dislocation which amplified other dimensions of insecurity, as communities once reliant on the trade in drugs resorted to trading their women and girls into the Thai sex industry (Feingold 2000).[8] Concentrated in the lowest rungs of the industry, many hill tribe women and girls contracted HIV, which, without preventative education, spread rapidly when they returned to their villages, further undermining the security of ethnic highland communities and increasing their vulnerability to trafficking and labor exploitation.

Thailand's response to these intersecting insecurities has long been driven by "national security" and "national interest" concerns aimed to protect the country's military, economic, and diplomatic interests, rather than ensuring and protecting people's rights. The country's history of military dictatorships and repression of social movement activism has created a militarized political field in which security frames tend to trump rights frames.

As some Thai women's NGOs observe, state deployment of national security to protect "national interests" has been used to legitimate the denial or violation of women's rights (Asia Pacific Forum on Women, Law and Development 2002). Indeed, women's advocates' early efforts to address exploitation in the commercial sex industry were inhibited by police corruption and official involvement in the sex industry and endorsement of sex tourism as a path to development. This historical context shapes the trajectory of contemporary antitrafficking reforms targeting Thailand's sex industry.

In the mid-1980s, middle-class women's activists and academics began to raise awareness about the socio-economic consequences of Thailand's sex industry, which had grown rapidly in the 1960s and 1970s to accommodate U.S. troops based in Thailand and on "Rest & Relaxation" leave from the Vietnam War (Boonchalaksi and Guest 1994).[9] When the troops pulled out, tourists began arriving from Europe and Japan, most of them male (Truong 1990). Thailand developed a reputation as the "sex capital of the world," and became a popular sex tourist destination.

When I asked Thai interviewees to identify the "causes" of trafficking, nearly every antitrafficking activist, shelter operator, and social worker with whom I spoke insisted on starting "from the beginning" to describe how the influx of American troops transformed the practice and meaning of prostitution in Thailand. Women's migration for sex work, the rise of military prostitution around U.S. bases in the rural northeast, and the development of sex entertainment districts in Bangkok and sex tourist destinations like Pattaya were attributed to the presence of American troops in Thailand during the Vietnam War (Phongpaichit 1982; Truong 1990; Skrobanek, Boonpakdi, and Janthakeero 1997). Although some women's activists acknowledged that local demand accounts for a greater number of women in sex work, they insisted that the scale of Thailand's sex industry and the normalization of such "immoral" work was a direct consequence of the foreign military presence and the "Americanization" of values among rural peasants. As one older Thai woman's advocate explained, "prostitution has always been here, but it was smaller and more discreet—girls did not hang out of the beer bars calling after men like they do now; they do it so they can buy new mobile phones or designer clothes."[10] The purchase, abuse, impregnation, and desertion of Thai women by American G.I.s during the Vietnam War featured prominently in narratives describing women's migration to work in the domestic sex trade as a precursor to trafficking into foreign sex industries.

Military prostitution was figured as a threat to Thai culture and the nation, representing foreign intervention and cultural decline. Prostitution was symbolic of both "the systematic degradation of the countryside that occurred in tandem with the drive for development and security and . . . the Westernization of Thailand through the arrival of American troops" (Jeffrey 2002, 29). Migratory sex work became a political issue representative of foreign domination and the exploitation of rural resources by both Thai and foreign elites. The increasing number of rural women in prostitution provided fodder not only for the nationalist social and economic critiques of the 1970s students' movement, but also for elites striving to reestablish authority through appeals to a disciplinary discourse of national identity, gender, and authentic Thai culture. Elite women invoked the prostitute as a sign of cultural upheaval and disorder, positioning themselves as the proper authorities to reassert correct cultural identity and guide peasant women through development (Jeffrey 2002). The continuing salience of the Vietnam-era sex trade in contemporary advocates' explanations of trafficking reflects how the bodies of Thai women prostituted to foreign men still bear significant cultural and political meaning, and can therefore be strategically securitized—both as referent objects of security in need of protection and as threats to social order and national identity in need of rehabilitation.

The following sections analyze selected examples of antitrafficking initiatives in Thailand. These examples demonstrate how advocates strategically securitized sex, bodies, and borders in order to identify women trafficked into the sex industry as referent objects of security; to provoke the government to take action to treat trafficked persons as victims, rather than criminals; and to implement reforms to promote the rights of trafficked women, children, and men. They also demonstrate how the consequences of such securitized interventions are not necessarily positive for the intended beneficiaries of those interventions.

Securitizing Bodies: Strategic Framing of Sexual Suffering and Exploitation

In the 1980s and 1990s, Thai activists and academics were central to the rise of transnational feminist advocacy networks from both antiprostitution and sex workers' rights camps.[11] Through visceral testimonials of sexual suffering, activists drew attention to the "sexploitation" of Thai women and children in both domestic and foreign commercial sex industries, exposing the social consequences of sex tourism as a path to development (Skrobanek 1983; Barry, Bunch, and Castley 1984).

International conferences helped Thai activists network with advocates and NGOs in the global North, which proved critical to Thai NGOs' ability to leverage a "boomerang effect" to pressure the Thai government to take action regarding forced prostitution and trafficking (Keck and Sikkink 1998). As one antitrafficking activist explained to me, "It was difficult to get the male politicians to see prostitution as a problem, because many of them go to prostitutes themselves."[12] To denaturalize prostitution in Thai society, antitrafficking activists strategically securitized the bodies of women and children exploited by *foreign* men—the bodies of Thai women and children became a front in a struggle against foreign intervention and influence. One legal activist who founded an organization to monitor child sex abuse cases and push for the conviction of offenders explained her strategy by noting "the only way I could get the authorities to pay attention to child prostitution and trafficking was to tell them stories about the rape of little boys by foreign pedophiles. The prostitution of young girls was so common, they didn't consider it a crime."[13]

Activists drew attention to forced and child prostitution by publicizing stories of young children from the countryside sold by their "ignorant," drug-addicted, or materialistic parents into Bangkok brothels to be raped by "foreign pedophiles" and depraved sex tourists.[14] Antitrafficking NGOs also exposed cases of sadistic sexual abuse suffered by Thai women who had migrated to find work in Japan to support their families, only to be trafficked by gangs of *yakuza* and enslaved in Japanese brothels and sex clubs (Skrobanek, Boonpakdi, and Janthakeero 1997). The sympathetic figures of the dutiful daughter and the innocent Thai child sexually and economically exploited by foreign men—combined with increasing sensitivity on the part of politicians to the threat such publicity posed to Thailand's international image, tourist industry, and foreign investment—spurred the government to pledge to crack down on trafficking and exploitation in the sex trade.

Because the security threat posed by trafficking and commercial sexual exploitation was both individual and cultural, victims were most likely to be respected when they also happened to be Thai. A 1993 Human Rights Watch (HRW) report, *A Modern Form of Slavery* found that "the main target of [Thailand's] highly publicized crackdown on forced and child prostitution has been the victims themselves," *Burmese* women and girls trafficked into Thai brothels.[15] Thai police and border guards were directly involved in trafficking, extorted free sex, and demanded bribes from traffickers and brothels, while authorities wrongfully arrested victims, detained them without charge or trial, and abused women and girls in detention before deporting them back to Burma. As one Thai prosecutor active in early antitrafficking advocacy observed, Thailand's selective enforcement of antitrafficking policies furthered its economic and political interests vis-à-vis Burma. He estimated that 30 percent of the Burmese workers in Thailand were prostitutes servicing undocumented Burmese laborers, and "both systems are profitable to the Thai government and are therefore tolerated."[16] The HRW report emphasized that the Thai government's treatment of Burmese trafficking victims "contrasts sharply with its efforts on behalf of Thai women trafficked into Japan and subsequently arrested as illegal immigrants," where Thai officials urged Japan not to imprison Thai migrants for illegal entry, to protect Thai women from "gangster bosses," and to pay for the costs of repatriating victims back to Thailand (Thomas, Asia Watch Committee [U.S.], and Women's Rights Project [Human Rights Watch] 1993).

However, the Thai government also instituted protectionist measures to prevent the trafficking of Thai women abroad by restricting their freedom of movement. For example, the U.S. Department of State's 1996 Thailand Report on Human Rights Practices noted that the Thai government had reinstituted enforcement of a statute dating to the previous century requiring a woman to obtain her husband's permission before traveling outside Thailand. In addition, female passport applicants under the age of thirty-six were required to submit to a series of interviews to determine their employment records and finances, and passport applications by single women were subject to the approval of the Department of Public Welfare. Thus, protectionist regulations aimed to reduce trafficking for the purposes of prostitution were implemented so as to infringe on the rights of adult women to travel freely, while increasing the costs and risks of migration. These responses illuminate how advocacy campaigns emphasizing migrant women's risk of personal insecurity and sexual exploitation can provoke state responses that aim to "protect women, rather than protecting their rights" (Miller 2004, 18).

The consequences of the Thai government's crackdown on forced and child prostitution and its cooptation of the trafficking issue to advance its own political and economic security agenda in dealing with its neighbors presented a challenge for women's NGOs. Advocates had successfully spurred the state to respond to trafficking, but the collateral damage suffered by migrant women and children "rescued" and deported evidenced the risks of making prostitution a security issue.

By the mid-1990s activists sought the reform of Thailand's antitrafficking and prostitution suppression laws to protect, rather than punish, victims of trafficking and commercial sexual exploitation. Replacing the punitive 1960 Prostitution Suppression Act, the 1996 Prevention and Suppression of Prostitution Act distinguished between voluntary and forced prostitution; strengthened penalties for promoting or patronizing underage prostitution; and imposed penalties on parents or guardians who "sold" children into prostitution. While prostitution remains officially illegal in Thailand, the 1996 Act essentially penalizes solicitation with a relatively low fine (approximately $25 USD), and rehabilitation is no longer compulsory. The following year, Thailand passed the Measures in Prevention and Suppression of Trafficking in Women and Children Act, which protected foreign victims as well as Thai nationals, providing for significant fines and six to twelve years in jail with even stiffer penalties if victims were minors. Notably, the 1997 law did not address male victims of trafficking, who remained outside the protection of the law until the passage of Thailand's Anti-Trafficking in Persons Act in 2008.

The emerging discourse of human security provided a framework to link the diverse forms of insecurity that fostered trafficking and sexual exploitation to the state's interest in protecting its borders and combating organized crime. Despite the growing role of civil society since the 1990s, the Thai military either *is* the government (as in the most recent in a long line of coups) or remains close to those in power, retaining influence over democratically elected governments. Consequently, the discourse of security resonates with the power brokers in Thai politics. Activists challenge state-centered notions of security by framing the diverse social, economic, and environmental issues that place people at risk of trafficking as sources of insecurity necessitating extraordinary measures and state resources. By securitizing a range of risk factors for trafficking, activists hope to draw attention to the variegated threats to human security that are both causes and effects of human trafficking. Further, strategic securitization positions advocates and SMOs as necessary partners in the governance of risk, as activists and NGOs facilitate access to targeted populations, implement programs to address sources of insecurity, and support traditional security projects, such as policing crime, by identifying victims and assisting them to testify as witnesses. But despite its politically strategic benefits, the human security framework proved less successful in transforming the state institutions that implemented antitrafficking laws, resulting in interventions that often undermine, rather than promote, the rights and security of both trafficked and voluntary migrants.

Securitizing Sex: Distinguishing "Willing Victims" and "Unwilling Victims"

Thailand has established "multidisciplinary," interagency task forces to coordinate the response to trafficking cases. NGOs and legal advocates partner with law enforcement, social workers, and medical officials to protect victims' rights and to support the prosecution of traffickers.

Antitrafficking, child rights, and women's rights advocates have positioned themselves as governance partners in Thailand's "war on trafficking" by providing social development programs and prevention services to ameliorate sources of human insecurity that give rise to trafficking. Simultaneously, they facilitated the state's law enforcement goals by managing victim-witnesses through shelter and rehabilitation services that promoted victims' cooperation with criminal justice officials. However, NGOs that collaborate with state agents to implement antitrafficking interventions must navigate the tension between their efforts to promote victims' rights and human security on the one hand, and the national security and criminal justice prerogatives that animate the official "war on trafficking" on the other.

When invoking the rhetoric of "human security" in the context of trafficking, both activists and policymakers emphasized the importance of transforming enforcement officials' perception of trafficked persons from criminals deserving punishment to victims entitled to basic human rights. One of the greatest challenges NGO advocates highlighted regarding their work with law enforcement officials involved the persistent perception of trafficked women in the sex trade as criminals who violated prostitution and immigration laws, rather than victims deserving protection and assistance. Securitizing sex is one strategy activists used to transform enforcement officials' understanding of human trafficking and commercial sexual exploitation.

Some NGOs developed training programs for low-level police officers that explained how human security issues could push women into prostitution. "The police see these girls in the brothels . . . as illegal aliens, because they can tell they are Burmese," explained one shelter worker in northern Thailand, "so [the police] automatically think, 'We should arrest them, fine them, and deport them,' but we try to teach them to look to see if they have been forced [into working in the brothel] and are really victims."[17] In training sessions with police officers, antitrafficking advocates challenged the assumption that women voluntarily engaged in sex work by emphasizing the frequency of sex, the types of sex acts performed, and the number of clients as evidence of trafficking. As one chief of police explained, "We can tell [the prostitutes] are victims by counting the condoms in the trash bin."[18] However, when I related this example to an activist who had worked with sex establishments to promote condom use in public health campaigns against HIV/AIDS, she cried out in frustration: "that could just as easily be a sign of safe sex practices! It might be an indicator of poor working conditions, but if the police start using condoms as evidence of trafficking, the owners will try to pressure the girls not to use them. This [tactic] could undermine years of our prevention work."[19]

Further complicating the development of human security approaches to trafficking are the diverse interests among antitrafficking actors: while NGO activists and social workers emphasize rights and rehabilitation, police and prosecutors focus on the arrest of traffickers and the dismantling of organized crime networks. To promote collaboration between NGOs and state agencies, many coordinators of antitrafficking task forces emphasized the instrumental benefits of respecting the rights of trafficked women and children in order to advance crime control agendas. As one antitrafficking task force leader told me, "If you explain to the investigator and the prosecutor that they are more likely to win their case if they stop treating victims like criminals, for example, by interrogating them in a 'big man' voice until they cry, then they start getting interested in victim's rights."[20]

The instrumental benefits to the state security apparatus may not always encourage respect for victims' rights or women's rights, however. As Zedner observes, "setting security as an object of policy has the tendency to sidestep the issue of whose security is being sought" (Zedner 2009, 147). The implementation of trafficking interventions, especially in the form of brothel raids, brings this problem into sharp relief

(Empower Chiang Mai 2003; Thrupkaew 2009a; Thrupkaew 2009b; Soderlund 2005; Pollack 2007; Empower 2012).

When I asked what happened to women who had voluntarily migrated to Thailand to engage in sex work who were detained in anti-trafficking raids, respondents relied on the discourse of security to set up a hierarchy of victims: some who deserved their plight and others who did not (Munro 2008). Although both trafficked women and voluntary migrants may come from the same communities and suffer similar threats to human security, securitizing discourses tend to essentialize women as victims or whores and erase the ways in which migrant women exercise agency—even under highly exploitative conditions (O'Connell Davidson 2008).

For example, advocates on one task force explained that after a brothel raid, women are detained at the police station and divided into different groups, depending on their (presumed) age and willingness to cooperate with investigators and serve as witnesses. Minors and "unwilling victims" forced into the sex trade who agreed to testify were housed in shelters and were eligible to receive state-led social assistance and rehabilitative services, including counseling and occupational training, for example sewing, hairdressing, and making handicrafts. Women who had knowingly migrated to Thailand, who refused to testify, or who wanted to continue working in the sex industry were deemed "willing victims" who were denied social services and detained as criminals. An advocate working with "rescued" women in shelter detention described rehabilitation programs attempting to transform "willing victims" into suitable victim-witnesses as follows:

> It took us two months to train and talk to them—to convince them they'd been used. The [rehabilitation] training was to help them relax so they could give testimony. We gave them guidance about how to live their life—to get married and have kids, [and] how to achieve in this life.[21]

This moralistic and heteronormative assessment reveals both the sociolegal construction of sexual victimhood and the class dynamics that animate interactions between some "rescued" women and their advocates. Moreover, the focus on women's consent to engage in sex work—rather than a focus on coercive migration or exploitative working conditions—sets up a dichotomy between innocent victims and criminal prostitutes. As one local women's advocate and antitrafficking activist explained to me, while "unwilling victims" are "forced to do immoral things," "women who are over eighteen and are willing are not *real* victims, because they agree to do illegal and immoral acts in prostitution," estimating that about one-half of the women detained in local brothel raids fell into this category.[22] "You can't trust the [willing victims]," she confided, because "the police and social workers are not sure they won't return to bad people . . . and they might become traffickers themselves."

The slippage between victim and criminal was evident in one of the most highly publicized "success stories" of antitrafficking initiatives while I was in Thailand: a Cambodian woman—reportedly herself a former victim of exploitation deported back home—was sentenced to eighty-five years in prison for trafficking underage Cambodian women through Thailand to Malaysia. Advocates reported that some migrant sex workers were afraid that they could be charged as traffickers themselves for helping friends or relatives safely migrate to Thailand and find work in the entertainment industry.

Antitrafficking campaigns that securitize commercial sex as risky or immoral can also legitimate discrimination against and coercion of voluntary sex workers by state officials, decreasing the likelihood that sex workers will report circumstances of abuse or exploitation in the future and creating barriers for those women seeking to exit the commercial sex industry. In lieu of individualized assessments to differentiate trafficked victims from voluntary workers, NGO advocates report that Thai officials continue to use documentation status as a proxy for identifying trafficking victims, applying different laws to different groups of women. Thai women arrested during raids are fined under prostitution laws, while migrant women without documents are presumed to be victims—and those who deny they are victims are instead detained to serve as witnesses in trafficking prosecutions (Global Alliance against Traffic in Women 2009, 50–51; Empower 2012, 81–84).

The emphasis on protecting "rescued" trafficking victims, in part to ensure their participation in criminal justice proceedings, has resulted in the involuntary detention of victims in state rehabilitation centers and private NGO "closed shelters" that employ restrictive practices to monitor victims and prevent escape (Gallagher and Pearson 2010). In the shelters I visited, victims were detained from months to years while waiting for court cases or repatriation, without the ability to challenge their detention or leave the shelter. Such efforts to "secure" and "protect" victims can actually operate to undermine their security, as they are unable to work, provide for their families, or enjoy basic freedoms. While some of these concerns are addressed by the passage of Thailand's new antitrafficking law in 2008 (for example, by authorizing temporary work permits for some victims and allowing victims to seek compensation from traffickers), both advocates and officials note that these provisions have yet to be effectively implemented by state agents.

Securitizing commercial sex as an exploitative practice entails constructing naïve, innocent victims. This was seen as a tactic to transform enforcement officials' understanding of prostitution and to promote a protective, as opposed to punitive, approach to women exploited in the sex trade. But the tendency still is to differentiate between deserving "unwilling victims" who are due social and legal services and undeserving "willing victims" who should be punished and reformed. Such assumptions obscure the common sources of insecurity that motivate women's migration, the gendered nature of labor markets, and the structural factors that create incentives for women to engage in commercial sex work.

Securitizing Borders: Trafficking and the War on Illegal Immigration

The "double identification" of the trafficked prostitute as both victim and criminal illegal migrant integrates her on a "continuum of danger" that links illegal immigration, organized crime, and prostitution; her rescue, rehabilitation, and repatriation serves to reconcile humanitarian and securitizing discourses about trafficking (Aradau 2004; Bernstein 2007; Bernstein 2010). Securitizing discourses about trafficking—even those grounded in human security—therefore tend to result in a focus on the breach of national borders by illegal immigrants.

Campaigns to raise awareness about trafficking in Thailand emphasized migrant criminality and organized crime as threats to social order and national security. As longtime antitrafficking activist Siriporn

Skrobanek observes, official antitrafficking campaigns have "justified the arbitrary arrest of both legal and illegal migrants under the pretext of antitrafficking concerns . . . [and exacerbated the] growing xenophobia and racial prejudice/discrimination against foreigners, making them scapegoats of national crime and unemployment" (Skrobanek 2003). Indeed, state bureaucrats and social workers gave me official awareness-raising materials that presented a large red hand and read: "STOP! Human trafficking threatens the security of the Nation." Although the flyers also identified "family violence," poverty, and a host of other human rights violations as contributing to trafficking, the phenomenon was presented as a pressing social problem because trafficked migrants undermined the security of local communities and the Thai nation.

The securitization of borders in antitrafficking campaigns is also reflected in advocacy efforts that focus on preventing trafficking by preventing migration. Antitrafficking activists in Thailand have strategically securitized borders by emphasizing how trafficking prevention and development programs can stymie irregular migration. When appealing for funding and political support for programs promoting education and job training opportunities for would-be migrant girls and women, activists emphasized how such programs would *prevent* migration in the first place, thereby promoting women's economic security as well as protecting Thailand's national borders.

The enrollment of NGO advocates in the rehabilitation and repatriation process also points to the tension between victims' rights and immigration control in trafficking interventions. Many rehabilitation programs were framed in terms of preventing remigration; trafficked women would receive "retraining" in "native" weaving, sewing, and traditional handicrafts to sell to tourists in the hope that women would remain in their countries of origin and not attempt to return to Thailand seeking work in the sex industry. Another NGO advocate on an antitrafficking task force explained that she had blindfolded victims during the drive back to Laos so the victims could not learn the way back to Thailand to return to work in the sex trade.[23] Legal advocates noted that proposed procedural and evidentiary reforms allowing adult victims to videotape their testimony before trial to avoid facing their exploiters in open court also served to facilitate repatriation, as the prosecution no longer needed victim-witnesses once officials had recorded their statements. Ironically, some reforms initially advanced to protect victims serve as a vehicle to hasten their (often involuntary) repatriation. When I asked whether some victims would like to participate in the trial to find some sort of closure or sense of justice, a legal advocate mused, "maybe they want to come back to hear the decision of the court, . . . [but] we don't want them to face the defendant, so they shouldn't come, because it will ruin the rehabilitation they've just had."[24]

Unfortunately, both repatriation and deportation practices can exacerbate the risk of trafficking and insecurity. In June 2010 Thailand launched a new crackdown on unregistered migrants. Some Thai officials developed schemes to extort deportees by delivering them to the Democratic Karen Buddhist Army in Burma, which in turn demanded bribes for release to labor brokers who arranged legal and illegal reentry to Thailand (Human Rights Watch 2010). Women unable to pay bribes were trafficked into the sex industry, while men were trafficked to serve as forced porters for the Burmese military. When I asked whether the deportation of migrant sex workers back to Myanmar was worrisome given the continuing violence and economic insecurity there, one social worker simply shrugged and said, "They are here illegally, and prostitution is not legal, so they have broken the law and they have to pay the consequences."[25] Thus, as immigration crackdowns intersect with the "war on trafficking," efforts to promote the human security of victims through traditional raid-rescue-repatriation interventions can paradoxically increase insecurity and retrafficking, as repatriated individuals are returned to areas plagued by conflict and economic hardship from which they will again try to escape by remigrating to Thailand.

Weighing the Risks of Securitization and Rights Violations in Thailand's War on Trafficking

Strategic securitization has provoked the state to respond to trafficking and forced prostitution, but has also exacerbated threats to the human security of both victims of sex trafficking and voluntary sex workers. The clandestine nature of migration and the difficulty of accessing many persons forced to labor in "hidden workplaces" incentivizes antitrafficking crackdowns focused on the sex industry (Pearson and ILO Mekong Subregional Project to Combat Trafficking in Children and Women 2005). The visibility and accessibility of commercial sex establishments makes sex workers easy targets for agencies charged with identifying victims, promoting overreporting in this sector (United Nations Office on Drugs and Crime 2009). Media attention to brothel raids and rescues of sex trafficking victims, the likelihood of netting a high percentage of "unwilling victims" per raid, and external pressure to "get results" all contribute to enforcement agents' emphasis on sex trafficking. As state-backed task forces receive funding from USAID, the antiprostitution approach endorsed by U.S. antitrafficking policies also encourages selective enforcement targeting the sex sector (Kinney 2006).[26]

Indeed, sex workers' rights organizations report that antitrafficking mandates allow police to "kill two birds with one stone" by raiding sex establishments at the same time migrant workers' permits expire and "entertainment places" are required to reregister (Puckmai 2010). Other activists note that Thailand's raid-rescue/arrest-detain-deport "vertical approach" to trafficking driven by the state's security and criminal justice interests produces untoward consequences for victims and voluntary workers alike. Veteran antitrafficking and women's rights activist Siriporn Skrobanek argues that the Thai government is focused on "changing existing and making new laws and national policies to suppress organized crime involved in human trafficking and restrict cross-border movement of other nationals," because "it is in the interest of [the] state to suppress [the] criminal aspect of human trafficking but not to protect [the] rights of trafficked women/children" (Skrobanek 2003).

NGOs promoting the rights of migrants and sex workers in northern Thailand have similarly criticized the focus on "sex trafficking," highlighting how trafficking interventions actually exacerbate the insecurity of migrant women vulnerable to abuse and exploitation. For example, one sex worker told me that it is difficult for "rescued" women to distinguish antitrafficking interventions from the periodic brothel raids carried out by police to arrest prostitutes and illegal migrants—oftentimes because the same police solicit bribes for "protection" or come as customers when they are off duty and demand free sex.[27]

Migrant and ethnic minority women at the sex workers' rights and empowerment organization EMPOWER have created awareness-raising art installations and a short film documenting the deleterious effects of "raid and rescue" antitrafficking interventions.[28] They highlight how brothel raids ostensibly intended to rescue trafficking victims create new sources of insecurity for migrant women working in the sex industry. "Rescue" can undermine economic security: "We lose our savings and belongings; we are not given compensation by anybody." Rescues also result in the violation of civil liberties and the right to privacy: "We are locked up; we are interrogated by many people; they force us to be witnesses; we are held until the court case; we are held till deportation; we are forced retraining [in rehabilitation programs]; strangers visit our villages telling people about us." Moreover, rescues undermine the security not just of individual women, but also that of their families back home: "Our family is in a panic; my family has a debt; our family must borrow money to survive while we wait [in detention]; the village and the soldiers cause our family problems; our family has to pay 'fines' or bribes to the soldiers." Faced with few other options, rescued sex workers must "find a way back to Thailand to start again" and are more vulnerable to exploitative smugglers because of their financial straits. Thus, raid-rescue-repatriate interventions can ultimately increase the pressure to remigrate under risky conditions and to accept even highly exploitative work.

Conclusion

Activists' strategic securitization of commercial sexual exploitation and human trafficking provoked a powerful response from the state. Since the 1980s activists have spurred Thailand to pass new laws, develop new operational guidelines, and provide legal and social assistance for trafficked persons. However, the collateral damage suffered by both trafficked persons and voluntary migrants in the "war on trafficking" illustrates the risks of engaging with the discourse of security to advance reforms. Even when interventions are framed as advancing the human security of victims and groups vulnerable to trafficking, such security frames tend to invite actions that might actually be harmful to trafficked persons. This is particularly likely when securitized frames are deployed in political and discursive opportunity structures dominated by militaristic state institutions and a "governing through crime" approach to social problems.

As part of its efforts to improve its record on human trafficking, Thailand replaced its 1997 antitrafficking law with the Anti-Human Trafficking Act in 2008. The 2008 Act reflects a response to critiques from NGOs and international organizations. It criminalizes a broad range of exploitative situations beyond forced prostitution, and enforcement officials are now investigating labor exploitation in other sectors (UNIAP 2010). The law aims to promote a "victim-centered" approach, establishing a fund to prevent and suppress trafficking and to improve victim assistance and welfare services. Custody periods are limited, and the law provides for temporary immigration relief during prosecution. Prosecutors are required to inform victims of the right to compensation and to the provision of legal aid, though legal aid is not guaranteed or funded by the state (2008 Anti-Trafficking Act, Section 34). Importantly, by recognizing men as potential trafficking victims, the 2008 Act implicitly acknowledges the common sources of insecurity and structural violence that motivate risky migration, while challenging the gendered assumption that womenandchildren are trafficked, while men are smuggled—a problematic framework that simultaneously infantilizes women and minimizes human rights violations against men. But despite these encouraging legal reforms, institutional reform is slow, and antitrafficking policies are being enacted in a political climate that is increasingly hostile toward migrants and refugees.[29] Both documented and undocumented migrants continue to suffer abuse at the hands of unscrupulous employers as well as state officials—in particular the police, who routinely arrest, abuse, and extort migrants. Thai authorities and military troops have forcibly "repatriated" ethnic minority refugees fleeing persecution in Laos and Burma back into active war zones.

Moreover, selective enforcement, discriminatory attitudes among state agents, and increased marginalization of workers in informal sectors—particularly in the sex industry—remain commonplace problems in antitrafficking initiatives, even those where NGOs partner with enforcement officials. Sex workers' rights NGOs report that the implementation of the 2008 Act has resulted in violations of fundamental human rights by both state and nonstate actors against voluntary migrant sex workers as well as women classified as trafficking victims (Empower Foundation and RATS-W Team 2012, vi). Relaxed warrant requirements incentivize raids; police (and some NGOs) routinely entrap sex workers; officials fail to notify people detained in trafficking raids of their rights as a victim, witness, or suspect; and "rescued" women continue to suffer extended involuntary detention in shelters and rehabilitation centers as they wait for court cases and repatriation (though trafficked men can work outside shelters) (Gallagher and Pearson 2010; Puckmai 2010; Empower Foundation and RATS-W Team 2012).

The current political environment in Thailand thus suggests that state agents will continue to use the "war on trafficking" as cover for more repressive criminal justice and anti-immigration initiatives, legitimized by the participation of antitrafficking and women's rights NGOs. Activists would do well to consider the potential consequences of strategic securitization in campaigns that aim to protect and promote the rights of women who are viewed as criminals—either as prostitutes or as illegal immigrants—by many state officials. While human security frames may provide activists entré into state institutions, such frames are also easily coopted by the state.

When deployed in the context of trafficking, security discourses trigger state policies emphasizing border control and prosecution, rather than policies addressing the exploitative conditions migrants face upon arrival at their destination, or the gendered sources of insecurity that place women at increased risk of exploitation. The pursuit of "human security" can generate new threats to the security of the very groups posited as victims of trafficking and exploitation. Although human rights and women's rights frames may be perceived as more radical and less resonant with political elites, the fallout of Thailand's "war on trafficking" should serve as a cautionary tale for movement strategists considering strategic securitization to advance women's rights and social justice reforms.

NOTES

1. Interview with Nancy, faith-based NGO activist.

2. Interview with Jane, Burmese migrants' rights NGO activist.

3. Field research was supported by a Fulbright Fellowship to Thailand, 2004–2005 and a dissertation research grant from the University of California, Berkeley. Interviews were conducted on condition of anonymity; quotes are referenced with a pseudonym and attributed to the role of the interviewee with respect to advocacy or antitrafficking initiatives.

4. Commission on Human Security (2003), at 4, available at http://www.human-security-chs.org/finalreport/index.html

5. The Bangkok Declaration issued after the Regional Meeting for Asia of the World Conference on Human Rights in 1993 "[stressed] the universality, objectivity and non-selectivity of all human rights and the need to avoid double standards in the implementation of human rights and its politicization." Reflecting hostility to the use of human rights as political leverage in trade and diplomatic relations by Western governments, Asian governments emphasized that human rights should be promoted cooperatively, rather than through confrontation, the "imposition of incompatible values," or conditioning development aid on human rights practices. *See* Report of the Regional Meeting for Asia of the World Conference on Human Rights, UN Doc. A/CONF.157/PC/59, at 3 (1993); Peerenboom 2004.

6. See, for example, the definition of trafficking in persons in Article 3(a) of the 2000 UN Protocol to Prevent, Suppress and Punish Trafficking in Persons, Especially Women and Children, Supplementing the UN Convention against Transnational Organized Crime.

7. The GMS contains incredibly diverse patterns of human trafficking with a range of victims and criminal profiles, including "internal and cross-border; highly organized and also small-scale; sex and labor, through both formal and informal recruitment mechanisms; and involving the victimization of men, women, boys, girls, and families." United Nations Inter-Agency Project on Human Trafficking, "Human Trafficking Background Information," http://www.no-trafficking.org/resources_background_what.html. Many explanations of sex trafficking emphasizing criminality and mechanisms of supply and demand "fail to consider the deep structural underpinnings of control, violence, and legitimated abuse of women" that shape the dynamics of trafficking and exploitation in the global sex trade (Dunlop 2008, 56).

8. See David Feingold's 2003 film, *Trading Women*, narrated by Angelina Jolie, produced by D. Slotar and D. Feingold, *available at* http://www.der.org/films/trading-women.html. Feingold observes that despite a thriving sex industry, in the 1980s there were no ethnic minority "hill tribe" girls working in the Thai sex trade, whereas in the 2010s they accounted for around 30 percent of the total number of sex workers in Thailand and were concentrated in the most exploitative parts of the industry (Feingold 2003; Feingold 2005).

9. Key organizations include Friends of Women, the Foundation for Women, and Empower (a sex workers' rights organization) (Tantiwiramanond and Pandey 1991).

10. Interview with Khun Sarakit, elite women's activist.

11. Thai activists presented evidence regarding official corruption, Thai women's global migration, and exploitation in the commercial sex industry to burgeoning transnational advocacy networks of both anti-prostitution and sex workers' rights feminists (Barry, Bunch, and Castley 1984; Pheterson 1989).

12. Interview with Aa, social worker and victim advocate.

13. Interview with Porntip, legal reform and child rights activist.

14. Interview with Suchada, child rights advocate.

15. The 1994 "Report by the UN Special Rapporteur on Violence against Women, Its Causes and Consequences" relied heavily on the HRW Report's examples of exploitation in Thailand's sex industry to characterize the harms of prostitution and human trafficking as VAW and human rights violations. (Thomas, Asia Watch Committee [U.S.], and Women's Rights Project [Human Rights Watch] 1993).

16. International Workshop on Migration and Traffic in Women, Chiang Mai, Thailand, 1994 (report on file with author).

17. Interview with Khun Siriporn, operator of a shelter for victims of domestic violence and trafficking.

18. Interview with Officer Wichit, police chief and member of antitrafficking task force.

19. Interview with Lulu, sex workers' rights advocate.

20. Interview with Banyat, CMM task force coordinator.

21. Interview with Khun Jeab, rehabilitation/shelter worker.

22. Interview with Khun Malee, women's advocate and antitrafficking activist.

23. Ibid.

24. Interview with Mu, legal advocate.

25. Interview with Ban, social worker at government shelter, rehabilitation, and vocational training facility.

26. USAID grant restrictions provide that "organizations advocating prostitution as an employment choice or which advocate or support the legalization of prostitution are not appropriate partners for USAID antitrafficking grants or contracts." USAID, "Trafficking in Persons, the USAID Strategy for Response," February 2003. U.S. policies restricting grants to organizations endorsing the antiprostitution pledge have hindered HIV/AIDS outreach and fractured alliances in the NGO community (Saunders 2004; Network of Sex Work Projects 2006).

27. Interview with Ping, sex worker activist.

28. Empower is a Thai NGO promoting the human rights of Thai and migrant sex workers, with centers throughout the country. Migrant sex workers at Empower have created several art installations to raise awareness about the collateral damage of law-and-order approaches to exploitation and trafficking in the sex industry. Pictures of an embroidered "Mida Tapestry" featured in their 2012 Hit and Run report and the 2012 film, The Last Rescue in Siam, illustrate migrant sex workers' experiences

regarding the diverse rights violations that attend raid-rescue-repatriate approaches to trafficking.

29. A recent Human Rights Watch report notes that the Thai government's policy toward migrant workers is "largely shaped by national security concerns," and government officials "often regard migrant workers from neighboring countries as a potential danger to Thai communities, the interests of Thai workers, and national sovereignty" (Robertson and Human Rights Watch 2010, 14).

REFERENCES

AFP. 2004. "Thailand Unveils War on Human Trafficking." *The Nation*, August 6. http://www.nationmultimedia.com/home/2004/08/06/latest%20news/Thailand-unveils-war-on-human-trafficking-103703.html.

Anti-Trafficking in Persons Act, B.E. 2551 (2008).

Aradau, Claudia. 2004. "The Perverse Politics of Four Letter Words: Risk and Pity in the Securitisation of Human Trafficking." *Millennium: Journal of International Studies* 33 (2):251–277.

Asia Pacific Forum on Women, Law and Development. 2002. *Human Security: Securing Women's Human Rights*. Bangkok, Thailand.

Barry, Kathleen, Charlotte Bunch, and Shirley Castley. 1984. *International Feminism: Networking against Female Sexual Slavery*. Report of the Global Feminist Workshop to Organize against Traffic in Women, April 6–15, 1983. Rotterdam, the Netherlands: International Women's Tribune Centre.

Bernstein, Elizabeth. 2007. "The Sexual Politics of the 'New Abolitionism.'" *Differences* 18 (3): 128–151.

———. 2010. "Militarized Humanitarianism Meets Carceral Feminism: The Politics of Sex, Rights, and Freedom in Contemporary Antitrafficking Campaigns." *Signs: Journal of Women in Culture and Society* 36 (1): 45–71.

Boonchalaksi, Wathinee, and Phillip Guest. 1994. *Prostitution in Thailand*. Nakhon Pathom, Thailand: Institute for Population and Social Research, Mahidol University.

Buzan, Barry, Ole Waever, and Jaap de Wilde. 1998. *Security: A New Framework for Analysis*. Boulder, Colo.: Lynne Rienner.

Bureau of Democracy, Human Rights, and Labor. 1997. "Thailand Report on Human Rights for 1996." Washington, D.C.: U.S. Department of State. http://www.state.gov/www/global/human_rights/1996_hrp_report/thailand.html

Duffield, Mark, and Nicholas Waddell. 2006. "Securing Humans in a Dangerous World." *International Politics* 43:1–23.

Dunlop, Karen. 2008. "Human Security, Sex Trafficking and Deep Structural Explanations." *Human Security Journal* 6:56–66.

Empower. 2012. *Last Rescue in Siam*. Empower Studios.

Empower Chiang Mai. 2003. *A Report by Empower Chiang Mai on the Human Rights Violations Women Are Subjected to When "Rescued" by Anti-Trafficking Groups Who Employ Methods Using Deception, Force and Coercion*.

Empower Foundation, and RATS-W Team. 2012. *Hit and Run: Sex Workers' Research on Anti-Trafficking in Thailand*. Chiang Mai, Thailand: Empower Foundation.

Feingold, David. 2000. "The Hell of Good Intentions: Some Preliminary Thoughts on Opium in the Political Ecology of the Trade in Girls and Women." In *Where China Meets Southeast Asia: Social & Cultural Change in the Border Regions*, edited by Grant Evans, Christopher Hutton, and Kuah Khun Eng. New York: St. Martin's Press.

———. 2003. *Trading Women*. Ophidian Films.

———. 2005. "Human Trafficking." *Foreign Policy*, October.

Gallagher, Anne, and Paul Holmes. 2008. "Developing an Effective Criminal Justice Response to Human Trafficking: Lessons from the Front Line." *International Criminal Justice Review* 18 (3) (September):318–343.

Gallagher, Anne, and Elaine Pearson. 2010. "The High Cost of Freedom: A Legal and Policy Analysis of Shelter Detention for Victims of Trafficking." *Human Rights Quarterly* 32:73–114.

Global Alliance against Traffic in Women. 2009. *Asia Regional Consultation Report, Godavari Village Resort, Kathmandu, Nepal, August 29–September 4, 2009*. Bangkok: Global Alliance against Trafficking in Women (GAATW).

Human Rights Watch. 2004. *Not Enough Graves: The War on Drugs, HIV/AIDS and Violations of Human Rights*. New York: Human Rights Watch.

———. 2010. "Open Letter Requesting Investigation of Claims by Migrants Deported from Thailand Facing Human Rights Abuses by DKBA." http://www.hrw.org/en/news/2010/07/19/open-letter-requesting-investigation-claims-migrants-deported-thailand-facing-human-.

Jeffrey, Leslie Ann. 2002. *Sex and Borders: Gender, National Identity, and Prostitution Policy in Thailand*. Vancouver: UBC Press.

Keck, Margaret, and Kathryn Sikkink. 1998. *Activists beyond Borders: Advocacy Networks in International Politics*. New York: Cornell University Press.

Kinney, Edi. 2006. "Appropriations for the Abolitionists: Undermining Effects of the U.S. Mandatory Anti-Prostitution Pledge in the Fight against Human Trafficking and HIV/AIDS." *Berkeley Journal of Gender, Law & Justice* 21:158–194.

Krause, Keith, and Michael Williams, eds. 1997. *Critical Security Studies: Concepts and Cases*. Minneapolis: University of Minnesota Press.

Measures in Prevention and Suppression of Trafficking in Women and Children Act B.E. 2540 (1997).

Miller, Alice M. 2004. "Sexuality, Violence against Women, and Human Rights: Women Make Demands and Ladies Get Protection." *Health and Human Rights* 7(4):17–47.

Munro, Vanessa. 2008. "Of Rights and Rhetoric: Discourses of Degradation and Exploitation in the Context of Sex Trafficking." *Journal of Law and Society* 35(2):240–264.

Network of Sex Work Projects. 2006. Taking the Pledge. Nesha Studio. http://blip.tv/sexworkerspresent/taking-the-pledge-185356.

O'Connell Davidson, Julia. 2008. "Trafficking, Modern Slavery and the Human Security Agenda." *Human Security Journal* 6:8–15.

Pavarini, Massimo. 1997. "Controlling Social Panic." In *Social Control and Political Order: European Perspectives at the End of the Century*, edited by Roberto Bergalli and Colin Sumner, 75–95. Thousand Oaks, Calif.: Sage.

Pearson, Elaine, and ILO Mekong Subregional Project to Combat Trafficking in Children and Women. 2005. *The Mekong Challenge—Human Trafficking: Redefining Demand*. Bangkok: ILO.

Peerenboom, Randall. 2004. *Asian Discourses of Rule of Law: Theories and Implementation of Rule of Law in Twelve Asian Countries, France, and the U.S.* Routledge Law in Asia Series. London: RoutledgeCurzon.

Pheterson, Gail. 1989. *A Vindication of the Rights of Whores*. Seattle, Wash.: Seal Press.

Phongpaichit, Pasuk. 1982. *From Peasant Girls to Bangkok Masseuses*. Women, Work and Development 2. Geneva: International Labour Office.

Pollack, Jackie. 2007. "Thailand." In *Collateral Damage: The Impact of Anti-Trafficking Measures on Human Rights around the World*, edited by Global Alliance against Traffic in Women, 171–202. Bangkok: Global Alliance against Traffic in Women.

Prevention and Suppression of Prostitution Act. B.E. 2539 (1996).

Puckmai, Pornpit. 2010. "Traditional Raids and Arrests." Empower Foundation. http://www.empowerfoundation.org/sexy_en.php?id=2#.

Robertson, Phil, and Human Rights Watch. 2010. *From the Tiger to the Crocodile: Abuse of Migrant Workers in Thailand*. New York: Human Rights Watch.

Saunders, Penelope. 2004. "Prohibiting Sex Worker Projects, Restricting Women's Rights: The International Impact of the 2003 U.S. Global AIDS Act." *Health and Human Rights: An International Journal* 7(2): 179–92.

Shan Human Rights Foundation, Shan Women's Action Network. 2002. *License to Rape: The Burmese Military Regime's Use of Sexual Violence in the Ongoing War in Shan State*.

Simon, Jonathan. 2007. *Governing through Crime: How the War on Crime Transformed American Democracy and Created a Culture of Fear*. New York: Oxford University Press.

Skrobanek, Siriporn. 1983. "The Transnational Sex-Exploitation of Thai Women." The Hague: Institute of Social Sciences.

———. 2003. "Human Trafficking: From Vertical to Horizontal Journey." Foundation for Women. http://www.womenthai.org/eng/trafficking.html.

Skrobanek, Siriporn, Nattaya Boonpakdi, and Chutima Janthakeero. 1997. *The Traffic in Women: Human Realities of the International Sex Trade*. New York: Zed Books.

Soderlund, Gretchen. 2005. "Running from the Rescuers: New U.S. Crusades against Sex Trafficking and the Rhetoric of Abolition." *Feminist Formations* 17(3):64–87.

Tantiwiramanond, Darunee, and Shashi Ranjan Pandey. 1991. *By Women, for Women: A Study of Women's Organizations in Thailand*. Singapore: ISEAS.

Thomas, Dorothy, Asia Watch Committee (U.S.), and Women's Rights Project (Human Rights Watch). 1993. *A Modern Form of Slavery: Trafficking of Burmese Women and Girls into Brothels in Thailand*. New York: Human Rights Watch.

Thrupkaew, Noy. 2009a. "The Crusade against Sex Trafficking." *The Nation*, October 5. http://www.thenation.com/article/crusade-against-sex-trafficking?page=full.

———. 2009b. "Beyond Rescue." *The Nation*, October 26. http://www.thenation.com/article/beyond-rescue?page=full.

Truong, Than-Dam. 1990. *Sex, Money and Morality: Prostitution and Tourism in South-East Asia*. London: Zed Books.

UNIAP. 2010. Books.m in South-Eon.com/article/beyond-rescue?page=full. icking?pStrategic Information Response Network. Bangkok: UNIAP.

United Nations Office on Drugs and Crime. 2009. *Global Report on Trafficking in Persons*. UNODC.

Waever, Ole. 1995. "Securitization and Desecuritization." In *On Security*, edited by R. D. Lipschutz, 46–86. New York: Columbia University Press.

Zedner, Lucia. 2009. *Security*. New York: Routledge.

5

Work and Love in the Gendered U.S. Insecurity State

LISA D. BRUSH

Conventional wisdom in the United States considers poverty in two ways (O'Connor 2001). The morally acceptable form of poverty is a temporary condition caused by circumstances beyond the individual's control. In this view, people are poor due to lack of income in old age after a lifetime of hard work, because of reduced earnings caused by a physical disability from a work-related injury, when they survive the death of a breadwinning man, or as a result of unemployment rooted in large-scale shifts in the economy, recession, competition from immigrants, or unfair trade policy and practices. These people are all considered the deserving poor (Katz 1989). For the poor deemed deserving, the United States provides a "safety net." The image of the safety net assumes that even Americans who work hard and play by the rules may occasionally fall into need and briefly accept public assistance without damaging their work ethic, family commitments, and sense of personal responsibility. The welfare state provides social insurance against the risk that hard-working individuals will suffer diminished earnings capacity due to old age, unemployment, or disability, or that dependent women and minor children suffer the death or disability of their family breadwinner.

Conventional wisdom views the stigmatized form of poverty, in contrast, as a long-term, intergenerational condition. This kind of poverty, conventional wisdom holds, is caused by individual failings of work ethic and sexual restraint and by government programs that erode initiative, undermine choice, and deter personal responsibility by rewarding cunning and failure instead of hard work and economic and sexual discipline. For everyone but the deserving poor, purveyors of conventional wisdom assert, welfare state programs are not a safety net but a moral hazard; welfare institutionalizes perverse incentives likely to change the behavior of both workers and employers. In this view of poverty, public provisions for income security and regulation of working conditions (including the minimum wage and protective labor legislation as well as welfare) not only keep poor people from responding rationally and responsibly to the consequences of their bad choices, They also keep businesses from creating jobs in a competitive global commercial environment (see, e.g., Collins and Mayer 2010; Hancock 2004; Schram 2006; Smith 2007).

Introducing Edna

Neither of these versions of the conventional wisdom about poverty captures the combination of personal and structural factors that led Edna[1] to apply for welfare. I met Edna in the summer of 2001 when she first enrolled in a mandatory job search/job readiness program. She enrolled in the program because doing so fulfilled one of the eligibility requirements for receiving in-kind and cash public assistance. Edna was so poor that she applied and qualified for the means-tested, time-limited, stigmatized Temporary Assistance for Needy Families (TANF) program Congress established through the Personal Responsibility Act of 1996.

Edna was poor and needed welfare because she faced many obstacles to finding and maintaining living-wage work. She was twenty-two years old and black in a city plagued by residential and occupational segregation, where black women made up a hugely disproportionate 65 percent of the female household heads and the racial gap in poverty rates for female-headed families was exceptionally wide (Bangs and Weldon 1998, 15; Davis 2006). At our initial retrospective interview, Edna had two children under age six with her ex-boyfriend; at a follow-up interview about a year later, Edna also had a three-month-old son with her new boyfriend. Edna left high school when she had her first baby and did not return. Most of her work experience was in the food service industry, which she said could be helpful for raising a family even if the wages were low, because, as Edna pointed out, "depending on the job, you can get food from restaurant work." She lived and tried to support her family in a country that sets the minimum wage below the poverty line even for full-time workers and also encourages employers to restrict workers' hours so they do not qualify for important benefits provided primarily through full-time employment.

In addition to common barriers to obtaining and maintaining family-supporting employment, such as truncated education, teen motherhood, no driver's license, and limited job opportunities in poorly paid consumer or producer services jobs, Edna had to deal with a further obstacle. The father of her two older children did not approve of her working. "He feels a guy should work and a mother should stay home with her kids," Edna remarked when asked about relationships and employment. He liked it that she worked because of the money she brought in, Edna observed, "but it was taking away from time with him, like a tug-a-war." Edna's ex-boyfriend enforced his feelings about traditional gender arrangements and tugged at Edna through surveillance and harassment that followed her from home to work. "He called and watched me at work," she explained, "and called in a bomb threat. I almost got fired. They traced his call and he went to jail." Edna had grown sufficiently tired of the abuse and harassment and was so afraid of what she called his "crazy talk," that she had petitioned for a restraining order against her ex-boyfriend, which was still in effect as she tried to make the transition from welfare to work. It did not much improve her sense of security to have protection through the courts, Edna noted, because "he doesn't pay any attention to that order." At her final follow-up interview, Edna was still having problems with her ex-boyfriend: "He has been vandalizing the house and it makes me feel unsafe. The police don't care and they don't do anything about it."

Along with thousands of women in the United States, Edna was trapped by poverty and abuse (Raphael 2009). Compared with their peers, physically abused women earn less, work fewer weeks, and more frequently work part-time involuntarily. Overall, a lifetime history of women's work effort's being sabotaged by men is coupled with both lifetime and recent hardships associated with poverty, such as homelessness and eviction, utility shut-offs, skipping meals or going to bed hungry, or having to choose between food and fuel (Brush 2004; Dodson 2009; Tolman, Danziger, and Rosen 2002). Current conventional wisdom in the United States holds that the way to escape both poverty and abuse is to get a job. Conventional wisdom also assumes that economic dependence is the main reason battered women stay and that like all responsible adults, battered women should earn their way to safety and self-sufficiency (Berns 2009).

Even my brief introduction of Edna shows that this conventional wisdom regarding work and personal responsibility as the escape route from the dual traps of poverty and abuse is inadequate. Edna is not personally responsible for her ex-boyfriend's ambivalence about her employment or his expectations for a proper girlfriend. Nor is she personally responsible for the dearth of family-supporting jobs, the segregation of the labor market, the high cost of quality child care, and the ability of food service industry employers to pay rock-bottom wages and expect workers to supplement their meager earnings with restaurant scraps. The retrograde notions of gender, race, and class that limit Edna's opportunities for education, training, and employment are not her fault. Edna was not old enough to vote in 1996 when Congress rescinded federal entitlements to welfare and instituted work requirements and time limits on eligibility for income assistance for poor mothers and their children. She is not personally responsible for the ways her ex-boyfriend tried to sabotage her employment and deter her from fulfilling work requirements, thereby jeopardizing her eligibility for welfare while simultaneously diminishing her earnings capacity.

Edna's story belongs in a book about gendered approaches to human security because it responds to the calls feminists have made to include the experiences and insights of ordinary people in the otherwise abstract debates over the meanings and practices of security (Tickner 1992). Feminists argue that security concerns extend beyond states, nuclear strategy, international treaties, and militias to everyday life, where there is no such thing as Universal Man. "Women's experiences of violence and their security needs differ significantly from those of men," Gunhild Hoogensen and Svein Vigeland Rottem note in their summary of reasons why gender identity should be central to the subject of security. They add, "Women are also usually the most insecure, disadvantaged and marginalized" (2004, 156). Economic security is an important factor in relationships and vulnerability to abuse. Trouble paying the bills can make women vulnerable to entering or staying in abusive relationships. Being in an abusive relationship makes it harder for women to keep track of bills and the money to pay them. Men sometimes deliberately withhold bills or money, or otherwise sabotage women's efforts to keep on top of their household budgets. Because of the gender dynamics of insecurity, disadvantage, and marginalization, it is important to document the ways in which women, in particular, experience the dual traps of poverty and abuse. Those traps are among the most serious on the perilous path to the "freedom from fear, freedom from want" that define human security (United Nations Development Program 1994, 24).

In this chapter, I analyze one dimension of the gendered organization of human security in the contemporary United States. I follow the suggestion of feminist security scholars and look for the gendered aspects of human security in the everyday experiences of women rendered vulnerable to and by fear and want. My interviews with Edna and the other women enrolled in her job search program demonstrate the centrality of gender (and race and class) to human security. Edna's identity, experiences, and social position as a young, black mother contributed to her frustration with school, her exploitation in the labor market, and her vulnerability to blandishments, threats, and stalking by her ex-boyfriend (Potter 2008). But I do not rely primarily on the *identity*-based notion of gender proposed by Hoogensen and Rottem and other feminist critics to counter the abstraction and gender-blindness of mainstream security studies. In order to contribute to new gendered perspectives on human security, I focus on the gendered *institutions* that, along with identities and interactions, generate the conditions for human security in the United States today.

Two U.S. Security States

The institutions I assess in this chapter are policies and practices of the two quite different security systems available to Edna. One involves the law-and-order state, and is central to the "freedom from fear" portion of the definition of human security: the police and courts. The other involves the social security state, and is key to any possibility of "freedom from want" for poor mothers and their children: cash and in-kind benefits. A gendered perspective on human security reveals how these two security systems organize gender relations when they produce and position plaintiffs and defendants, cops and complainants, worthy battered women and welfare cheats. At the same time, a gendered perspective on human security highlights the ways in which ideas about masculinity and femininity, citizenship and dependency, responsibility and vulnerability all contribute to the gendered organization of the U.S. insecurity state. Sensibly, given her situation, Edna appealed to both branches of the state in her quest for freedom from fear and freedom from want.

The *law-and-order state* to which Edna appealed consists of policies, practices, and personnel of law enforcement, public safety and security, and criminal justice. The principal components of the U.S. law-and-order security state are proarrest and proprosecution provisions, complemented by a system of interstate enforcement of protective orders for dealing with partner-perpetrated violence. *Proarrest policies* allow or require security officers to make warrantless arrests at the scene if there is reasonable evidence of a crime even if the police did not witness it (Buzawa and Hirschel 2009). Also known as evidence-based or no-drop prosecution policies, *proprosecution provisions* give prosecutors the ability to pursue criminal assault and other charges against alleged perpetrators without testimony from the victim and even against her wishes (Maxwell, Robinson, and Klein 2009).

In addition to proarrest and proprosecution policies, law-and-order state resources for battered women include restraining orders against the perpetrator to be enforced by security officers anywhere in the country under the full faith and credit provisions of the Violence against Women Act (VAWA) of the Violent Crime Control and Law Enforcement Act of 1994 (Pub. L. No. 103-322). This was the step Edna (along with a quarter of the forty women enrolled with her in the job readiness program) had taken. All these law-and-order state policies and practices send a strong message to perpetrators: police and the courts take battering seriously, and abusers face consequences. Restraining orders also provide documentation of women's efforts to protect themselves and their children from stalking and abuse, and give victims an alternative to criminal prosecution in those cases where either the woman or the prosecutor declines to pursue charges (Saunders 2009). Moreover, VAWA provisions tend not to stigmatize at least those women who conform to the image of the "good victim"—the woman who turns to the forces of law and order only after suffering persistent physical abuse, without defending herself, after taking heroic measures to preserve her relationship, primarily in the name of protecting her children (Berns 2009).

The security system established by the police and courts is far from perfect. It builds the penal state at the expense of the social welfare state. It expects (mainly poor and racial-ethnic minority) women to police men marginalized from even the low end of the labor market, and consequently has different effects on women from different social and demographic groups. For instance, the intimate partner-perpetrated homicide numbers for three U.S. groups—black men, black women, and white men—fell significantly between 1976 and the early 1990s (and have remained roughly steady since Congress passed the VAWA in 1994). The percentage of all men killed by their wife or girlfriend fell from 10.4 percent in 1980 to 4.9 percent in 2008, a 53 percent drop. For women, the percentage killed by their husband or boyfriend increased 5 percent across the same period (Cooper and Smith 2011, 18). The number of black men killed by intimates dropped by 83 percent, white men by 61 percent, and black women by 52 percent. In contrast, the number of white women killed by an intimate partner in 2005 was only 51 fewer than the number of white women killed by an intimate partner in 1976, a decline of a mere 6 percent (Bureau of Justice Statistics n.d.; Cooper and Smith 2011; Rennison 2003; Stark 2007). In other words, the lives saved by the law-and-order security apparatus are disproportionately men's, and (as with the rest of U.S. society) starkly differentiated by race. Arguably, the gendered pattern in the decline in partner-perpetrated homicides is a result of the feminist movement to shelter battered women,[2] which has given both black and white women a viable alternative to intimate partner homicide for escaping abuse. The glaring racial disparity in the decline in partner-perpetrated homicides is part of the racialized constitution of hegemonic masculinity in the United

States, including the vast differential in the ways the law-and-order security state oversees and confines black and white men (Potter 2008; for extended analysis and discussion, see Stark 2007). Although it may save lives, in many cases the law-and-order state provides only an illusion of security in an insecure world; as Edna points out, law enforcement is effective neither in stopping her ex-boyfriend's vandalism nor in promoting her freedom from fear.

The other branch of the U.S. security state to which women trapped by poverty and trapped by abuse can appeal is the *social security system*, specifically the Temporary Assistance for Needy Families (TANF) program for poor mothers included in the Personal Responsibility Act of 1996 (Pub. L. No. 104-193). Over the same decades that Congress has augmented the law-and-order state, politicians and pundits have attacked and diminished the social security state by rescinding entitlements, slashing benefits, and intensifying state surveillance and control of poor women (Alexander 2010; Wacquant 2009). In response to battering, the state security apparatus offers women police intervention and protection, including enforceable no-contact orders, efforts to keep controlling and coercive men from discovering the whereabouts of battered women when they flee their homes, and provisions to register and confiscate abusers' firearms. In response to poverty, the social security system offers mothers meager cash and in-kind benefits, simultaneously imposing work requirements and an intrusive system of surveillance to enforce strict compliance with high expectations of deferred gratification, discipline, competition, and selective compliance with racialized gender norms (Brush 2003b; Collins and Mayer 2010; Morgen, Acker, and Weigt 2010). Welfare benefits are obviously part of securing freedom from want. To the extent that they increase women's leverage within or ability to leave abusive relationships, they can also be an important part of battered women's achieving freedom from fear (Brandwein 1999; Davis 1999). However, the erosion of the value of cash benefits, the "diversion" of eligible potential recipients—even mothers of very young children—from welfare into low-wage and part-time employment, and the imposition of work requirements, time limits, and mandatory child support provisions can increase women's vulnerability to both poverty and abuse (Brush 2011; Hetling and Born 2005). Increasingly strict eligibility requirements increase the burden of care on mothers of children with disabilities and restrict support for women with their own serious physical and mental health challenges (Scott 2010).

Both the welfare and the law-and-order branches of the U.S. security state draw on similar notions of what causes poverty and battering and the central roles of gendered personal responsibility and women's employment as the principal routes to safety and solvency. Bolstering the penal security state and attacking the social security state are complementary strategies, both rooted in the rhetoric of empowerment, individual initiative, and personal responsibility. Conventional wisdom holds that women's employment, especially the virtues and resources that working women cultivate in themselves and model and provide for their children, is the best way to reduce both poverty and partner-perpetrated coercive control and violence against women. Congress institutionalized this conventional wisdom, which Frank Ridzi (2009) calls "'work-first' common sense," in the work requirements, time limits, and minimalist employment supports of the Personal Responsibility Act. When poor women go to work, according to work-first common sense, they join mainstream society, build their human capital, bring resources into their households, and break the intergenerational cycle of poverty.

Similarly, the system of police intervention and court-ordered protection institutionalizes what Nancy Berns (2009) calls "victim empowerment folklore," which holds that the cause of battering is the fact that the victim "takes" or "puts up with" abuse and offers waged work as the material and emotional basis of safety for battered women. Victim empowerment folklore asserts that when battered women stand up on their own behalf and establish themselves at work, especially with backup from law enforcement, they can support themselves and their children and live happily ever after. Together, work-first common sense and victim empowerment folklore constitute emblematic features of contemporary U.S. politics. Both are built into the security systems that symbolically offer poor and battered women freedom from fear and want.

Gendered (In)security

Gender is a key organizational principle in both branches of the U.S. security state. That is, eligibility criteria, hierarchical distributions of personnel and power, routines, and other characteristics of welfare and law-and-order policies and practices have different logics rooted in three incorrigible propositions that constitute gender as a principle of social organization. The first incorrigible proposition is the notion that men and women, masculinity and femininity, are opposites. The second is that men and masculinity set the standard for being human (as workers or citizens, for instance) and women and femininity are exceptional, diminished, peripheral, or invisible; men and masculinity are privileged over women and femininity. The third incorrigible proposition is that the differences between women and men and the resulting patterns of masculine dominance and feminine subordination are rooted in reproductive biology and therefore are natural, healthy, and desirable as well as immutable and inevitable (Bem 1993; Crawley, Foley, and Shehan 2008; Ridgeway 2011).

Human security in the contemporary United States is gendered at the institutional level, where the law-and-order and social security branches of the state to which Edna appealed are organized according to all three incorrigible propositions. For example, the definition of "family violence," the instrumental and structural[3] masculinization of law enforcement and the judicial system, and other features of the law-and-order state institutionalize differences between women and men and naturalize expectations about men's aggression and women's subordination, dependence, and domesticity. Similarly, in the policies and practices of the welfare state, the stigmatization of dependency emphasizes distinct normative expectations for men and women. The welfare system exploits and reinforces sex segregated labor markets that produce women's subordination. The differential regulation of men's and women's personal responsibility for work and family builds ideas about men's and women's putatively natural roles as breadwinners and mothers into the welfare state. The effects of the gendered organization of the two security apparatuses of the state are evident in Edna's everyday experiences. Her *identity* is not as important as the organization of penal/justice and welfare *institutions* and the rules of the game they take for granted and impose on welfare bureaucrats and applicants, plaintiffs and defendants, prosecutors and beat cops, and feminist advocates alike. In myriad ways, the policies and practices of the institutions of the welfare and law-and-order states produce and position women and men, masculinity and femininity, as mutually exclusive, exhaustive, complementary, and unequal (Brush 2003a).

How do the gendered policies and practices supposed to promote human security play out in the lives of poor and battered women who appeal to the two branches of the U.S. security state? The consequences show up in high relief in the everyday experiences of women like Edna and Larnice, another twenty-two-year-old black mother enrolled in the same work-first program. Larnice had a run-in at the courthouse with her former boyfriend, who was angry about having to pay for the blood test to establish paternity that was required for Larnice's application for welfare to support their three-year-old child. His anger and jealousy prompted Larnice's ex-boyfriend to try to strangle her after he saw her getting out of the car with her new boyfriend. Her efforts to find freedom from want by appealing to the welfare state contradicted Larnice's ability to find freedom from fear because mandatory paternity establishment requirements aggravated her ex-boyfriend's jealousy and anger (Brush 2011, 43). Tonya, a divorced forty-one-year-old mother of two, who self-identified as black, Irish, and Indian, faced a similar contradiction. Tonya, who showed up for her interview wearing a neck brace after a blow from her ex-husband sent her to the emergency room, was supposed to attend the mandatory work-first program in order to maintain her welfare eligibility *at the same time* that she was supposed to appear in family court to petition for a protective order against her ex-husband (Brush 2011, 18).

The gendered dynamics of the security state are on display as well in the ways in which poor women write about both crisis points in their lives and how the vastly expanded law-and-order state and shrunken and misshapen welfare state produce gendered insecurity. For example, Nikki was in her early thirties when we met. She participated in a community literacy project designed to help current and former welfare recipients enter meaningfully into public deliberation about poverty, woman battering, and work that activist-rhetorician Lorraine Higgins and I ran. Like Edna and Larnice, Nikki was a black woman who became a mother in her teens and who had received welfare. Unlike Edna and Larnice, Nikki was married to the father of her children and was still in the relationship when she participated in the literacy project, although they had lived separately at several points during their rocky union. Along with the other participants in the community literacy project, Nikki learned to articulate her feelings and analyses in terms both audible and legible to the mainstream and otherwise transform complaints and conflicts into stories and arguments that could receive at least a serious, if not sympathetic, hearing from mainstream audiences. Nikki's narrative and analyses illustrate the gendered insecurity she and many poor women confront.

Nikki, who entitled her story "Black Butterfly," needed a backup plan when her husband failed to support her through a difficult pregnancy, two-timed her with another woman, stole her money and her dignity, and left her to care for their children and his own ailing grandmother. In narrating her story in the third person, Nikki describes how she found herself having a complicated second pregnancy that required her to "go on bed rest, . . . [h]er husband assured her that they could make it, but that turned out to be what she called a lie from the bottom of the pit of hell."[4] While she was at home on her doctor's orders, Nikki had to cope with repeated harassing visits from their landlord, and after two months "her husband told her that they needed to move out, because money was very tight." In fact, they lost their apartment because her husband had taken Nikki's share of the rent each month and spent it on "drinking and hanging out with friends." Her husband moved Nikki into his grandmother's house and told her "he would be working a lot more, maybe two jobs, to pay his grandmother's rent." Nikki wound up living with and caring for an older relative by marriage, whose behavior became increasingly erratic and abusive. Moreover, as it turned out, Nikki's husband was not, in fact, working two jobs, but was frequently staying overnight with a woman in the neighborhood other than his pregnant wife.

Nikki had a healthy but premature baby and moved in with her own parents for the first year of her new baby's life. Then she moved back in with her ailing grandmother-in-law because "Her husband had begged her to come back to him, because he couldn't live without her, and Nikki agreed if he would be there for her and the kids." Five months later, feeling sick, Nikki went to the doctor and found out she was pregnant again. When she learned of this third, unintended, and unwanted pregnancy, her narrative continues, "Nikki was so upset that she started crying. She felt like her husband was trying to trap her. *He knows I'll leave him if he cheats again, but I'll have to stay if I am pregnant. What else can I do? He's entrapping me with this pregnancy*, she thought." Not only was Nikki five months pregnant, caring for two young children, and feeling trapped by her husband; the doctor simultaneously delivered the news that Nikki had cervical cancer.

Nikki's life with her husband carried many of the classic markers of what sociologists call "hard living" (Kurz 1995): Her husband was frequently absent, he stole her share of the rent money, he drank, he betrayed his marriage vows, and he manipulated her emotions. She felt that he used money, housing, emotional blackmail, and pregnancy to keep her dependent and in the relationship—a formidable mix. Writing about unstable relationships as a contributing factor in her going on welfare, Nikki says, "I moved to low-income housing and went on welfare to get on my feet, because I wanted my own place. Getting subsidized housing meant I could afford my own rent even if my husband was not reliable."

Nikki's narrative describes her experiences of gendered insecurity and demonstrates the shortcomings of the conventional wisdom concerning poverty and abuse. On the one hand, "'work-first' commonsense" fails to recognize the obstacles to family-supporting employment that both Nikki and her husband face. Her difficulties obtaining and maintaining living-wage work are rooted in problem pregnancies, care responsibilities for both children and needy adults (such as her grandmother-in-law), and a husband who lied to her, robbed her, and cheated on her. Her difficulties were not due to her lack of incentives to work or her lack of personal responsibility. On the other hand, Nikki's situation put her under the radar of the standard mechanisms of the criminal justice, welfare, and shelter systems. Protective orders, a police system designed to deal primarily with episodic misdemeanor-level physical violence, and an overburdened nonprofit system of shelters for battered women are poorly suited to address Nikki's experiences of dependency, betrayal, and loss of control over her housing, finances, health, and fertility.

Welfare offered Nikki little freedom from want. The legal system offered her little freedom from fear. Nikki was harassed by her landlord and robbed and manipulated by her husband. She grew tired of cleaning up after her incontinent, "money hungry," alcoholic grandmother-in-law (who accused Nikki of "sleeping with her man, the man that Nikki called grandpa"). Nikki formally separated from her husband and decided: *"I'm going to pack my shit and get the kids together and move to a shelter away from all these crazy sons of bitches."* Nikki was then hassled and threatened by residents in the public housing project to which she fled.

Toward Human Security through Work and Love

In their visions of what could be different, Nikki and the other community literacy project participants carefully balanced accountability for themselves and the men in their lives, calling both for women to take action on their own behalf and for men to respond with respect. They called for changes in gender socialization, the division of care work, relationships with men, and social respect for women. They also made a strong collective case for the transforming effects of their having more options for their life projects.

When they spoke and wrote about the importance of enhanced options for pursuing lives of their own design, the participants in the community literacy project invoked two key substantive examples. Both are fundamental to understanding the gendered dynamics of insecurity in the United States today. The first involved marriage, motherhood, fertility, and birth control. Motherhood remains central to how women think about themselves, how the media portray women and their lives, and how politicians, policymakers, and other experts think and talk about and treat women. Marriage—a marker of heterosexual desire and desirability—remains a vital component of normative femininity; for many, marriage gives the cultural stamp of approval to women's sexuality and fertility. As a consequence of the significance of marriage and motherhood to gendered insecurity, women's control over their sexual selves and their fertility is one important means to their leading safe and solvent lives in which they have hope of following the life paths they determine toward freedom from want and freedom from fear.

For instance, when envisioning the factors that might have made a difference in their life outcomes, the community literacy project participants speculated about the availability of birth control and their enhanced ability to use it and other resources to make sound decisions about relationships, family, and fertility:

> What if . . . ? Young women and men were more savvy about using protection that works for them? THEN they would have more control over their finances and future. (Jule)

> What if . . . ? Jule hadn't felt so lonely when she met the men who fathered her children? Having good friends and a supportive family can help with the pain of isolation. THEN maybe she would have waited for a man ready to commit to her and the children. What if Jule found enjoyable and safe ways of meeting men? (Jule)

> What if . . . ? Nikki had other methods of birth control available and had used them? What if she alone had made the choice whether to have children or not? THEN maybe she would not have felt so trapped. Maybe she would have had one less worry in her tumultuous life. (Nikki)

Combined with the evidence from their everyday lives and narratives, these women's speculative imaginings of other life outcomes and their conditions of possibility make it clear that as long as motherhood remains one of the defining elements of femininity, human security will be gendered. This is true both in terms of women's identities and also in terms of the broader social organization of sex education, health care and medicine, heterosexual relationships, employment, and welfare, all of which influence women's ability to pursue self-determined life projects free from fear and want.

The second set of substantive issues the community literacy project participants raised concerned education, training, and work. They wrote about the tight constraints and unforgiving circumstances under which poor women make decisions and choose between very limited alternatives. They described the cramped sense of possibilities and life options that contributes to women's depression and vulnerability to both addiction and abuse. For example, Red (a black participant in the community literacy project who was in her mid-thirties) wondered how things might be different if she had not blindly followed her mother's example and trained as a health aid, if she had known she would have such a strong negative reaction to many of her work tasks, or if she could have had a "second chance."

> What if . . . ? We could have more chances to figure out what we want to do in life? THEN we wouldn't be stuck if the first thing we trained to do turned out not to make us happy. If we had more options for jobs and education, we wouldn't feel so stuck.

> What if . . . ? Caseworkers or job counselors could modify or adapt education, job training, and placement to help people find more agreeable jobs? What if we had better vocational training and career planning? THEN people would have more options and would be able to change later.

Similarly, in line with her vision of increased independence for young women, Nikki connected issues of education and work directly to issues of relationships and sexuality:

> What if . . . ? Young women and men got the training and education necessary to support and feel good about themselves before entering into a life partnership with another person? THEN maybe each person in a serious relationship would be more empowered to make good decisions for themselves.

Nikki invoked the language and ideas of empowerment for good personal decision-making, illuminating both the possibilities and the limits of this discourse. The limits are set by the degree to which her focus is relentlessly on individual responsibility rather than structural change. But Nikki's rhetoric also refers to possibilities; she highlights the basic claim to personhood for poor women, a fundamental gendered issue in human security. The combination of limits and possibilities in Nikki's framing of her experiences of insecurity makes it important to distinguish the notion of women's right to pursue self-determined life projects from the conventional language of empowerment in folklore about battered women and especially from the formulation of personal responsibility in the welfare legislation of 1996. In the United States, experts and pundits talk about poverty and battering in ways that tend to devolve responsibility and blame for success and failure to the individual. The current policies and practices of insecurity require that the individual citizen discipline herself in every realm, including money, sex, work, education, motherhood, and relationships. This is another reason to attend to and then go beyond the focus on identity called for by feminist critics of security discourse.

Poor women's emphasis on changing gender relations and expanding their life options around motherhood, marriage, and employment makes a lot of sense. Work is central to the rules and rhetoric of welfare and shelter systems. Since Congress rescinded welfare entitlements, there is more emphasis on women's work than ever before. Everywhere they turn, poor women encounter program staff, media coverage, and political talk that barrage them with "'work-first' common sense" and "victim empowerment folklore." These symbolic and logistic elements of the law-and-order and welfare branches of the U.S. state are all the more pernicious because they generate consent by coopting the ways ordinary people think, talk, and feel about their lives. In this case, the rhetoric, policies, and practices around poverty and battering incorporate the basic human insight that, as Sigmund Freud is supposed to have put it, "Work and love are the cornerstones of our humanness." That life options about family and employment would take pride of place in current and former welfare recipients' accounts of change, hope, and aspiration is hardly surprising.

The demand to expand women's life options is susceptible to assimilation into conventional notions of individual responsibility and limited, identity-based theories of gender. However, expansive concerns with women's agency and options also connect the experiences of women like Nikki, Larnice, and Edna to discourses of human rights and security that recognize women as persons and as effective actors in their own lives (Libal and Parekh 2009; Stark 2007). The demand to increase women's options for fulfilling their self-determined life projects illuminates the limited and limiting ways the simple-minded focus on jobs and protective orders draws poor and battered women into the welfare and law-and-order branches of the state. Women who are writing about welfare and work and the roles each play in crises in their lives seek a broader range of options that will expand their abilities to determine and strive toward their own life projects. Poverty, battering, and the misplaced insistence on employment as the sole and universal marker of personal responsibility make it more difficult for women to pursue these basic elements of human security.

In the decade since the attacks of September 11, 2001, politicians have pumped money and political capital into an increasingly militarized U.S. national security state. But the promises of the security state ring hollow. Attacks on welfare recipients and the institutions, programs, and people who serve them have led to a paltry and confusing patchwork of under-funded public, subsidized private for-profit, and stripped down nonprofit legal and social services. For battered women and poor mothers, the result is frustrating, with delays and interruptions in services and ben-efits that they can ill afford. Welfare workers are pressured by increased caseloads and escalating performance criteria. Local welfare adminis-trators lead departments, espouse ideologies, and implement dramatic restructuring plans with diminished resources and controversial man-dates simultaneously to improve outcomes, slash spending, and shrink the size and scope of government. Overcrowded prisons inspire building sprees that undermine state budgets and pervert public priorities. Staff and administrators of organizations dedicated to serving battered women have to substitute professionalized fund-raising and creative accounting for strategizing and mobilizing to prevent violence and promote social change. Advocates find themselves trying to help bureaucratic welfare offices and law enforcement agencies implement a welter of incongru-ous work requirements, time limits, exemptions, safety plans, recov-ery efforts, sanction schemes, and mandatory court appearances. Local Workforce Development Boards face a race to the bottom that truncates their vision and squeezes them between the rock of market pressures and the hard place of political accountability. Mushrooming private program providers wind up tempted to cut corners and succumb to nepotism and profiteering (Brush 2011; Collins and Mayer 2010).

New gendered perspectives on human security highlight these devel-opments and dynamics. Theorizing and investigating gender primarily as an individual identity or basis for group membership and solidar-ity, and focusing on the everyday lives of the most vulnerable— poor and battered women—is necessary but not sufficient to establishing the new gendered perspectives feminists need to analyze human security. New gendered perspectives on human security show how the institutions of the welfare and law-and-order branches of the state create and constrain freedom from want and freedom from fear and construct and construe men, women, and their potential for making lives and communities through work and love.

In the end, Edna's story belongs in a book about gendered perspectives on human security because poor and battered women do not need a safety net, a handout, punitive sanctions, or a lecture about personal responsibility. In interviews and their own descriptions and diagnoses of their situation, Edna, Larnice, Nikki, and women like them tell researchers, policymakers, and advocates what they need to pursue life paths of their own design. To find a measure of human security, Edna and women like her say they need civil and labor rights and ways to join with other workers to organize for jobs that make a living. They demand care arrangements that value mothers and others who do care work, whether for love at home or for money in the market. They want an educational system that protects and values all children. They clamor for not just access to affordable, quality health care services for themselves and their children, parents, and grandparents, but remedies for the conditions that undermine the health of poor and battered women (Collins and Mayer 2010, 20; Dodson 2009, 196–200). They say they want work and love that allow them to challenge conventional notions of feminine domesticity and dependency without fearing punishment from employers, police, welfare bureaucrats, or coercive and controlling men. They want to build communities of care that will encourage them to flourish as they determine their own life projects and pursue work and love free of want and fear.

NOTES

1. Edna is the pseudonym of one of forty Allegheny County welfare recipients enrolled simultaneously in a "work-first" program to fulfill the requirements Congress instituted when they rescinded federal income support entitlements with the Personal Responsibility Act (PRA) of 1996. Material in quotes attributed to Edna and other interviewees comes from interviews and researchers' field notes by the author and graduate research assistants (now Drs.) Danielle Ficco and Lisa H. Ruchti; excerpts

from Nikki's narrative and Jule and Red's "talking back" writings are from the community literacy project designed and led by Lorraine Higgins (Worcester Polytechnic Institute). The interview and community literacy projects received expedited review and approval from the University of Pittsburgh Institutional Review Board (IRB #001097). The research was funded through Grant No. 2000-WT-VX-0009 awarded by the National Institute of Justice, Office of Justice Programs, U.S. Department of Justice. Points of view in this chapter are those of the author and do not necessarily represent the official position or policies of the U.S. Department of Justice.

2. I suspect credit is due to the feminist movement to shelter, mobilize, and advocate for battered women rather than criminalization or other elements of the security state response, because most of the drop in partner-perpetrated homicides occurred between 1974 and the early 1990s, before Congress passed VAWA and established its proarrest, proprosecution, and protective order policies and practices (Bureau of Justice Statistics n.d.; Stark 2007).

3. The people "manning" the positions in the law-and-order state are mostly men, increasingly so at the upper reaches of the hierarchy. The institutionalized point of view, assumptions, rules of order, etc., in the law-and-order state present as neutral, natural, and objective but in fact reproduce men's privileged access to women's sexuality and instantiate men's experiences and point of view at the expense of women's experience and interpretations (MacKinnon 1983).

4. Unlike the other participants in the community literacy project, Nikki wrote her narrative in the third person. It was the easiest way for her to write about events that still upset her. On obstacles to creating narratives and strategies for supporting people ordinarily excluded from democratic deliberation about their lives and public policy, see Higgins and Brush (2006).

REFERENCES

Alexander, Michelle. 2010. *The New Jim Crow: Mass Incarceration in the Age of Color-blindness*. New York: New Press.

Bangs, Ralph, and S. Laurel Weldon. 1998. *Economic Benchmarks: Indices for the City of Pittsburgh and Allegheny County*. Pittsburgh, Pa.: University [of Pittsburgh] Center for Social and Urban Research.

Bem, Sandra Lipsitz. 1993. *The Lenses of Gender: Transforming the Debate on Sexual Inequality*. New Haven: Yale University Press.

Berns, Nancy. 2009. "Domestic Violence and Victim Empowerment Folklore in Popular Culture." In *Violence against Women in Families and Relationships*, edited by Evan Stark and Eve S. Buzawa. Vol. 4: *The Media and Cultural Attitudes*, 105–124. Santa Barbara, Calif.; Denver, Colo.; Oxford, U.K.: Praeger/ABC-CLIO.

Brandwein, Ruth A. 1999. "Family Violence and Welfare Use: Report from the Field." In *Battered Women, Children, and Welfare Reform: The Ties That Bind*, edited by Ruth A. Brandwein, 45–58. Thousand Oaks, Calif.: Sage.

Brush, Lisa D. 2003a. *Gender and Governance*. Walnut Creek, Calif.: AltaMira Press.

———. 2003b. "Impacts of Welfare Reform." *Race, Gender and Class* 10:137–192.

———. 2004. "Battering and the Poverty Trap." *Journal of Poverty* 8:23–43.

———. 2011. *Poverty, Battered Women, and Work in U.S. Public Policy*. Oxford, U.K.: Oxford University Press.

Bureau of Justice Statistics. n.d. *Intimate Partner Homicides*. Retrieved November 27, 2010 from http://bjs.ojp.usdoj.gov/content/homicide/intimates.cfm#intprop.

Buzawa, Eve S., and David Hirschel. 2009. "Evolution of the Police Response to Domestic Violence." In *Violence against Women in Families and Relationships*, edited by Evan Stark and Eve S. Buzawa. Vol. 3: *Criminal Justice and the Law*, 69–89. Santa Barbara, Calif.; Denver, Colo.; Oxford, U.K.: Praeger/ABC-CLIO.

Collins, Jane L., and Victoria Mayer. 2010. *Both Hands Tied: Welfare Reform and the Race to the Bottom of the Low-Wage Labor Market*. Chicago: University of Chicago Press.

Cooper, Alexia, and Erica L. Smith. 2011. *Homicide Trends in the United States, 1980–2008*. Retrieved February 24, 2012 from http://bjs.ojp.usdoj.gov/content/pub/pdf/htus8008.pdf.

Crawley, Sara L., Lara J. Foley, and Constance L. Shehan. 2008. *Gendering Bodies*. Lanham, Md.: Rowman & Littlefield.

Davis, Dana-Ain. 2006. *Battered Black Women and Welfare Reform: Between a Rock and a Hard Place*. Albany: State University of New York Press.

Davis, Martha F. 1999. "The Economics of Abuse: How Violence Perpetuates Women's Poverty." In *Battered Women, Children, and Welfare Reform: The Ties That Bind*, edited by Ruth A. Brandwein, 17–30. Thousand Oaks, Calif.: Sage.

Dodson, Lisa. 2009. *The Moral Underground: How Ordinary Americans Subvert an Unfair Economy*. New York: New Press.

Hancock, Ange-Marie. 2004. *The Politics of Disgust: The Public Identity of the Welfare Queen*. New York: NYU Press.

Hetling, Andrea, and Catherine E. Born. 2005. "Examining the Impact of the Family Violence Option on Women's Efforts to Leave Welfare." *Research on Social Work Practice* 15:143–153.

Higgins, Lorraine, and Lisa D. Brush. 2006. "Personal Experience Narrative and Public Debate: Writing the Wrongs of Welfare." *College Composition and Communication* 57:694–729.

Hoogensen, Gunhild, and Svein Vigeland Rottem. 2004. "Gender Identity and the Subject of Security." *Security Dialogue* 35:155–171.

Katz, Michael B. 1989. *The Undeserving Poor: From the War on Poverty to the War on Welfare*. New York: Pantheon Books.

Kurz, Demie. 1995. *For Richer, for Poorer: Mothers Confront Divorce*. New York: Routledge.

Libal, Kathryn, and Serena Parekh. 2009. "Reframing Violence against Women as a Human Rights Violation: Evan Stark's Coercive Control." *Violence against Women* 15:1477–1489.

MacKinnon, Catharine A. 1983. "Feminism, Marxism, Method, and the State: Toward a Feminist Jurisprudence." *Signs: Journal of Women in Culture and Society* 8:635–658.

Maxwell, Christopher D., Amanda L. Robinson, and Andrew R. Klein. 2009. "The Prosecution of Domestic Violence across Time." In *Violence against Women in Families and Relationships*, edited by Evan Stark and Eve S. Buzawa. Vol. 3: *Criminal Justice and the Law*, 91–113. Santa Barbara, Calif.; Denver, Colo.; Oxford, U.K.: Praeger/ABC-CLIO.

Morgen, Sandra, Joan Acker, and Jill Weigt. 2010. *Stretched Thin: Poor Families, Welfare Work, and Welfare Reform*. Ithaca, N.Y.: Cornell University Press.

O'Connor, Alice. 2001. *Poverty Knowledge: Social Science, Social Policy, and the Poor in Twentieth-Century U.S. History*. Princeton: Princeton University Press.

Potter, Hillary. 2008. *Battle Cries: Black Women and Intimate Partner Abuse*. New York: NYU Press.

Raphael, Jody. 2009. "The Trapping Effects of Poverty and Violence." In *Violence against Women in Families and Relationships*, edited by Evan Stark and Eve S. Buzawa. Vol. 1: *Victimization and the Community Response*, 93–110. Santa Barbara, Calif.; Denver, Colo.; Oxford, U.K.: Praeger/ABC-CLIO.

Rennison, Callie M. 2003. *Intimate Partner Violence, 1993–2001* (NCJ No. 197838). Washington, D.C.: Bureau of Justice Statistics, U.S. Department of Justice. Retrieved November 27, 2010 from: http://bjs.ojp.usdoj.gov/index. cfm?ty=pbdetailandiid=1001.

Ridgeway, Cecilia L. 2011. *Framed by Gender: How Gender Inequality Persists in the Modern World*. Oxford, U.K.: Oxford University Press.

Ridzi, Frank. 2009. *Selling Welfare Reform: Work-First and the New Common Sense of Employment*. New York: NYU Press.

Saunders, Hilary. 2009. "Securing Safety for Abused Women and Children in the Family Courts." In *Violence against Women in Families and Relationships*, edited by Evan Stark and Eve S. Buzawa. Vol. 2: *The Family Context*, 41–65. Santa Barbara, Calif.; Denver, Colo.; Oxford, England: Praeger, ABC-CLIO.

Schram, Sanford F. 2006. *Welfare Discipline: Discourse, Governance, and Globalization*. Philadelphia: Temple University Press.

Scott, Ellen K. 2010. "'I Feel as If I Am the One Who Is Disabled': The Emotional Impact of Changed Employment Trajectories of Mothers Caring for Children with Disabilities." *Gender & Society* 24:672–696.

Smith, Anna Marie. 2007. *Welfare Reform and Sexual Regulation*. Cambridge, U.K.: Cambridge University Press.

Stark, Evan. 2007. *Coercive Control: How Men Entrap Women in Personal Life*. Oxford, U.K.: Oxford University Press.

Tickner, Ann. 1992. *Gender in International Relations*. New York: Columbia University Press.

Tolman, Richard, Sheldon K. Danziger, and Daniel Rosen. 2002. *Domestic Violence and Economic Well-Being of Current and Former Welfare Recipients.* Joint Center for Poverty Research Working Paper 304.

United Nations Development Program. 1994. *Human Development Report 1994.* New York and Oxford: Oxford University Press; available at http://hdr.undp.org/reports/global/1994/en/. (July 18, 2011).

Wacquant, Loïc. 2009. *Punishing the Poor: The Neoliberal Government of Social Insecurity.* Durham and London: Duke University Press.

6

A Struggle for Rites

Masculinity, Violence, and Livelihoods in Karamoja, Uganda

ELIZABETH STITES

A group of young men in the district of Nakapiripirit in northeastern Uganda sit under a tree and talk about their lives and the challenges of recent years. We discuss the repeated years of drought, the health of their animals, the abuse suffered at the hands of the military, and the lack of economic options as their predominately livestock-based livelihood system has eroded. These are commonplace conversations in this area, and the young men are relaxed and languid. We segue to the topic of insecurity and the pervasive violence in the region, violence that is usually carried out by young men such as these. The tempo of our dialogue increases, and the men talk over each other. "Hunger!" they explain, "Hunger is behind this violence; people are stealing for survival!" "But life here has always been difficult," I say, "so why has the insecurity worsened since your fathers were young men like yourselves?" This leads us to the relations with their fathers and other male elders, and the associated fundamental shift in the social order that has determined the place and role of male youth within society.

This chapter examines the role of violence in the livelihoods of male youth and power struggles among generations of men. Using data collected from 2005 to 2009, I argue that violence has become entrenched within the livelihoods of male youth seeking to establish hallmarks of normative manhood against a backdrop of the erosion of traditional livelihood options and customary authority. Stagnation of customary succession rites means that few males are heralded into the realm of adult men and thus lack recognition and voice within the customary systems. Alternative means of achieving status and providing for families have emerged, and these means often include violence. These violent strategies in turn exacerbate the conditions leading to livelihood loss, creating a cycle of conflict, which has serious impacts on the human security of all demographic groups. Violence is further institutionalized in the government's official policy response of forced disarmament. Lack of protection by the state security forces, the stripping of men's ability to protect their families, and the erosion of their cultural role as keepers of livestock combine to undermine both masculine identity and human security in the region.

Positive human security requires that basic and essential needs not only be met, but also that the ability to fulfill these needs not be under constant threat. Violence has increased in Karamoja since the 1970s both in prevalence and in the range of those affected (Adan and Pkalya 2005; Gray et al. 2003; Jabs 2007; Mirzeler and Young 2000). Pervasive insecurity has long been part of life in the region, particularly in rural areas, and it shapes the strategies that people use to graze animals, to access water, to gather wild foods, and to design their homesteads. As violence has intensified and spread its reach, however, these strategies that previously allowed for a modicum of physical security are undermined. Enemies now regularly breach the high thorny homestead walls that once deterred attack and, once inside, steal essential and productive household goods such as sheets, clothing, and cooking utensils. Physical violence is common in these incursions. International agencies have been delivering food relief to the region for more than thirty years, but collecting food from distributions has become risky, as thieves wait in the bushes for women coming from the distribution points or attack recipient villages after dark. Women in some areas report that these thieves are local youth, stealing from members of their own communities. Intergroup allegiances that once served as social protection mechanisms in times of hardship and drought have crumbled in certain areas, with groups formerly considered "brothers" engaged in simmering but violent hostilities. Livestock, the backbone and currency of the traditional economic, social, and political systems, have decreased in numbers and ownership is less equitable among households (Ocan 1992). The Karamoja of recent years is one in which human security is severely lacking: it is a daily struggle to procure subsistence, to move about freely without fear of attack, and to raise children with the hope of future sustainable livelihoods.

Karamoja: The Context

Life in Karamoja has never been easy—populations contend with an often inhospitable and highly unpredictable natural environment and survive through a careful balance with their animal herds and maintenance of social relations. The terms of these relations fluctuate through periods of strategic alliance, peace, small-scale but regular thefts, and widespread raiding verging on warfare. Cattle raids—often violent— have long been a part of the social, political, and economic fabric in pastoral regions in eastern Africa, and allowed for the redistribution of herds after drought and disease (Fleisher 2000a; Gray 2000; Markakis 2004; MaCabe 2004). Since the 1970s in Karamoja, violence has become inherent within livelihood strategies, the nature of vulnerability, and in national military policies toward the region.

Violence in Karamoja is multifaceted and driven by a range of social, economic, and political processes. This chapter focuses on those who are both the main perpetrators and the primary victims of armed violence—young men.[1] Examining the intersection of customary authority and masculinity in conflict, I posit that the deterioration of pastoral livelihoods has resulted in an escalation of armed violence perpetrated by male youth as part of a response to livelihood change and stagnation of political succession. In turn, violence has become an integral part of today's livelihood strategies, creating a cyclical relationship between livelihoods and conflict, and with profound effects on human security for men, women, and children.

This analysis draws upon primary data collected in seven field trips to Karamoja between December 2006 and November 2009 by a team of Tufts University researchers and local research assistants. We used nonprobability purposive sampling and qualitative methods (including focus group discussions, semistructured individual interviews, key informant interviews, participant observation, timelines, map making, and proportional piling) and spoke to a roughly equal number of men and women of all ages. We conducted a total of 228 interviews, including individual interviews and focus groups. Fieldwork in this time period took place in Moroto, Nakapiripirit, and Kotido districts. The data referenced in this chapter are from Moroto and Nakapiripirit districts.

The Karamoja region of northeastern Uganda consists of seven districts and is populated by approximately 1.2 million people.[2] The region is semiarid and subject to extreme climate variability. Often collectively referred to as the Karimojong, the three largest ethnic groups are the Dodoth, the Jie, and the Karimojong, and these groups are further divided into territorial units, clans, and subgroups. This chapter focuses on the Karimojong of southern and central Karamoja, comprising the territorial units of the Bokora, Pian, and Matheniko.

Pastoralism formed the basis of traditional livelihoods in Karamoja, with opportunistic cultivation when and where conditions allowed. A combination of processes and policies in the twentieth century constrained livelihood strategies for pastoralists in the region and across eastern Africa. These processes included environmental degradation, tightened border controls, more stringent land-use regulations and loss of available land for pastoralism, competition for natural resources, agricultural encroachment, taxation by colonial and postcolonial powers, and an increase in conflict among groups (Dietz 1993; Fratkin 2001; Gray et al. 2002; Jabs 2007; Kandagor 2005; Markakis 2004). In Karamoja, the closure of traditional migratory routes placed increased pressure on natural resources, as herders were no longer able to migrate in response to the regular and frequent droughts, and poorly orchestrated government and donor interventions undermined the pastoral economy (Mamdani, Kasoma, and Katende 1992; Walker 2002).

Pastoral livelihoods in East Africa have always included a relatively high degree of diversity as part of an advanced system of coping mechanisms, including seasonal cultivation, migration, trade and foraging (Babiker 2002; Fratkin 2001; Mkutu 2003). As mobility became restricted and land access more limited in Karamoja, households further diversified their livelihood strategies in response to the increasing challenges of pastoral production. People moved to urban areas, sought to plant more crops where conditions allowed, outmigrated from the region (usually as individuals as opposed to households) (Gray 2000; Stites, Mazurana, and Akabwai 2007), sought wage labor where possible, and engaged in petty trade both within the region and beyond. In response to culminating stresses on livelihoods since the early 2000s, a growing number of people have decreased their reliance on animal husbandry. This has been an intentional decision in some instances to reduce vulnerability to cattle raids, but is more often the result of animal loss from disease, theft, and impoverishment. Government policies that promote agriculture—as opposed to more ecologically appropriate livestock-based strategies—have led to increased migration to the western and southern areas of Karamoja that receive slightly greater annual rainfall.[3]

Masculinity: Achieved and Socially Recognized

Masculinity, like femininity, is socially constructed and context specific. The lived reality of culturally specific manhood evolves and changes in a given place and time. While contextually and temporally specific, some broad commonalities of masculinity can be discussed. Perhaps most importantly, manhood must be achieved and socially recognized (Barker and Ricardo 2006). This process occurs in socially and culturally specific ways, but almost always involves informal and/or formal rites, peer recognition, inter-generational acknowledgment of a new status, and ongoing efforts to maintain status once acquired. The trappings of normative manhood with the broadest cultural resonance are having a family and being able to provide for (including to protect) this family (Correia and Bannon 2006; Dolan 2002). Failure to achieve this socially recognized normative state results in a perpetual state of boyhood.

In Karamoja, the most important process for achieving manhood is the rite of initiation. Male elders control this process, determining the timetable and ritual calendar. Until undergoing this rite of passage, a man is excluded from decision making and is not an official member of the political order (Knighton 2005). The second most important aspect of manhood is marriage. Although attracting a woman and producing children are important trappings of male status in many cultures (Barker and Ricardo 2006), it is the ability to make these acts and accompanying status *official* that often carries the greatest weight, i.e., people ask, does the man have what it takes to marry? In Karamoja, official marriage requires the payment of bridewealth to the woman's family and clan. Informal unions continue to occur, but the father has no claim to children born out of such relationships until bridewealth is paid. Even virility does not contribute to masculine status in the absence of official marriage.

Initiation ceremonies in Karamoja have all but ceased due to a crisis in generational relations and authority. Official marriage is next to impossible for most young men due to high bridewealth expectations (Gray et al. 2003; Jabs 2007). Already in a lower position after being unable to muster the resources for official marriage, men struggle to provide for their families due to widespread impoverishment, growing inequity in cattle ownership, and the loss of animals through raids, disease, and frequent drought. Those who do have animals struggle to manage their herds in the face of military intervention, loss of access to pasture, restrictions on mobility, and insecurity. Limited economic development, lack of infrastructure, and extremely low levels of formal education make it difficult for men to move into more diversified livelihoods not based on livestock.

As hallmarks central to achieving socially recognized masculinity in Karamoja—primarily initiation, marriage, and cattle ownership—became increasingly difficult to realize, violence has become more entrenched within livelihood strategies as a means to an end. Since the 1970s, cattle raids, banditry, and, more recently, looting of domestic goods have become both more violent and increasingly tied to male status. When successful, these violent strategies can result in livestock for marriage, social exchange, or trade and, in times of hardship, the acquisition of basic assets to support households. In addition, prowess as a raider traditionally brought recognition from the larger community for strength and bravery (Kandagor 2005; McCabe 2004). Raiding today is usually more commercial and individualistic and lacks sanction from the wider community (Adan and Pkalya 2005; Akabwai and Ateyo 2007; Hendrickson, Armon, and Mearns 1998), but brings important respect from within a young man's peer group. Thus, successful raids allow men to provide for their families, officially marry, and establish status—all critical aspects of normative masculinity. Raiding and the fruits thereof become mechanisms for coping with livelihood erosion and the stagnation of rites of passage. The violence inherent in these strategies, however, further undermines a pastoral production system that relies on social allegiances, shared access to resources, and mobility. As such, violent raiding can be seen as a maladaptive coping strategy that creates a negative cycle of livelihoods and conflict (Gray et al. 2003; Jabs 2007; Young 2009).

Livelihoods, Authority, and Violence

Pressures on pastoral livelihoods and related insecurity have made livestock more difficult to acquire, to protect once owned, and to manage effectively. The most basic tenets of masculine identity—providing for and protecting one's family and assets—are severely undermined as a result. A related and simultaneous development is the erosion of formal rites of passage that allowed for the transfer of authority and heralded male youth into the realm of adult men. These shifts have profoundly altered the perception and experience of manhood and have led to increased violence. The remainder of this chapter examines three interlinked processes: the erosion of traditional male livelihoods and associated gender-specific roles, the stagnation of the customary authority system that allowed young men to achieve power and recognition, and the increase in violence as young men seek to develop alternative forms of status and recognition. Lastly, a brief discussion of the Ugandan military's disarmament program shows how this policy response further impacts masculinity and entrenches violence.

Cattle and Manhood

Within a pastoral production system, accruing livestock is central to both the livelihood strategies and the status of men (Kandagor 2005). Although all members of a household or community have specific and important roles (Hodgson 2000; Lydall 2005; Dyson-Hudson 1972), male youth are the backbone of pastoral production. They travel long distances with herds for dry season grazing, scout for grassland or water sources, protect both animal and human populations, diagnose and treat veterinary diseases, and make important decisions about trade and exchange of animals for barter, sale, or social exchange.

Livestock, and cattle in particular, are part and parcel of the rituals through which young males move into recognized manhood. Animals can be obtained through reproduction, trade, purchase, social exchange, or raiding. Cattle are the central commodity in bridewealth and are presented at key points in the extended courtship phase, such as to support children born prior to official marriage, to signify intention to marry, and to maintain positive relations with prospective in-laws (and to discourage them from looking more favorably on another suitor). Exchanges of cattle also maintain one's standing with older generations, and young men are regularly required or requested to make offerings of cattle out of respect or deference to the male elders (Knighton 2005). Horizontal exchanges of animals among males build critical social and economic ties and ensure future reciprocity (Dyson-Hudson 1966; Kandagor 2005).

Pressures on pastoral production in Karamoja include both external shocks, such as droughts, disease, and the closure of borders to animal migrations, as well as internal processes, such as raiding, distress sales, and increased inequity in animal ownership. For male youth, the declining viability of animal husbandry and the decimation of herds have had a profound impact on their social and economic role within their communities. Male and female respondents in multiple locations spoke of young men as "redundant" and "idle" in the absence of their livestock and the erosion of their duties as herders. As a young Matheniko man explained:

> The enemy took the animals and sent most people home. There was some killing, but mostly they just took animals. We are now reduced to living with total shame. There is nothing we are doing.[4]

Not only are men idle, but they struggle to provide for their families without their herds. Having animals allowed communities an important insurance against hardship and hunger. Animals provided milk in the wet season and blood in the dry season, and they could be sold or traded when necessary to purchase cereals or other necessities. Men managed this balance and decided what animals should be sold. As household herds diminish, women are taking on increased and disproportionate responsibilities in feeding their families through the collection and sale of natural resources, including wild fruits and vegetables (Stites and Fries 2010). Women's more intensive gathering of natural resources increases their exposure to risk of violent attack, as they must spend more time in the remote and often insecure bush areas situated between hostile groups (Jabs 2007).

Disarmament campaigns (the most recent began in 2006) by the Uganda People's Defense Force (UPDF) have left many communities defenseless to attackers, with respondents complaining that disarmament is uneven and incomplete, leaving some populations armed (see Bevan 2008; Human Rights Watch 2007; Stites and Akabwai 2009). Young men, normally in charge of protecting their communities, have borne the brunt of the UPDF's disarmament. While livestock are housed in protected kraals near barracks, no protection is provided for disarmed villages. Attacks on assets, property, and individuals have increased.[5] Multiple male and female respondents equated the loss of the ability to protect with a shift in gender status for men, saying, "The men are like women now. Their guns were taken and there is no protection,"[6] and "The increase in pouring of blood has been increased by disarmament. The enemies know that our side has become women and they take advantage of this. We can't put up any resistance."[7] Young men find themselves unable to provide for or protect their families. Making matters worse, they also find themselves unrecognized as official "men" within the traditional authority system and unable to secure their claim over women and children. The very premise of manhood has been undermined from multiple directions.

Locating Male Authority

Similar to other East African pastoral societies, authority in Karamoja is based on a gerontocratic system (Gulliver 1953; Kertzer 1978; Knighton 2005; Legesse 1973; Morton 1979), whereby the senior generation of males (known as a generation-set) holds power at a given time. Only two generation-sets can officially exist at any one time: the senior generation-set, which consists of those in power, and the junior generation-set, which will eventually assume power. Generation-set identification passes from grandfather to grandson, and a man cannot be in the same generation-set as his father (with a few exceptions, see Dyson-Hudson 1966). At present, the senior generation-set in Karamoja is the *Ngimoru* (Mountains) and the junior generation-set is the *Ngigete* (Gazelles) (Dyson-Hudson 1966; Knighton 2005). Generation-sets are further divided into age-sets, and a generation-set must be "open" in order to accept initiates. Age-sets for women existed historically, but there is disagreement in the literature and local impressions as to the continuation of the female system today.[8]

For men, initiation marks the transition to adulthood: a man is only considered an adult and able to fully participate in the social and political order after he has been initiated. Men join the junior generation-set upon initiation into the appropriate open age-set. On the broader political level, the symbolic, ritual, and real passing of power occur when the senior generation-set of male elders steps down and promotes the junior generation-set in a succession ceremony. This succession opens space for a new generation-set (the new "juniors") and initiation into age-sets begins for the next generation. Elders control the time frame for both initiations and for the succession of power from one generation-set to the next. A year with sufficient harvests is required for initiations in order that there be enough oxen, grain, and brew for the ceremonies (Knighton 2005; Lamphear 1976). Peace is an additional requirement for succession from the seniors to the juniors, as this must happen in coordination and with shared participation across the Matheniko, Bokora, and Pian territorial units—groups that have engaged in periods of sporadic but often brutal conflict since the 1970s.

Based on oral and recorded history, generation-sets in Karamoja held power for approximately twenty-five to thirty years (Dyson-Hudson 1966).[9] The *Ngimoru* generation-set took the reins of control in the senior position in 1956–1958,[10] heralding their sons as initiates into the first age-set of the *Ngigete* generation-set. These two generation-sets, *Ngimoru* and *Ngigete*, have occupied the senior and junior position for the intervening fifty-plus years, approximately twice as long as indicated in the historical record. A variety of factors contribute to this delay, including enmity between groups, who must engage in a unified succession ceremony, and the lack of peace and prosperity to ensure auspicious conditions in the year slated for the handover. In the absence of a power transition, initiations have all but ceased, as there is no open age-set for the sons and grandsons of *Ngigete*.[11] As Gray notes:

> A number of male informants, who were in their late middle age in 1998–1999, complained that they were nothing more than "rats" (*ngidoi*), or uninitiated men, without a formal identity in the traditional power structure of Karimojong society. (2000, 408)

This large group of men in their twenties, thirties, forties, and even fifties are technically not adults and are thus not able to participate in decision making and hold no authority. The term for these male "youth," *ngikaracuna*, translates as "they of the apron," indicating that their status is akin to that of women (Gulliver 1953, 148; Knighton 2005, 135).

The current stagnation of succession and initiation rites excludes these men from the normative social, political, and economic order. This exclusion has widespread repercussions, leading to conflict between generations of men as well as an ongoing and evolving struggle by these male "youth" to establish and define their own systems for status and respect. Occurring against the backdrop of a society already marred by heavy violence, these systems themselves often entail and further perpetuate the very violence that stands as an obstacle to succession.

The elders' reluctance to hand over authority has suspended the nominal, political, and symbolic transfer of power and has created a disconnect in relations between the generations. Some respondents believe that the elders have lost the ability to control the youth, thereby contributing to the escalation in violence. Knighton posits that this process is not unique, and that the "rule of the elders . . . necessarily goes through a crisis" before a succession ceremony can take place (2005, 145). He believes that this very behavior of the younger generations, including the possible use of violence, assists in pushing the seniors toward succession. The juniors are eventually promoted and their sons can be initiated into the next generation-set. When this happens, the former young "troublemakers" conform to the established patterns of allocated roles and reemphasize the hierarchy of the age-class system (Dyson-Hudson 1966, 199).

Regardless of the historical antecedents, male youth in Karamoja today perceive the system to be working against them, and they are chafing against the existing structures of traditional authority. This can be seen in the nature of respect paid toward the elders and in the elders' ability to influence the actions of the youth (Simala and Amutabi 2005). Rituals to demonstrate respect are central to a seniority-based authority system. In Karamoja, youth traditionally offer sacrificial animals as tributes to their elders. The youth offer the meat to their "grandfathers" in the senior generation-set, with the ceremonially most important pieces of the animal doled out based on seniority (Knighton 2005). However, as youth in Lorengedwat subcounty explained, so few *Ngimoru* remain alive that the youth now share offerings with "our fathers, the *Ngigete,* not our grandfathers," as it is the *Ngigete* who now preside at rituals.[12] This illustrates the *de facto* authority adopted by the junior generation-set in the absence of succession of power. A young district official in Nakapiripirit described the circuitous nature of the situation thus:

> The Mountains have been in power for fifty-one years and have robbed the next two generations of their authority. As a result, these younger ones say, "Don't talk to us of this power! You have refused to hand over power so we do not listen to you!" The Mountains will say to the Gazelles, "It is you who are not organizing [controlling] your children!" But the Gazelles reply, "But it is your fault! You have the power and you have not handed over power so we cannot sanction or condemn our youth!"[13]

Importantly, in many cases the fathers of the youth are themselves not initiated, meaning that fathers and sons have the same official status, thereby upsetting the hierarchical system of tributes and respect. As explained below, youth are also no longer offering bounty from raids to the senior generations, as these raids are no longer occurring with the knowledge or blessing of the elders.

The elders' most important means of exercising authority is through the ability to curse or bless (Mkutu 2008a). A curse is the most serious form of approbation, particularly when levied collectively by the elders (Dyson-Hudson 1966).[14] Perhaps not surprisingly, views of male respondents regarding the current strength of the elders' curse differed by generation, with older men adamant that they still have the power to bless or curse at will, while younger men were more likely to question the strength of such actions.[15] Views also differed by group within the study population.[16] Pian respondents in southern Karamoja—both elders and youth—were more likely to stress the collapse of these mechanisms of exercising control. For instance, when asked if the senior generation still cursed their youth, a group of young Pian men responded:

> No, the power to curse has ceased! We look around and we don't see anyone with the power to curse. Maybe this is because they have been weakened by the violence . . . Cursing has also failed in [the neighboring districts]. There is no one who can command their children anymore, even when the [children] do something bad in another area. When we were boys the elders had the power to curse us. We don't know what has happened to this. We think the gun took away the power to curse.[17]

Pian elders in Kakomongole subcounty said that while elders attempted to curse the raiding "children" from other groups, they would not curse their own children.[18] Of the three groups in the study population (Matheniko, Bokora, and Pian), the Pian have experienced the most recent and pronounced internal strife and, at the time of a field visit in May 2009, Pian-Pian raids were frequent. This internal conflict may account for the more strident view by both elders and youth on the decline of the power to curse. In comparison, a group of Matheniko male youth was convinced that the curse of the elders still remained strong; strong enough, in fact, to alter the harvest in a given year (thereby affecting the necessary conditions for initiation):

> At present they are refusing to hand over power. The *Ngimoru* have power to command. When they hear murmuring from the youth that they want to have more initiations they curse *the year*—they have done this many times up until now! When they curse the year there can be no initiations![19]

Another group of Matheniko youth pondered the stagnation in succession and initiations, but felt that the power of the elders on this issue remained absolute: "Nothing can be done to resolve this. The elders have the power to curse us. We will never be able to take power unless they hand it to us."[20]

Some male respondents, both young and old, believed that the elders still had the ability to curse but said that they were no longer using this power to prevent raids. When asked why this might be the case, one young man said that the elders "have the power to curse the raids, but they don't use it. This is because of the gun—the elders fear the power of the gun."[21] Still others felt that the elders had lost the power to curse and were only able to offer blessings, including those secretly offered for raids in exchange for gifts of stolen cattle.

For our discussion, it is not the veracity of the provision of sanction or condemnation that matters, but the very fact that this traditional role of the elders is a topic of debate, as indicated by the differences of opinion expressed above. The younger generations are pushing against and at times questioning the established dynamics of authority and control. Part of this process entails the creation of new parameters of respect, status, and power. Frequently grounded in the acquisition of assets (both material and social), these new parameters often entail violent measures. Thefts and raids acquire livestock that can be liquidated for cash, jewelry, and new clothes or transferred as bridewealth. Compare this to the traditional system, whereby raided cattle would be offered to the elders as a tribute of respect and in appreciation for the approval and blessing of the raid. This reciprocal exchange of sanction and respect allowed the elders to have a degree of influence in the raids of the youth, and this influence could result in moderation in the use of violence or in the occurrence of the raid itself (Almagor 1979; Mkutu 2003, 2008a). In contrast, livestock seized in raids that do not have the blessing of the elders are usually sold quickly on the market (Mkutu 2008a; Akabwai and Ateyo 2007) distributed among age-mates or transferred to the family of a wife (to whom bridewealth is being slowly paid), who will then sell or transfer the cattle onward.

Violence and the Quest for Masculine Identity

Violence in Karamoja is not new. Cattle raiding has long been an "intrinsic feature of competition between groups" in the harsh environments of pastoral societies in East Africa (Hendrickson, Armon, and

Mearns 1998, 186), and numerous ethnographers and anthropologists have touched on this issue (as discussed in Fleisher 2000b). Raiding, however, followed specific and understood patterns (Adan and Pkalya 2005; Akabwai and Ateyo 2007) and deaths from raiding were relatively few and were compensated through a transfer of cattle to the victim's family (Mkutu 2003). The transformation of cattle raiding to a more commercial, individualistic, and often violent endeavor has received more attention in recent years, with some of the most extensive work by Fleisher among the Kuria in Tanzania and Kenya (Fleisher 1998, 1999, 2000a, 2000b; Fleisher and Holloway 2004). Although long a fact of life, armed violence in Karamoja began to increase in the early 1970s due to poorly planned economic interventions, ecological crisis, and intensified internal raiding (Gray et al. 2003). These factors were exacerbated by the increased availability of small arms in the region (Mkutu 2003, 2006, 2008a), and the uneven distribution of weapons after the Matheniko overran the Moroto armory in 1979 on the heels of the departure of Idi Amin's forces. The nature of the violence changed along with the intensity, including the rise in banditry and road ambushes, increased mortality among individuals not directly involved in raids, and, more recently, stripping of essential and productive assets during attacks within homes and in the bush.

It is oversimplistic to blame the rise in violence solely upon the increase of small arms (Eaton 2008), but is important to note how increased access to these weapons for young men has altered the political dynamic between male generations. Prior to the widespread availability of small arms in the second half of the twentieth century, a household would own one "family gun," the use of which was controlled and regulated by the patriarch (Akabwai and Ateyo 2007). The tight control over the use of guns diminished as weapons became available from multiple sources and much more affordable. Mkutu researched price changes in the cost of weapons and found that, as reported by Matheniko informants, a gun that had cost twenty head of cattle in 1979 was available for two head of cattle in 2004 (Mkutu 2008a, 73). Cash, as opposed to cattle, was also being used for the purchase of guns for the first time. Within our study population, elders in Rupa subcounty discussed the many ways young men acquire their guns, including the killing of an armed enemy, theft from "defeated rebel groups," and purchase from traders or army personnel. The elders explained, "Such guns have no traditional control like the family gun that was bought by the father! And these are the guns that our youth use to steal cattle from the neighbors!" The youth transport the animals quickly to the nearest cattle market to avoid being found with the looted animals.[22] As elders lost control over the means of force they also lost control over the assets of the raids—the cattle. This process parallels the rise in raiding for commercial purposes.

A better understanding of commercial raiding is relevant here as evidence of the increased independence of young men from the traditional authority system, and how this intergenerational cleavage relates to the increased violence as part of livelihood strategies. For the purposes of this discussion, commercial raiding entails theft of livestock for market gain as opposed to building or restocking herds.[23] In pastoral societies, a man who owns cattle is economically wealthy as well as politically and socially powerful through his ability to loan, bequest, and bestow cattle upon associates and kin. The influence of the monetized economy, however, has spread into Karamoja and other pastoral areas that were once more remote and isolated from these economic processes. Young men engage in this economy both through the sale of their labor in towns and trading centers and through the sale of livestock (Mkutu 2006). Observers link the growth in livestock markets in Karamoja since the 1970s and 1980s to the expansion of commercial raiding.[24]

Male youth raiding for commercial purposes operate in small groups and without the sanction of their communities (Adan and Pkalya 2005; Simala and Amutabi 2005). These raids are often opportunistic and unplanned, and respondents associate this spontaneity with increased violence, including an expansion of the types of people likely to be killed or injured in raids. While young men engaged in raiding are still most likely to experience casualties (Gray et al. 2003), women and young shepherds who were normally spared in the past are today more likely to be victims of violence (Simala and Amutabi 2005). This was discussed by a group of Matheniko young men, who were referencing their experience of mutual raiding with the Pokot:

> In the past there was a culture that said you would not kill someone who was just collecting wood or poles or charcoal in the bush. This is no

longer the case. Also, in the past you might take a shepherd hostage temporarily but you would not kill him, you would let him go free . . . .Today, people kill those they come across in the bush and also the shepherds because they don't want to be reported as having guns and traced.[25]

Violent assaults, including sexual assaults, against women appear to be more common than killing and are explained, in part, by the greater interaction between women and perpetrators during more intensive harvesting of natural resources as well as the intentional targeting of assets other than livestock, including charcoal, food, and clothing. Women who encounter enemies in the bush may also be attacked to force them to disclose the location of animals or they may be killed to prevent them from alerting their communities to a potential impending raid. In addition, as animals become scarcer and are kept closer to homes for greater protection, the means of acquiring them have become more violent, with more impacts on women and children. The increase in violence and casualties is perpetuated in a cycle of revenge and retaliatory attacks (Eaton 2008). As discussed by Akabwai, raiders engage in reciprocal brutality against the other group. This may also explain, in part, the increase in sexual violence against women. As Akabwai explains:

> Any raided community . . . will never forget to pay back, moreover in a big way, against the group that raided them. It may take those five years to build on the strength in the form of guns and ammunitions. When they are ready, they simply march to strike the unsuspecting neighbor and during that combat they will be singing war songs that vividly point out that they are coming to take back their cattle which the enemy raided five years ago! In addition, they will pay back exactly what the enemy did to them during that raid. For instance there would be abduction of children, raping and physical killing of women and children. (Akabwai 2008, 9)

Through commercial raiding, males in Karamoja are able to acquire trappings of status that afford them respect among their peers. Raiding as an act in and of itself has always brought status for young men. Writing on the Jie, the Karimojongs' neighbors to the north, Lamphear explained:

Personal bravery was geatly [sic] admired and encouraged, and men who killed an enemy in battle were honoured with a "battle name," and were allowed to scar their breasts and shoulders and to cut the ears of their oxen in a special way. Men of outstanding courage and physical prowess became "battle-leaders" to whom a band of twenty or so warriors might attach themselves as a kind of "private company." (1976, 207)

Mkutu quotes a respected Matheniko elder commenting on the direct link between raids and status: "Young warriors were compelled to accumulate cows in order to gain status. Their respect depended on the number of successful raids" (2008a, 17). Prowess gained as a raider is remembered and passed down. Over the course of our fieldwork, respondents and key informants often mentioned "sharp-shooters," who were famed for their gun skills and raiding capabilities. These references marked time (e.g., a woman explained that her children were born "around the time of the death of the famous sharp-shooter"),[26] important character traits (an old man introduced as a former "highly respected sharp-shooter"),[27] and served as explanations for the amassing of wealth. Sharp-shooter Kete reportedly used the financial gains he made with his skills to build the first shops in the now bustling market town of Matany.[28] These examples show that raids have always been linked to status, but were previously regulated by the system of generational governance. Today's raids take place beyond the oversight of this system, and seek to bolster a status recognized not by the traditional hierarchy, but within the perceptions of other uninitiated men. As Simala and Amutabi explain, "Contemporary raiding is sometimes carried out merely for military reputation and prestige. A new hierarchy based on the capacity to amass and use modern arms has replaced the authority of the elders" (2005, 214).

Violence and masculinity also intersect in the process and institution of marriage (Meekers 1992; Mkutu 2008a, 2008b). In order to officially marry, a man must transfer bridewealth to the woman's clan. This transfer can take place over many years but, upon its completion, the man has rights to the woman's reproductive and domestic labor, and any children born of the union are members of the man's clan. Prior to the full transfer of bridewealth, children born to a woman belong to her father's clan, and the woman usually continues to reside within her natal homestead.[29] The woman is not contractually bound to the father of her children until bridewealth has been paid: another suitor with sufficient wealth can offer bridewealth for both the woman and her children from previous unions (Jabs 2007), and, upon payment, they become part of his family. As a successful and independent adult, a man in Karamoja should be able to secure his claim over his wife or wives and their offspring. Before this is done, the man remains a youth in an extended phase of courtship, visiting his bride at night and returning to his own home each morning.

When asked about the most important rituals in a man's life, men of all ages say "initiation and marriage," in that order. Marriage can take place prior to initiation or vice versa, though the preference is for initiation before marriage (Knighton 2005). As the prevalence of initiations has waned in the absence of open age-sets for initiates, the importance of marriage as a rite of passage defining masculine identity has increased (Barker and Ricardo 2006; Howe and Uvin 2009). Unlike initiation, which occurs at the behest and will of the elders, men have a great deal more autonomy and control over the process of marriage. Men cannot initiate but they *can,* with adequate resources, marry, thereby acquiring at least some of the socially recognized trappings of official manhood.[30] Through official marriage, men also have recognized independence and contractual control over their women and children. In turn, women push men to marry for the benefit of their natal clans, including brothers who may be waiting for the transfer of cattle so that they themselves may marry (Fleisher 1999). This gives women the respect and privileges (such as protection by the man's clan) of a married woman, as opposed to that of a "concubine" (*akapukupukut).* Marriage is an important factor behind cattle raids, as indicated by one of Mkutu's respondents:

> Senior women in Rupa noted that "Women would tell the men who did not go raiding: you are not a man. Women encourage raids because all her peers are fully married, and they would tell the man why are you still sitting here? [G]o for raids and marry me." (2008b, 242)

As Gray points out, bridewealth payments that may once have taken several years can today be "acquired as a result of a single successful raid" (2000, 406). Marriage as a rite of passage still does not grant full adulthood or entrance into the company of adult men, but it is a process that men themselves can control beyond the scope of the elders. A group of Matheniko elders recognized this and linked it to the rise in gun violence:

> Young men wanting to marry and tired of being abused as useless decided to pick up AK47s for raiding cattle so that they can also marry. From then on they used the power of the barrel and no longer respect their elders. They only bow to us during initiation.[31]

The role of violence in commercial raiding and as part of the quest for status and to marry illustrates the functional nature of violence. Knighton explains that there is also an important symbolic reason for the violence, as a generation (or generations) of men engage in violence to apply pressure upon the elders to cede power. According to Knighton, this violence, including the increased use of force in raids, is a natural and even expected part of the process of succession from one generation-set to the next. Knighton references Dyson-Hudson to explain how raiding becomes a natural part of the "crisis" within the system of authority:

> Older uninitiated men drift into raiding, as the only means whereby they can increase their standing in the community. The junior generation of initiated men, which itself contains men older than the most junior age-set of the senior generation, is itching for power. They will show, short of revolution, various displays indicating that power should now be handed over to them, while some rituals fall into abeyance for lack of elders, and men move their herds totally independently. (2005, 114)

Raiding to establish standing within the community and to signal dissatisfaction with the existing power structures may be cyclical and as such, predictable. In the current situation, however, it is the duration in which there has been no handover of power combined with the increased availability of small arms along with the deterioration of traditional livelihoods and coping mechanisms that have fomented a violent struggle over the nature of masculinity. The younger generations of men are disillusioned with the power of their elders and thus do not respect the system, further eroding the efficacy of traditional curbs and restrictions on violence. As Mkutu explains:

> The erosion of traditional governance institutions among the pastoralist communities has weakened the ability of community elders to exercise control over young men. Indeed, "eldership" can now be attained by wealth, and youth are often well positioned to attain wealth if they can gain access to guns. Elders now have to "negotiate" with such youth in a way that has not been the case in the past. (2003, 11)

Although the "negotiations" between the youth and their elders are most visible in the increase in violence, the struggle is essentially over the definition of manhood in a system where the normal rites of passage are no longer attainable.

State Responses: Entrenching Violence and Further Undermining Masculinity

The erosion of customary authority and the increase in violence as perpetrated by young men have occurred in a region where there is a near complete absence of state law and order or justice mechanisms. Successive governments in Kampala have long sought to curtail violence in Karamoja through control of weapons and have launched repeated punitive disarmament campaigns over the past century (Bevan 2008). While these campaigns have often quelled raiding (Knighton 2003), the frequency of the disarmament campaigns illustrates the short-term nature of their success. The current extended disarmament campaign began its active phase in 2006; it is the second forced disarmament campaign of the decade.

Disarmament in Karamoja has been covered in depth elsewhere (Human Rights Watch 2007; Saferworld 2010; Stites and Akabwai 2009), and the current campaign has decreased the number of road ambushes, thereby improving road access for traders and allowing entrance and programming by the national and international organizations that previously avoided the region. However, violence and the threat of violence continue to have profound effects upon the livelihoods and human security of households and communities. Households, as opposed to livestock, are increasingly targeted, resulting in an increase in female and child victims. Sexual assault is becoming more common in the attacks within the homesteads and in attacks on women collecting fire-wood and other natural resources. The rape of women directly under-cuts the masculine role and identity of their male partners and relatives (Allen 1996; Stiglmayer 1994), highlighting again the inability of men to protect their families and to live up to the expectations of normative manhood.

Asset-stripping of productive and essential assets, including food stores, continued to be widespread as of late 2010. Male respondents describe their helplessness as their household goods and food supplies are removed by enemies still in possession of weapons. The Uganda People's Defense Force (UPDF) created cattle enclosures at their bar-racks in 2006 to provide protection for animals. While decreasing losses to raids, men found their role as managers of herds supplanted, and respondents in all areas complained of being idle (Stites and Akab-wai 2009). The changes experienced by men as a result of the military disarmament campaign, however, go far beyond the loss of their liveli-hood role. Men's dominance and control over their cattle, the critical cultural identifier for pastoralists (Broch-Due 1999; Gray et al. 2003; Jabs 2007), has been supplanted. In addition, men have been forced (often through brutal and humiliating means) to give up the weapons that are themselves hallmarks of masculinity (Adan and Pkalya 2005). Disarmament has been a direct and effective attack on male honor and status, and violence characterizes many of the attempts to reclaim and reestablish the culturally prescribed masculinity (Moritz 2008).

The UPDF is the most visible arm of the central government in Kar-amoja, and its violent tactics and pervasive presence have established it as the major power broker in the region. Male and female respondents across all population groups speak of the military as their adversary and complain of the repeated brutality experienced as part of disarma-ment.[32] Most interactions with the military (and, by proxy, the state) are characterized by force, and violence has become entrenched within both the political and social currency in the region. Furthermore, as documented by Mkutu, "Militaristic approaches such as those taken during disarmament have further ingrained the patterns of arms acqui-sition," leading to an increase in the value and trade of weapons (2006,

69). In the absence of protection and effective law and order and justice mechanisms, the previous patterns of disarmament followed by rearming are likely to hold true. Combined with the undermining of masculine honor through disarmament, the erosion of customary authority, the stagnation of generational succession, and the lack of alternative viable livelihoods, violence perpetrated by young men will continue in Karamoja in the absence of concentrated efforts by all parties to address the political, social, and economic causes of the violence.

Conclusion

Discussing gun violence in America, Michael Kimmel argues that violence by men is driven by "entitlement unfulfilled" (2005, 3) and by the powerlessness that men feel when faced with daily realities that do not live up to the promises implicit in their societies, promises of eventually achieving a position of power, status, and respect. Men come of age believing they have entitlements to power, and that the steps to this power—whether these steps are marked by securing an office job, buying a house, or killing a ceremonial bull upon initiation—can be realized by following the path of generations of men before them. In Karamoja, there is no longer a clear and defined path to recognized manhood. The rites required to become an adult male and proud member of society have ceased to occur in a predictable pattern and young men have limited agency to resurrect these rites. Making matters worse, the actions taken by young men to redefine their status erode the very peace and prosperity that is needed to create the conditions that would allow for the renewal of passage of authority.

Gender and violence intersect in multiple ways in Karamoja. Men are more likely to be casualties in raids on livestock, but women increasingly bear the brunt of violent attacks taking place within their homes and in the bush, where women encounter enemies while trying to access essential natural resources. Likewise, while men are the perpetrators of the violence, women also bear some culpability for the cyclical insecurity that plagues the region. Most women want to be officially married through the transfer of bridewealth to their families, and men state that they feel pressure to raid in order to acquire animals for their in-laws (Adan and Pkalya 2005). Furthermore, raiding has historically brought status to men for their strength and bravery, and the blessings and involvement of women were central to these communal rituals and laudations (McCabe 2004). Women today, and peacemakers targeting women, often speak of women's ambivalence in wanting an end to the bloodshed while at the same time eager for the economic and social benefits brought through official marriage for themselves and their daughters or the status of having a brave warrior for a son (Akabwai 2008).

Relations between genders in Karamoja are evolving with the shift in livelihood strategies away from male-dominated animal husbandry and toward petty trade, migration for casual labor, and natural resource exploitation—activities performed primarily by women. Women's economic role in their households and communities is increasing at the same time that men are losing their ability to provide for and protect their families. Women are also residing for longer periods with their natal kin prior to the transfer of bridewealth payments. While research has yet to be conducted on the specific impacts of these and other trends upon gender relations within households, we can assume from the available data that roles are evolving and are likely being repeatedly negotiated at the interpersonal level.

This chapter focuses on one aspect of gendered conflict: the ways in which power relations between generations of men contribute to the perpetuation of violence in society. Viewing this struggle through a gender lens allows us to see how the quest for recognition of masculine identity has ripple effects upon the human security of all demographic groups. Human security, which relates to the overall well-being of the population, is undermined both by violence and by the pervasive threat of violence. The threat of violence curtails the ability of women to gather natural resources to feed their families, limits trade on roads (leading to overpriced and undersupplied markets), inhibits the mobility critical for livestock health and production systems, and allows the government to justify decades of underdevelopment and marginalization of the region. Violence in the region since the 1970s has shaped all aspects of life, leading to higher rates of mortality and morbidity through direct and indirect causes, a more congested settlement pattern as people cluster together for safety, and the outmigration of male and female youth in search of better economic opportunities and improved security.

Although other factors contribute to low levels of human security in the region (such as repeated harsh droughts and livestock epidemics), the pervasiveness of violence has had a profound impact on people's ability to cope with and weather these shocks. Resilience is critical for survival in the harsh environment of Karamoja, and it is the inverse relationship between violence and resilience that stands to have the most serious and long-term impact on human security in the region.

Kimmel would likely argue that the case of Karamoja is not so dissimilar from that of the west: men come of age and realize that power is, in fact, not so easily obtainable. Men struggle to create new identities and to exercise agency over that which they have some power to control. Often this process is fraught with violence. In Karamoja, the violent strategies of male youth seeking to build respect, exercise their rights over women, and establish a name and reputation for themselves further damage the pastoral livelihood systems that the men lament losing. Raids lead to more raids, and stolen cattle are sold quickly and transported out of the region. Impoverishment accompanies the steady decrease in livestock numbers, and skills developed in raids are used in road ambushes and in thefts of household assets. Banditry spills over into neighboring districts, and political pressure mounts on the government to disarm the region. Disarmament is brutal and violent, and men are stripped of their ability to protect and provide. Control over livestock is ceded to the soldiers, but weapons markets begin to quietly reemerge. Elders, already reluctant to relinquish their remaining authority, refuse to hand over power in a time of chaos, stressing the unpropitious conditions for passing the baton.

On a positive note, however, change is inevitable. The elder generation is dying off, and power will either be ceded by the few remaining elders or will pass, de facto, to the next generation. It will then be up to the next generation to resurrect or abandon the rites of succession. When asked how the seemingly intractable problems in Karamoja can be solved, young men increasingly speak of the need to halt the cycle of violence that has so long characterized their region. Peace, they say, will allow the animal herds to recover, will allow for the sharing of natural resources, will allow for cultivation and trade, and will allow engagement between hostile neighbors in order to set the stage for the succession of power to the next generation.

NOTES

1. The terms "young men" and "male youth" are used interchangeably in this essay. This group includes males from puberty into their thirties and even early forties and is determined by initiation status, as will be discussed in more detail below.

2. The seven districts are Abim, Amudat, Kaabong, Kotido, Moroto, Napak, and Nakapiripirit. Amudat and Napak were created after 2009. Citations of interview data in this chapter refer to the name of the district at the time the interviews were conducted.

3. The Karamoja Action Plan for Food Security, for instance, focuses primarily on increased crop production (Office of the Prime Minister 2010). "Resettlement" sites in the so-called "green belt" have attracted numerous migrants, but most of these areas lack any services and given their susceptibility to frequent and prolonged droughts, are unlikely to be able to support agriculture over an extended period. In comparison, see the food security recommendations for pastoral areas in COMESA's "Policy Framework for Food Security in Pastoralist Areas" (COMESA 2009).

4. Interview with Matheniko male youth, Nadunget subcounty, Moroto, July 8, 2008.

5. The increase in attacks since the start of the most recent disarmament campaign was reported in all but one or two study locations from July 2008 onward.

6. Interview with Matheniko woman, Rupa subcounty, Moroto, July 8, 2008.

7. Interview with Matheniko male youth, Nadunget subcounty, Moroto, February 15, 2009.

8. The system of age-classes for women traditionally mirrored that of the men, but Sandra Gray's research shows that the last women's age-class was initiated in the 1940s and that this system has since fallen into disuse. See Sandra Gray, "A Memory of Loss: Ecological Politics, Local History, and the Evolution of Karimojong Violence," *Human Organization* 59 (4) Winter 2000:401–418. This was also the impression of three of our key informants, both male and female. Ben Knighton, on the other hand, says that the female age-class system is still functioning. He explains that while the initiation for men requires the spearing of oxen, for women a marriage with cattle was the central facet of initiation. See Knighton (2005, 252–253) for a detailed discussion on the ceremonies for the initiation of women.

9. There is disagreement in the literature on the length of time between succession, with Dyson-Hudson claiming twenty-five to thirty years, Lamphear (1976) stating thirty-five to forty years, and Knighton (2005) stating fifty to sixty years. Based on discussion with key informants and academics (Sandra Gray, personal correspondence, June 10, 2011), I posit that the Dyson-Hudson model is likely the most accurate.

10. There is debate over the precise date—usually given as 1957—because the Pian carried out a separate ceremony, breaking from the rest of the Karamojong groups (Gray 2000).

11. This is best illustrated with an example: Suppose a man was eighteen in 1958 when power was last transferred from one generation-set to the next. The *Ngigete* generation-set became the junior set, the first age-class within the *Ngigete* was opened, and this young man initiated. This man is now seventy-one years of age; his eldest sons are approaching their fifties, and their sons are nearly thirty and likely to have sons of their own. But because there has been no handover of power to the *Ngigete* since 1958, this seventy-one-year-old man remains in the junior grouping and cannot initiate his sons, as sons cannot be in the same generation-set as their father. His sons are well into middle age yet still technically "youth"; *their* sons are nearly thirty and have no hope of being initiated for many years to come.

12. Interview with Pian male youth, Lorengedwat subcounty, Nakapiripirit, May 14, 2009.

13. Interview with Ilukol Jobs Lomenen, Nakapiripirit, February 17, 2009.

14. Spencer posits that the elders' curse can lead to the death of young men who go against their will (1973).

15. Views on the power to curse also differ in the academic literature. Knighton (2005) is adamant that the elders still have the power to censure their youth.

16. As the qualitative methods did not seek to be representative, this trend reflects patterns in the data and is not absolute.

17. Interview with Pian male youth, Lolachat subcounty, Nakapiripirit, May 9, 2009.

18. Interview with Pian male youth, Kakomongole subcounty, Nakapiripirit, May 10, 2009.

19. Interview with Matheniko male youth, Katikekile subcounty, Moroto, July 11, 2008.

20. Interview with Matheniko male youth, Nadunget subcounty, Moroto, February 15, 2009.

21. Interview with Pian male youth, Namalu subcounty, Nakapiripirit, May 11, 2009.

22. Interview with Matheniko male elders, Rupa subcounty, Moroto, July 8, 2008. Interview with key informants #1 and #4, Moroto, July 11, 2008.

23. As such, commercial raiding can refer to raids orchestrated, funded, or supported by outside interests, such as businessmen, politicians, or traders (see Mkutu 2003; Mafabi 2008), as well as those undertaken for a quick cash sale for more individual uses.

24. Interview with key informant #4, Moroto, 11 July 2008. Livestock were traditionally sold only in times of extreme hardship or in order to raise cash for medical treatment or (in some areas) school fees.

25. Interview with Matheniko male youth, Nadunget subcounty, Moroto, July 11, 2008.

26. Interview with Matheniko woman, Rupa subcounty, Moroto, December 2, 2006.

27. Introduction at Lokunoi kraal, Rupa subcounty, Moroto, March 11, 2007.

28. Interview with key informant #1, July 15, 2008.

29. As the prevalence of official marriage in Karamoja wanes due to difficulties in amassing cattle to pay bridewealth, some young women are moving to their husbands' homesteads prior to the full transfer of bridewealth.

30. The acquisition and transfer of the requisite bridewealth is today largely up to the man himself. This is in contrast to the traditional model, in which a father and other male relatives made gifts of cattle toward the total needed to secure a wife (this applied to the first wife; later marriages were more likely to be the responsibility of the individual alone) (Mkutu 2006).

31. Interview with Matheniko elders, Rupa subcounty, July 10, 2008.

32. Knighton (2003) finds that the state—in the form of the military—is understood in terms used for a raider.

REFERENCES

Adan, Mohamud, and Ruto Pkalya. 2005. "Closed to Progress: An Assessment of the Socio-Economic Impacts of Conflict on Pastoral and Semi-Pastoral Economies in Kenya and Uganda." *Practical Action*, May 2005.

Akabwai, Darlington. 2008. "Promoting Peace among the Members of the Karamoja Cluster." Unpublished paper presented at meeting on pastoral mobility, Addis Ababa, November 10–14, 2008.

Akabwai, Darlington, and Priscillar Ateyo. 2007. *The Scramble for Cattle, Power and Guns in Karamoja*. Medford, Mass.: Feinstein International Center, Tufts University.

Allen, Beverly. 1996. *Rape Warfare: The Hidden Genocide in Bosnia-Herzegovina and Croatia*. Minneapolis: University of Minnesota Press.

Almagor, Uri. 1979. "Raiders and Elders: A Confrontation of Generations among the Dassanetch." In *Warfare among East African Herders*, edited by K. Fukui and D. Turton. Osaka: National Museum of Ethnology.

Babiker, Mustafa. 2002. "From Decline to Survival in East African Drylands: An Introduction." In *Regional Workshops on East African Drylands. Khartoum and Addis Ababa: Organization for Social Science Research in Eastern and Southern Africa* (OSSREA).

Barker, Gary, and Christine Ricardo. 2006. "Young Men and the Construction of Masculinity in Sub-Saharan Africa: Implications for HIV/AIDS, Conflict and Violence." In *The Other Half of Gender: Men's Issues in Development*, edited by I. Bannon and M. C. Correia. Washington, D.C.: World Bank.

Bevan, James. 2008. *Crisis in Karamoja: Armed Violence and the Failure of Disarmament in Uganda's Most Deprived Region*. Geneva: Small Arms Survey.

Broch-Due, Vigdis. 1999. "Remembered Cattle, Forgotten People: The Morality of Exchange and Exclusion of the Turkana Poor." In *The Poor Are Not Us: Poverty and Pastoralistm in Eastern Africa*, edited by V. Broch-Due and D. M. Anderson. Oxford: James Currey.

COMESA. 2009. "Policy Framework for Food Security in Pastoralist Areas: Consultative Draft," December 2009. Common Market for Eastern and Southern Africa, Comprehensive African Agriculture Development Programme (CAADP) Pillar III.

Correia, Maria C., and Ian Bannon. 2006. "Gender and Its Discontents: Moving to Men-Streaming Development." In *The Other Half of Gender: Men's Issues in Development*, edited by I. Bannon and M. C. Correia. Washington D.C.: World Bank.

Dietz, Tom. 1993. "The State, the Market, and the Decline of Pastoralism." In *Conflict and the Decline of Pastoralism in the Horn of Africa,* edited by J. Markakis. London: Macmillan.

Dolan, Chris. 2002. "Collapsing Masculinities and Weak States: A Case Study of Northern Uganda." In *Masculinities Matter! Men, Gender and Development*, edited by F. Cleaver. London: Zed Books.

Dyson-Hudson, Neville. 1966. *Karimojong Politics*. Oxford: Oxford University Press.

Dyson-Hudson, Rada. 1972. "Pastoralism: Self Image and Behavioral Reality." *Journal of Asian and African Studies* 7:30–47.

Eaton, David. 2008. "The Business of Peace: Raiding and Peace Work along the Kenya–Uganda Border (Part I)." *African Affairs* 107:89–110.

Fleisher, Michael L. 1998. "Cattle Raiding and Its Correlates: The Cultural-Ecological Consequences of Market-Oriented Cattle Raiding among the Kuria of Tanzania." *Human Ecology* 26(4):547–572.

———. 1999. "Cattle Raiding and Household Demography among the Kuria of Tanzania." *Journal of the International African Institute* 69(2):238–255.

———. 2000a. *Kuria Cattle Raiders: Violence and Vigilantism on the Tanzania/Kenya Frontier.* Ann Arbor, Mich.: University of Michigan Press.

———. 2000b. "Kuria Cattle Raiding: Capitalist Transformation Commoditization and Crime Formation among an East African Agro-Pastoral People." *Comparative Studies in Society and History* 42(4):745–769.

Fleisher, Michael L., and Garth J. Holloway. 2004. "The Problem with Boys: Bridewealth Accumulation, Sibling Gender, and the Propensity to Participate in Cattle Raiding among the Kuria of Tanzania." *Current Anthropology* 45(2):284–288.

Fratkin, Elliot. 2001. "East African Pastoralism in Transition: Maasai, Boran, and Rendille Cases." *African Studies Review* 44(3):1–25.

Gray, Sandra J. 2000. "A Memory of Loss: Ecological Politics, Local History, and the Evolution of Karimojong Violence." *Human Organization* 59(4):401–418.

Gray, Sandra, Paul Leslie, Helen Alinga Akol, R. Leonard William, and H. Crawford Michael. 2002. "Uncertain Disaster: Environmental Instability, Colonial Policy, and Resilience of East African Pastoral Systems." In *Human Biology of Pastoral Populations*, edited by Anonymous. Cambridge: Cambridge University Press.

Gray, Sandra, Mary Sundal, Brandi Wiebusch, Michael A. Little, Paul W. Leslie, and Ivy L. Pike. 2003. "Cattle Raiding, Cultural Survival, and Adaptability of East African Pastoralists." *Current Anthropology* 44 (S5):3–30.

Gulliver, P. H. 1953. "The Age Set Organization of the Jie Tribe." *Journal of the Royal Anthropological Institute of Great Britain and Ireland* 83(2):147–168.

Hendrickson, Dylan, Jeremy Armon, and Robin Mearns. 1998. "The Changing Nature of Conflict and Famine Vulnerability: The Case of Livestock Raiding in Turkana District, Kenya." *Disasters* 22(3):185–199.

Hodgson, Dorothy L., ed. 2000. *Rethinking Pastoralism in Africa: Gender, Culture & the Myth of the Patriarchal Pastoralist*. Oxford: J. Currey.

Howe, Kim, and Peter Uvin. 2009. "I Want to Marry a Dynamic Girl: On Changing Gender Expectations in Burundi." In *Life after Violence: A People's Story of Burundi*, edited by P. Uvin. London: Zed Books.

Human Rights Watch. 2007. "'Get the Gun!' Human Rights Violations by Uganda's National Army in Law Enforcement Operations in Karamoja Region." New York: Human Rights Watch.

Jabs, Lorelle. 2007. "When Two Elephants Meet, the Grass Suffers: A Case Study of Intractable Conflict in Karamoja, Uganda." *American Behavioral Scientist* 50(11):1498–1519.

Kandagor, Daniel Rotich. 2005. "Rethinking Pastoralism and African Development: A Case Study of the Horn of Africa." Njoro, Kenya: Department of History, Egerton University.

Kertzer, David I. 1978. "Theoretical Development in the Study of Age-Group Systems." *American Ethnologist* 5:368–374.

Kimmel, Michael. 2005. "Masculinities and Gun Violence: The Personal Meets the Political." Paper read at UN Session on "Men, Women and Gun Violence." July 14, 2005.

Knighton, Ben. 2003. "The State as Raider among the Karimojong: 'Where There Are No Guns, They Use the Threat of Guns.'" *Africa* 73:439–446.

———. 2005. *The Vitality of the Karamojong Religion: Dying Tradition or Living Faith?* Hants, U.K.: Ashgate.

Lamphear, John. 1976. *The Traditional History of the Jie of Uganda*. Oxford: Clarendon Press.

Legesse, Asmarom. 1973. *Gada*. New York: Free Press.

Lydall, Jean. 2005. "The Power of Women in an Ostensibly Male-Dominated Agro-Pastoral Society." In *Property and Equality: Encapsulation, Commercialisation, Discrimination*, edited by T. Widlok and W. G. Tadesse. Oxford: Berghahn Books.

Mafabi, David. 2008. "Moroto District Councillors Named in Cattle Rustling." *Daily Monitor*, June 17.

Mamdani, M., P. M. B. Kasoma, and A. B. Katende. 1992. *Karamoja: Ecology and History*. Kampala: Centre for Basic Research.

Markakis, John. 2004. *Pastoralism on the Margin*. London: Minority Rights Group International.

McCabe, J. Terrence. 2004. *Cattle Bring Us to Our Enemies: Turkana Ecology, Politics and Raiding in a Disequilibrium System*. Ann Arbor: University of Michigan Press.

Meekers, Dominique. 1992. "The Process of Marriage in African Societies: A Multiple Indicator Approach." *Population and Development Review* 18(1):61–78.

Mirzeler, Mustafa, and Crawford Young. 2000. "Pastoral Politics in the Northeast Periphery in Uganda: AK-47 as Change Agent." *Journal of Modern African Studies* 38(3):407–429.

Mkutu, Kennedy Agade. 2003. *Pastoral Conflict and Small Arms: The Kenya-Uganda Border Region.* London: Saferworld.

———. 2006. "Small Arms and Light Weapons among Pastoral Groups in the Kenya-Uganda Area." *African Affairs* 106(102):47–70.

———. 2008a. *Guns & Governance in the Rift Valley: Pastoralist Conflict & Small Arms,* African Issues. Bloomington, Ind.: Indiana University Press.

———. 2008b. "Uganda: Pastoral Conflict & Gender Relations." *Review of African Political Economy* 35(116):237–254.

Moritz, Mark. 2008. "A Critical Examination of Honor Cultures and Herding Societies in Africa." *African Studies Review* 51(2):99–117.

Morton, R. F. 1979. "The Structure of East African Age-Set Systems (Masai, Arusha, Nandi and Kikuyu)." *PULA: Botswana Journal of African Studies* 1(2):77–102.

Ocan, Charles Emunyu. 1992. "Pastoral Crisis in Northeastern Uganda: The Changing Significance of Cattle Raids. Kampala." Centre for Basic Research, Working Paper 21.

Office of the Prime Minister. 2010. *Karamoja Action Plan for Food Security (2010–2015).* Development of Karamoja Agricultural and Production Zones. Republic of Uganda.

Saferworld. 2010. *Karamoja Conflict and Security Assessment.* Kampala: Saferworld.

Simala, Kenneth I., and Maurice Amutabi. 2005. "Small Arms, Cattle Raiding and Borderlands: The Ilemi Triangle." In *Illicit Flows and Criminal Things: States, Borders and the Other Side of Globalization,* edited by W. van Schendel and I. Abraham. Bloomington, Ind.: Indiana University Press.

Spencer, Paul. 1973. *Nomads in Alliance.* Oxford: Oxford University Press.

Stiglmayer, Alexandra. 1994. "The Rapes in Bosnia-Herzegovina." In *Mass Rape: The War against Women in Bosnia-Herzegovina,* edited by A. Stiglmayer. Lincoln: University of Nebraska Press.

Stites, Elizabeth, and Darlington Akabwai. 2009. "Changing Roles, Shifting Risks: Livelihood Impacts of Disarmament in Karamoja, Uganda." Medford, Mass.: Feinstein International Center, Tufts University.

Stites, Elizabeth, and Lorin Fries. 2010. "Foraging and Fighting: Community Perspectives on Natural Resources and Conflict in Southern Karamoja." Medford, Mass.: Feinstein International Center, Tufts University.

Stites, Elizabeth, Dyan Mazurana, and Darlington Akabwai. 2007. "Out-Migration, Return and Resettlement in Karamoja, Uganda: The Case of Kobulin, Bokora County." Medford, Mass.: Feinstein International Center, Tufts University.

Walker, Robert. 2002. "Anti-Pastoralism and the Growth of Poverty and Insecurity in Karamoja: Disarmament and Development Dilemmas." A Report for DFID East Africa (Uganda).

Young, Helen. 2009. "The Conflict-Livelihoods Cycle: Reducing Vulnerability through Understanding Maladaptive Livelihoods." In *Environment and Conflict in Africa: Reflections on Darfur,* edited by M. Leroy. Addis Ababa: University for Peace.

7

From German Bus Stop to Academy Award Nomination

The Honor Killing as Simulacrum

KATHERINE PRATT EWING

In the past few years, honor crimes have become a global cause célè-bre among activists and scholars concerned about the rights and security of Muslim women. Headlines like "The Rise of Honor Killings in America" (Frank 2011) and "Ehrenmorde: Warum Töchter für die Ehre sterben müssen" (Honor Killing: Why Daughters Must Die for Honor) (Pagel 2011) proliferate across Europe and North America. No one can argue against the importance of protecting victims of domestic violence. But the transnational media frenzy about "honor killing" is a distinct phenomenon that must be examined in its own right, especially when right wing anti-Muslim bloggers such as Pamela Geller vociferously take up this campaign.[1] Media visibility of honor killing is based on a few dramatic cases but is reinforced by the decision by organizations such as the World Health Organization, Human Rights Watch, and Terre des Femmes (a German women's rights organization) to make "honor killing" a focal point for their campaigns. Through this rhetorical move, women's murders have been categorized as manifestations of Muslim tradition, stoking public anger against Turkish immigrants in Germany and other parts of Europe.

This campaign to protect Muslim women has itself become a source of insecurity, both for Muslim minorities who face growing stigmatization and for a European public whose perspectives on Muslims are distorted by fear.

I focus on the 2005 murder of Hatun Sürücü at a bus stop in Berlin, Germany, a murder that became "Germany's most famous honor killing" (3SAT 2012). I describe how her murder became the model for the film *Die Fremde* ("When We Leave" in its English-language release) and how the intense media discussion attached to this murder was used to generate horror, fear, and anger among Germans directed at the Turkish immigrants in their midst.

Such media frenzy about "honor killing" is different from simple concern for preventing violence against women. The concept "honor killing" obscures the sources of actual, specific acts of violence against women by creating a simulacrum—a representation that bears an illusory and even deceptive resemblance to something that is claimed to be its original. By calling honor killing a simulacrum, I emphasize the disjunction between actual murders and the phenomenon of the "honor killing" circulating in the media, a disjunction created by casting the murder as a manifestation of an alien cultural tradition. The term also highlights the power that any simulacrum acquires through its claim to being an accurate representation or a "good copy" of a real phenomenon.

What is an "honor killing"? At a demonstration she helped organize at the site of Sürücü's murder, Sibylle Schreiber from Terre des Femmes explained what she thought makes an honor killing different from a crime of passion and why this murder "could have been" an honor killing:

> In many cases, it's planned. It is something that has been discussed for a long time, and how it's done is coordinated in depth. Often, the youngest in the family is chosen, since the sentence will be lighter. It's very strategic. And then it's really about extinguishing this woman, and in many cases, even if the murder is not discussed with the entire family, there's a sort of quiet acceptance and consent that the murder was justified. And this is something that was observed in the case of Hatun Sürücü, that it could have been that way. (Wessel 2009)

Because Hatun Sürücü's murder fits the definition of honor killing given by this and other human rights activists, it has become an ideal vehicle for the propagation of the "honor killing" scenario as a drama that accurately represents Muslim practice: an ostensibly "good copy" of a "bad tradition."

I argue that the media engagement around this particular murder is linked to the representational power of a simulacrum. The simulacrum anchors a political imaginary to a specific moment as a real event. My goal here is to track the production and proliferation of the honor killing as simulacrum through the murder of Hatun Sürücü. I trace the points at which representations of the event diverge, are contested, and congeal into new forms. By examining how this drama positions its various actors, I foreground its paradoxical gendered effects. These include an alliance between liberal supporters of women's rights and conservative anti-immigrant politicians, the reiteration of stereotyped and limiting scripts for women's options within immigrant families, new and highly publicized role models for young immigrant boys angling for respect for their masculinity, and the portrayal of Muslim men as unassimilable into western societies. Rather than increasing Muslim women's safety, it has reduced the security of many immigrant families by deepening the stigmatization of Muslim minorities and heightening public distrust of trying to integrate Muslims into modern secular democracies. It both contributes to the marginalization of Muslims, especially in Europe, and reinforces the "clash of civilizations" postulated between Islam and the West.

The "Honor Killing" as Simulacrum

For a long time, the story of honor killing goes, Muslim women have been segregated and isolated in their homes, subject to violence by male family members who must uphold cultural tradition and their own honor by punishing wives and daughters for sexual impropriety. According to this story, feminist activists have struggled for women's equality over the past several decades, and their gradual success has brought the problem of brutal violence against Muslim women by their families into public view. Activists are creating new mechanisms for protecting these women, increasing state punishments for violence by these men, and educating and civilizing a population whose traditional masculinity is said to rest on a culture of honor and violence associated with Islam. These aims appear admirable, but this story is problematic in many ways.

This generic story about the prevalence of honor killing as Islamic "tradition" has been questioned from several angles (see Abu-Lughod 2002, 2011; Ewing 2008; Volpp 2000). Few men resort to such forms of violence since problems of domestic violence are more effectively countered in other terms and troubled families themselves typically seek other solutions to family conflict. To justify an escalating international campaign against honor killing despite the paucity of data, one Human Rights Watch researcher stated, "Many don't get reported, or they happen in remote areas, or they get classified as something else" (Dahl 2012). But Lila Abu-Lughod has convincingly questioned both the category of honor killing and much of the empirical evidence that is often cited in anti–honor killing literature. She argues that the honor crime functions as "a comforting phantasm that empowers the West and those who identify with it" (Abu-Lughod 2011, 36). Leti Volpp has challenged how the concept of honor killing conflates culture and "bad behavior" (Volpp 2000). In previous work, I have shown how activism focused on protecting Muslim women traffics in entrenched stereotypes about honor that stigmatize and marginalize Muslim men. Most Muslims themselves vigorously assert that honor killing is against Islam.

Yet this story of honor killing continues to intensify as a global political issue, despite its rather tenuous relationship to the violence it is meant to represent. The term (but not the practice) has become increasingly widespread as Muslims become more visible to a broader public in both Europe and North America. Honor killing is a simulacrum that has taken on its own dynamic, shaping public culture in ways that hinder rather than help solve the problem of violence against women who are Muslim.

The concept of simulacrum can be traced back to Plato, who distinguished a good copy of a true idea from this false one. Though in this post–platonic era the very notion of true and false copies and the primacy of an original over a copy have been undermined (e.g., Deleuze 1983, 47), modern politics still mobilizes publics by claiming that only some individuals and their social practices are "good copies" of a group's original founders. By appealing to the interlocutor's own point of view and emotions in order to weave convincing fantasies about the outsider, the simulacrum is a powerful illusion that obscures the phantasmic nature of such political claims (Audouard n.d.). The concept of honor killing convincingly marks non-Muslim publics as modern, rational, democratic subjects and Muslims as traditional and violent oppressors of women. It thus operates as a simulacrum that is linked to emotionally loaded fantasies misrecognized as truth.

The Case of Hatun Sürücü

Twenty-three-year-old Hatun Sürücü was killed by several shots to the face and torso at a Berlin bus stop at around 11 P.M. on Monday, February 7, 2005. The police immediately suspected that the assailant had been known to the victim because she was not robbed during the act. Some (but not all) of the earliest articles in local daily newspapers reproduced the tone of a police report, simply laying out what been learned at the crime scene (e.g., Laninger 2005). But a simulacrum began forming, even though police denounced a tabloid story headlined: "Murdered Because She Threw Away Her Headscarf" (*Bild* 2005) as "cheap propaganda" (*Tageszeitung* 2005).[2] But even after her brothers had been identified as suspects, the characterization of it as a "headscarf murder" was generally rejected by respectable German news sources.

Some in the Muslim community were angered by the association of the Islamically prescribed headscarf with a murder, which Muslim spokespersons asserted is a violation of the principles of Islam. The European edition of an Islamically oriented Turkish-language newspaper published the first of several articles about the case on February 11, two days before the assailants had been identified. The article, "Mutlu Sürücü: My Sister Uncovered Her Head 5 Years Ago, Why Would She Be Killed Now for Not Wearing a Headscarf?" contested coverage in the German and secular Turkish press (*Zaman* 2005a) by extensively quoting her brother Mutlu (the eldest). Mutlu argued that the German reporters interviewing the family never asked about a headscarf and that the wife of one of his uncles, like Hatun, wore no headscarf.

Mutlu and two other brothers were arrested a few days later on a tip from the youngest brother's girlfriend, who claimed knowledge of a plot to murder Hatun. Before the arrest, Mutlu, though asserting ignorance of the perpetrator, had suggested to the *Zaman* reporter that the murder was probably caused by the fact that Hatun had been involved with three or four men, and perhaps more, over the course of a few months:

> She began to fight with mother, father, and us. Once she even called the police because she was supposedly under pressure. After this she went to a home and lived there for a time. Meanwhile I maintained our contact and extended the offer of returning to our family. But I never received a positive answer. I broke contact three years ago. At that time, my sister had begun living like a foreigner. She had created a new friend circle for herself. She said that she wanted to find a partner herself. We know that she was with three or four people that we knew of for four or five months. During that time, it is possible that the number of people that she had met was even greater. It was after that point that we were confronted with the fact of her murder (*Zaman* 2005a, my translation).

According to later testimony by her youngest brother at the trial, she had shouted, "I'll fuck whoever I want to fuck" just before he shot her. This was not a "headscarf" issue. Sexual activity and not wearing a headscarf are not the same thing, but there was ready slippage between them. Though from a German perspective, there may be little difference between murdering a woman for abandoning the headscarf and murdering her for "promiscuity," emphasizing the former exoticized the murder and her brothers, and moved the story into an existing public discourse focused on headscarves.

In a typical newspaper report about three weeks after the murder, "When Freedom Gets the Death Sentence," the circumstances of the murder were summarized, crystallizing a story of the Turkish woman as victim:

> All Hatin [*sic*] was doing was leading her life the way she wanted.
> But it was a choice she paid for with her life. On Feb. 7, 23-year-old Hatin Sürücü was gunned down at the aforementioned bus stop. She died on the spot. Shortly afterwards, three of her brothers—who reportedly had long been threatening her—were arrested.

Investigators suspect it was a so-called "honor killing," given the fact that Sürücü's ultra-conservative Turkish-Kurdish family strongly disapproved of her modern and "un-Islamic" life.

Sürücü grew up in Berlin and was married off at 16 to a cousin in Istanbul. After a few years, she returned to the German capital with her young son, moved into a home for single mothers, completed school and began to train as an electrician. She stopped wearing a headscarf and was said to be outgoing and vivacious. (Phalnikar 2005)

The elements of her life that this news story, like many, stressed were the conservatism of her family, including her threatening brothers, her marriage at a young age to a cousin back in Turkey, and her rejection of this life, including the headscarf, all of which were contrasted with free choice, a career, independence as a single mother, and an outgoing personality.

Yet in the earliest reports, before the label "honor killing" had been attached, there had been hints that Hatun's social life may have been unusually "outgoing" (e.g., Bakirdögen and Laninger 2005). In a lengthy article in *Die Zeit*, her love life was mentioned but soft-pedaled: "She had many friends, liked to go out, and had a few love stories, also with German men" (Lau 2005). As the image of Hatun Sürücü crystallized into a symbol for a cause, any hint that she might have been *too* fun-loving for some German tastes disappeared. The documentary "Mord im Namen der Ehre? Der Tod von Hatun Sürücü" (Murder in the Name of Honor? The Death of Hatun Sürücü) (Monheim 2005) emphasized her close relationship with one German man, a recasting of her life that suggests that a woman the German public would find virtuous makes a more sympathetic heroine. Scenes of her worksite and images of her holding her son were presented, but not sites where she socialized. Hatun's life was reimagined as a working single mother involved in a long-term relationship.

But this was later. It took several weeks for the individual murder to erupt into a generalized problem. When the story did eventually become a focus of national media attention, *Der Spiegel*, Germany's most respectable weekly news magazine, now echoed earlier tabloid speculations intimating a connection between the headscarf and murder: "The percent of schoolgirls wearing headscarves in the Berlin district where Hatin was killed has gone from virtually none to about 40 percent in the past three years. Which one of today's smiling schoolgirls . . . will be next year's victim of honor?" (Biehl 2005) Something had changed in media representations, redefining one killing to be a symbol of generalized threat.

Turkish Schoolboys Perform Violence

After the usual several weeks of local police and media attention, this particular murder suddenly exploded into international concern. Labeled an "honor killing," the BBC and NPR covered the story on March 29 as the most recent, dramatic evidence that the integration of Turks—even third-generation Turks—into German society had "failed."

What drew local and international media attention was less the murder than the comments of several fourteen-year-old boys of Turkish background during a school discussion several days later. One boy was quoted (in many newspapers over several weeks) as saying, "She deserved what she got—the whore lived like a German" (Phalnikar 2005; *Frankfurter Allgemeine* 2005). Another said, "She had only herself to blame." These comments were taken as evidence that Hatun's murderous brothers were just typical young Turkish men. Now "honor killing" seemed to enact Turkish Muslim culture and these boys to represent typical Turks living in Germany. By appearing to present how Turkish men treat women, Hatun Sürücü's murder had turned into a simulacrum representing Turkish brutality and indifference.

International media attention was drawn to the schoolboys' statements by the director of the school, who had sent a letter out not only to his students and their parents but to teachers across Germany, castigating the students and warning that the school would not tolerate "incitement against freedom" (Phalnikar 2005). Eventually, the boys were punished for their comments. Some declared it was the boys' parents who should be punished, but others argued that the boys were just trying to provoke their teachers and draw attention to themselves (Vieth-Entus et al. 2005).

This kind of schoolboy performance of aggressive masculinity as provocative play was publicly demonstrated two years later in a different context. In 2007, Berlin teachers invited reporters into a minority school to film graphic images of violence. Scandal—and media coverage—erupted when it was learned that a reporter had paid for students to create a riot for the camera—truly a simulacrum of student violence. In the flurry of coverage, a reporter in front of a TV camera asked a crowd of teenage boys at another school: "How integrated do you feel in Germany?" The students—all male and probably Turkish—laugh and shout replies; one pulls out a large knife and briefly holds it at another student's throat, simulating the violence that he imagines a German audience expects of him.[3]

In the wake of the media attention to the schoolboys' comments about Hatun Sürücü, a highly publicized "solemn vigil" was held at the bus stop where Sürücü had been murdered. As one reporter emphasized, the vigil was called "not by the city's Muslim community but a gay and lesbian organization" (Phalnikar 2005), suggesting that Sürücü represented a cause around which the German public was mobilizing while the Muslim community was indifferent. Another reporter wrote: "At a memorial vigil held a few weeks after Hatin's death, a mere 120 people showed up. Almost none were Turkish. In fact most were from a lesbian and gay organization that—outraged by the crime—organized the make-shift ceremony" (Biehl 2005, 2). German journalists and the international press took this as a sign that the Muslim community cared little about (now generic) honor killings. "It is often not the Muslim community that expresses outrage over how its women live, but those on the outside" (Biehl 2005).

The press used the occasion to contrast Muslim and German without considering whether the small number of Turks at a vigil organized by a gay rights group might have other causes. Just as the press equated removing the headscarf and sexual promiscuity, its rhetoric now created an equivalence between rejecting honor killing and expressing solidarity with a gay rights organization. The press demanded that the Turkish Muslim community in Berlin "prove" itself to be against honor killing, no matter what.

The *Jouissance* of Taboo and Horror

As coverage escalated, public discourse was presented as positively transformed in several stages: this honor killing became a "wake-up call" to the German community, so that "taboo" issues were being discussed "at last," and Germans were responding with growing "horror." Journalists claimed that as a result of Hatun Sürücü's murder, Germany "turned its attention to previously taboo subjects, such as forced marriage and violence against women in Turkish homes" (*Frankfurter Allgemeine* 2005). The images of "taboo" and "wake-up call" were used to signal that public discourse was shifting, as the media thought appropriate, acknowledging a festering social problem that had been ignored and pressing for a change in policy.

However, there had already been significant media attention to what it defined as the plight of Muslim women and Muslim cultural difference. Common themes were the threatening emergence of a "parallel society," in which Muslims "sink into their own hidden world," so that "most Germans never get a look inside of the life of their friendly Turkish baker, butcher or green grocer" (Spiegel Online 2004). The subject of Turkish women as victims of their men and their culture had also been highly visible before the murder in newspaper articles, in an extensive social work literature, and in movies (see Ewing 2008). Despite all this prior concern, the idea of a taboo being broken came up repeatedly as the reaction to Sürücü's murder grew. In Germany, the concepts of taboo, wake-up call, and horror are associated with deep silences surrounding the memory of the Nazi period and deliberately invoke ongoing sensitivities that shape German historical memory.

Among those claiming to violate a taboo were three prominent feminist activist-authors of Turkish background: Serap Çileli (2002), Seyran Ateş (2003), and Necla Kelek (2005). Each had written books about the oppression of Turkish Muslim women and played a prominent role in organizations assisting women to escape their families' control. By positioning themselves as escapees from this archaic culture of violence, the three had gained new opportunities and elite status. One or all of them are usually interviewed as experts whenever an issue related to headscarves, honor killings, or other aspects of the situation of Muslim women is discussed. Ateş commented to the press that she had considered using Sürücü's final words, "I'll fuck whoever I want to fuck," as the title of a book (Spiegel Online 2009).

For German audiences, these activists serve as models of how other Muslim women might be thinking if given the opportunity to speak.

They have used the murder of Hatun Sürücü as a platform for urging policy changes and new legislation involving closer public scrutiny of Muslim immigrants, banning headscarves in classrooms, and barring "forced" marriages.[4] They frequently and explicitly use imagery that evokes the German public's relationship to Nazism and draws an analogy with it, emphasizing the "enslavement" of thousands of Muslim women by their husbands. They present honor killing as if it were a common and accepted practice, accusing ordinary Germans of passively ignoring these routine atrocities as they ignored the Nazi genocide. By implicitly linking their cause and the fate of Muslim women with the victims of the Holocaust, these spokespersons have drawn on one of the most powerful images available in German national discourse.

The idea of taboo breaking was taken up by the public. It was expressed, for example, at a parents' meeting at the school where the students had infamously said that Hatun Sürücü deserved death, organized following the eruption of the controversy.[5] The teachers expressed a sense of relief and even pleasure associated with breaking a taboo. The German School Senator Klaus Böger spoke:

> "We have let our cultural values be pushed away for too long, we have become too little aware of ourselves." He strikes a nerve in the teachers present. "Yes! That is it!" one cries out, relieved. As though a weight were falling from her, as though someone had finally pushed open the school gates behind which she had despaired for years. (Bauer 2005)

The pleasure of venting is palpable in this snippet of public dialogue. Another article expressed similar sentiments: "If the reason were not so tragic, one could feel relieved that the beating around the bush has finally come to an end" (Lau 2005). Report after report suggests that the floodgates of outrage have opened, resulting in determination to expose this secret world of horrific practices. The sense of relief that people expressed suggests that they were experiencing a social fantasy that involved an enactment of transgressive pleasure made acceptable through a sense of moral outrage. In Lacan's terms, violating a taboo while experiencing horror points to a site of *jouissance*, or transgressive, even painful, enjoyment as an outraged public (Lacan 1997: 191–203; Zizek 1997).

Horror also became a recurring motif attached to Sürücü's murder as it became more generalized and less individual. An article published at the end of February in the German weekly news journal *Die Zeit* noted that "the horror has increased with distance from the event" as "the horror over the act itself has become mixed with the horror over the moral brutality of the young men who approved of the act and thus feel themselves as consistent with the values of their community" (Lau 2005). The motif of horror was also used to characterize the violence of the staged school riot. To react with horror short-circuits thought.

Horror also justifies rage. The Turkish schoolboys who condoned the killing were taken as horrifying enough to legitimate a highly emotional, angry tone in mainstream media. One journalist wrote of "murderous macho patriotism" in families where "women are treated little better than slaves" (Biehl 2005, 1). Another portrayed Hatun's killing as only the tip of the iceberg, a hint of the situation of "thousands—perhaps even tens of thousands—of Turkish women who live in virtual enslavement in a 'hidden world' in ghettos at the heart of German cities" (Spiegel Online 2004). Imagining a huge potential for similar violence on the basis of one action is indicative of fantasies associated with breaking a taboo. The trope of a "wake-up call" operated along with the fantasy of breaking a taboo and the emotion of horror it legitimated to make the fierce and angry rhetoric of mainstream journalism seem reasonable, intensifying the stigmatization of the Muslim community in Germany.

These fantasies about the ever-lurking presence of honor killing had the power to shape public discourse because they used a simulacrum of a real event linked to a specific person and an identifiable public spot, the bus stop, as their focal point. They subtly transformed the event from a single act to a concern that resonated with national and transnational preoccupations.

Redefining the Past and Reframing the Future

The publicity surrounding Hatun Sürücü's murder generated a sense of crisis. That her murder was designated by some journalists as the sixth "honor killing" in Berlin within the space of four or five months fed public fears that a practice thought to be declining was on the rise. This perceived increase, along with the infamous schoolboy comments, was used to suggest that Turks cling to traditional, patriarchal ways, despite their residence in Germany for two or three generations. Press accounts suggested that Turks were becoming less integrated and more isolated in their ghettos, creating a "parallel society" operating on principles inconsistent with German values.

But this supposed spate of "honor killings" in Berlin was an artifact of classification: a range of murders committed under various circumstances were retrospectively labeled "honor killings." Most of the murders were cases of Turkish husbands attacking their wives, a pattern that could at least partially be explained by endemic jealousy and domestic violence; even the Berlin police psychologist emphasized, "It is generally known that German men commit murder out of jealousy as well" (Lau 2005:1).

Only after the murder of Hatun Sürücü crystallized in public discourse were the other murders recast as honor killings. Although still defined by one reporter as "slayings arranged by families who believe that their reputations have been stained" (Fleishman 2005), this definition of "honor killing" does not fit these earlier reclassified murders by husbands. However, Germans began to chastise themselves and the Muslim community for not noticing these earlier murders or publicizing the names of the victims. Activists charged that these earlier murders had been "covered up" because they hadn't been turned into a public spectacle.

Turning back from the simulacrum to the actual case, a year after the murder Hatun Sürücü's three brothers were put on trial for killing her. Before the start of the trial, her youngest brother Ayhan confessed to shooting his sister at close range. The trial began in early March 2006, and concluded on April 26, 2006, with the sentencing of Ayhan as a juvenile because he was eighteen at the time of the murder. The press interpreted the fact that the youngest brother had committed the murder as indicating the typical pattern of an honor killing and provided the public with further evidence that the family had strategically and heartlessly planned the murder together, even though the two older brothers Alpaslan and Mutlu, ages twenty-five and twenty-six respectively, were acquitted. Their complicity in the murder could not be proven, though both had been accused of planning and supporting the crime.

Other perspectives emerged outside the political mainstream (see Ewing 2008, 167–172), but there was remarkable consistency about the trial in the mainstream German media. One quote from Ayhan's testimony was included in most stories:

> Ayhan Sürücü told prosecutors he was appalled by her Western lifestyle and concerned about his nephew. As a result, he had visited his sister at home before walking with her to the nearby bus stop. When she defended her way of life, he pulled out the gun he said he had bought off a Russian seller and killed her. "It was too much for me," he told the court. "I grabbed the pistol and pulled the trigger. I don't even understand what I did any more." (*Deutsche Welle* 2006)

Whatever he may have meant by "her way of life," months of media coverage had constructed a public interpretation that emphasized her efforts to build an independent life for herself as an employed single mother. Ayhan's statement emphasized his own blind rage, but the public was not convinced that Ayhan acted on impulse. Ayhan was an instrument of a culturally backward family who had coldly planned the crime.

Segments of the Turkish and Muslim population formed a counterpublic that objected to the German media campaign in the wake of Hatun Sürücü's murder, complaining that all Turks were now being "recognized through Hatun" (Fleishman 2005), and challenging the German press's uncritical quotation of activists Çileli, Ateş, Kelek as expert, especially their conflation of Islam and murder. In contrast, the Islamic press often drew on the work of Germans who offered social and economic rather than cultural or religious explanations for the murders now all labeled "honor killings" (e.g., *Zaman* 2005b). Despite their efforts, the simulacrum of "the honor killing" was firmly attached to the murder of Hatun Sürücü, and the vivid image of this death as the manifestation of Muslim culture now served as a site for displays of horror, rejection, and exclusion by Germans against Turkish men.

Rejection and exclusion now drove responses to Hatun's individual killing, too. Immediately following the sentencing of Ayhan as a juvenile, media voices questioned whether the sentence was adequate to send a message to "the community" that the German government-would not tolerate honor killings. Plans by Hatun's younger sister Arzu to apply for custody of Hatun's young son prompted more headlines: "German Politicians Outraged by Custody Demands: Politicians have condemned the idea that the boy grow up in the family responsible for his mother's death" (Doeleke and Schröder 2006). Though the judgment explicitly found Ayhan solely responsible for the murder and the older brothers not guilty, near-consensus appeared in the German public (including both liberal and conservative politicians and church leaders) that the entire "clan" was to blame for the murder. So it followed that Hatun's son must be rescued from them. A spokesman for the Social Democrats said that turning him over to the family could not be considered, while a Christian Democrat legal expert opined, "That would be like putting a fox in charge of the henhouse" (*Deutsche Welle* 2006). Arzu's request was rejected by the German courts, and Hatun's son remained in foster care.

In August, 2007, a German federal court ordered that the older brothers be retried as accessories to murder (Spiegel Online International 2007), but by that time they had moved to Turkey. Turkey did not extradite the brothers to Germany, and Germany did not seek to have them tried in Turkey.[6] This was taken as a sign by activists that neither state was doing enough to protect women and punish the perpetrators of honor killings. Hatun's killing was now about a different kind of honor, having become a piece in the game of negotiating a relationship between Muslim-majority Turkey and the West as instantiated in the European Union. Mutlu, filmed in Turkey for a German television documentary, was now described as a "radicalized, strict Muslim" (Deiß and Goll 2011).

Imperfect Copies: A Memorial and a Prize-Winning Film

Hatun's murder continues to be a paradigmatic symbol of "honor killing" in Germany. Several TV documentaries, TV interviews with her acquaintances, other TV programs, a play, and countless newspaper and magazine articles have been produced.[7] The bus stop where she died has become the site of annual commemorations and demonstrations organized by Terre des Femmes, a German organization that has been a driving force in keeping the issue of honor killings in the public eye. Their website describes their mission as "women's rights":

> In 1981, a group of concerned women were inspired to act after reading a disturbing article in *Brigitte* magazine about the horrible fate of women in the Middle East. The women contacted Sentinelles, the Swiss human rights organization that had published the report "Princesses mortes" on which the article was based. ... [In] May 1981, the idea of founding a women's rights organization in Germany was born. (Terre des Femmes)

Based on little more than their reactions to a magazine article, these German women were moved to act. The murder of Hatun Sürücü gave them a focus for a renewed campaign that problematically divides the world between the liberal democratic subject and the Muslim bearer of patriarchal tradition.

Three years after the murder, a memorial stone was laid at the site. The plaque on the memorial states that "she was murdered because she did not want to be oppressed by her family" and it is "a memorial to all the other victims of violence in this city." These statements simultaneously define her murder as an honor killing ("family oppression") and universalize her victimhood. The plaque also got the date of her birth wrong by a year (Wessel 2009). Though apparently a trivial detail, the error signifies the gap between Hatun's life and her various simulacra. Her memorial was created by people who did not know her but sought to make her famous for their own complex purposes without even stopping to get basic facts correct.

At the fourth anniversary demonstration, both Necla Kelek and Seyran Ateş were featured. Ateş used the occasion to argue that many women are still "suffering under the same antiquated and archaic traditions." By also emphasizing that Sürücü's murder had made German society more open about honor killings, she claimed success for Terre des Femmes but a continuing need for the tireless activities of educated, secular women like them. She embraced the intensely waged conservative argument in Europe against multiculturalism by arguing that the United States was "covering up" its own honor killing problem, because "the air of political correctness" is a bit more "stifling" there (Wessel 2009).

What makes women insecure in their homes is framed for public consumption as a simulacrum in film as well. Here the cross-cultural differences in the telling matter. Germany's 2011 nomination for an Academy Award in the Foreign Language Film category was Feo Aladağ's *Die Fremde*, released in the United States with the English-language title, "When We Leave." Roughly based on the murder of Hatun Sürücü, the film is about honor-related violence within a family whose members and marriages span Turkey and Germany. The main character Umay's life story closely parallels Hatun's life. But there is a significant difference between the film's title in English, "When We Leave," and the German title, which can mean "female foreigner," "foreigners (plural)," or "foreign land." The ambiguity in the English title is between the woman's decision to leave her abusive husband, foregrounding the problem of domestic violence, and the dislocations of migration from leaving Turkey. Only the German title emphasizes the barrier between Turkish and German cultures: the Turk is a "foreigner" in Germany, and when a Turkish woman is sexually active she becomes a foreigner, an outsider, to her family and community. This emphasis on a cultural divide echoes European political rhetoric that focuses on a clash of cultures rather than on everyday obstacles to integration or on the stresses that accompany migration.

Though *Die Fremde* did not make the Academy Award short list, the film won a number of prizes in both the United States (at the Tribeca film festival) and Europe, including the 2010 LUX Cinema prize awarded by the European Parliament. The published criteria for the LUX prize are that it "illustrate the founding values of European identity, explore cultural diversity or contribute insights to the EU integration debate, explore and question European shared values, look at the level of support for the project of building Europe and address cross-border concerns such as immigration, justice, solidarity, public freedoms and fundamental rights" (Lux Film Prize 2011). The prize affirms the European Parliament's social vision of transcending national borders, forging a European identity, and promoting justice and human rights, goals which a vocal segment of the public across the EU perceives to be threatened by large immigrant minorities. This film is ostensibly about violence against women: it opens with several scenes of Umay the heroine being slapped around by a husband who makes no effort to control his temper, and it ends with a paradigmatic attempt at honor killing, as this is imagined by women's rights activists. Given the self-evident laudability of fighting for the rights of all women, it is very difficult to challenge the validation of the filmmaker and the adulation that this film has received. It is awkward to question the politics of victimhood.

Yet the film garnered a number of negative comments from North American critics, which suggests that the American press and public do not view Muslim culture quite as those in Germany do. One American review, "Trapped in a Clash of Cultures," described it as "A powerhouse melodrama that feels didactic and manipulative even as it rips your heart out" (Burr 2011). Another noted that "'When We Leave' has a predetermined arc that almost chokes its life, but for frustrated witnesses to this passion play, Kekilli [the lead actress] offers redemption" (Williams 2011). Such comments suggest that the film did not win prizes on its artistic merits as much as on its power as a simulacrum that resonated with the media-cultivated sentiments of German and European viewers. The predictable didacticism criticized by the American reviewers points to the film's ritual quality. As anthropologist Victor Turner long ago recognized, participants in both rituals and aesthetic performances enact and reconstruct culture in ways that also stir and restructure the experience and emotional responses of participants themselves (Turner 1980). The German viewers saw a simulacrum of Hatun Sürücü that presented an idealized version of her. They also experienced a demonized and unredeemable Muslim man and the *jouisssance* of watching a predictable "horror" unfold. The inevitability of Umay's death is foregrounded by the opening scene when we see the moment when she is about to be shot.

In discussing her motivation for directing this film, the film's Austrian director Feo Aladağ said in a 2011 interview for a global feminist blog: "I figured out that I didn't necessarily have to go to very far away countries in order to talk about certain dynamics. They were happening right in front of my door, they were going on in Europe, and they were going on in Germany. When I started doing the research there was already a very high rate of 'honor-crimes' in Berlin. In four months, there were five honor killings just in Berlin. There was even more of a validation that it was okay and necessary to tell a story like this" (Bachan 2011).

The quote demonstrates clearly how the "very high rate of 'honor-crimes' in Berlin" had become a truth that, in turn, generated new simulacra. The film now represents honor killing as the almost inevitable outcome of a Turkish woman's resistance to family expectations. It presents Turkish family and community expectations as rigid cultural norms grounded in honor and pitted against individual needs and wishes, especially those of women but also those of men forced by these norms to sacrifice a daughter or sister to the demands of family honor. The film represents both Turks and Germans through stereotypes that emphasize the oppression of young Turkish women by their families, epitomized by male violence based on traditional ideas of honor. It closely parallels earlier cinematic depictions of Turkish daughters who free themselves from their families in the face of male violence: the female protagonist crosses between two distinct cultural worlds and defiantly stands up for her right to act as an individual capable of making her own decisions.[8]

The Turkish men in these films are constrained by a traditional form of masculinity rooted in honor, violence, and conformity. Nearly every Turkish man in *Die Fremde* performs more than one act of physical violence, repetitively lashing out whenever he is challenged. Turkish cultural practices are presented in unambiguously negative terms, as is Turkey itself.[9] Yet several Germans who have spoken with me about the film see the representation of Turkish men as nuanced simply because the father shows love for his daughter and expresses conflict about having to reject her, wishing she had been a boy instead. The key divergence between the lives of Hatun and Umay occurs in the last moments of the film. Where Hatun purportedly screamed at her youngest brother, Umay looks steadily and silently into his eyes. Umay's younger brother fails to shoot her. He loses his nerve, drops the gun, and runs.

These moments of ambivalence recall similar scenes from earlier films such as *Yasemin* (Bohm 1988) when a father or brother hesitates and then lets her escape to be with a German. The men are shown as troubled by conflict between their love for the women in the family and the rigidity of traditional Turkish values. In Umay's case, her older brother then steps in to stab her, a scene emphasizing the family's collective planning. *Die Fremde* ends in pathos: he accidently stabs her son instead, and brother and sister stare at each other in misery until she runs screaming down the street bearing her dead son.

The film also reflects the common German perception that Turkish women are more open to integration than are Turkish men, enticed by the chance to continue studying and avoid early marriage. Like other simulacra of Hatun that have proliferated over the years, Umay is presented as a virtuous heroine. She explicitly preaches women's equality and freedom to her mother and sister. After she leaves home, she antagonizes her family by showing up at her sister's wedding, but she does so to fulfill a promise to her sister. At the wedding, she publicly humiliates her family by making a speech, thereby triggering the family's decision to kill her, while the speech also makes her a mouthpiece for feminist ideals and human rights. Umay's employer, also a Turkish woman, similarly serves as mouthpiece for German values when she chastises Umay's father, saying, "You should care for all your children." As an assimilated immigrant, she also criticizes his interpretation of Islam as demanding honor killing by saying, "You leave God out of this—He has nothing to do with it." Umay and her employer, representatives of modern feminism, are presented as more German-friendly and so more civilized than the men of their own community.

The film reassures Germans that they are saviors of Turkish women, whether in the form of the police who rescue Umay from her family, or the girlfriend and boyfriend who provide safe havens. In earlier films such as *Yasemin,* Germans serve as embodiments of democracy, equality, and human rights who confront the Turkish Muslim other. In this film, western civilization is itself presented as unproblematically good, and all its representatives as noble and just. Violence against women becomes a cue for the audience to recoil in self-righteous horror; presenting Muslim culture as barbaric justifies the exclusion and vilification of Turkish men.

Conclusion

As the story of a young single mother estranged from her family, living a more "German" life complete with dancing at clubs, barhopping, and multiple boyfriends, Hatun Sürücü's life and death were reconstructed as a morality tale. Her murder was transformed into its simulacrum, a typical honor killing, and presented as justification for anti-immigrant politics in Germany. This simulacrum still operates in Germany as a dense signifier that obscures its workings by means of its illusory and phantasmic links to Hatun herself. The confusing details that make any life unreadable as a simple morality tale quickly dropped out of the news, while aspects of the story came to the fore that could be used as evidence for the family's depraved and unrepentant rejection of this young woman.

While human security as a gendered issue often is understood as mobilizing cultural resistance to violence against women, the horror and anger generated have other, less visible effects than protecting women from physical harm. I have traced the formation of the "honor killing" as a simulacrum of Hatun Sürücü in order to point to the political effects of such media frenzy. The immediate and unspectacular response to the specific act of violence was transformed into a cultural enactment of good versus evil through the rhetorical force of a drama of victimhood and rescue. Muslim women lose their specific humanity and become comprehensible only as victims who are eager to be rescued from patriarchy and the incorrigible violence of the stereotypical Muslim man (see Abu-Lughod 2002). The honor killing as simulacrum is staged as the sequel to the uncertain and uneasy triumph of (our, western) gender equality over (their, traditional) patriarchy. In this drama news reporters express shock and outrage to discover that oppression of women has reemerged in Europe and North America, brought by growing populations of immigrant Muslims. Feminist activists are enlisted in the cause of stigmatizing Muslim men as the exponents of a now-archaic and un-European patriarchy. With the mobilization against honor killings as its justification, Muslim communities are represented as stifling cages of violence, the image of Islam as a violent religion is reinforced, and the immigration of Muslims becomes a threat to human security.

Although there are global dimensions to the movement against honor killings and even to the simulacrum of Hatun Sürücü, the cultural mobilization has specific local effects. In Germany, with its large but economically struggling Turkish minority, the iteration and reiteration of the story of Hatun Sürücü has helped to crystallize a public perception of the policy of multiculturalism as a failure. "The Muslim community" was held to be responsible, even though Muslim and

Turkish organizations in Germany condemned German-Turkish youth for espousing "self-administered justice" and publicly deplored violence against women. The political right in Germany connected "honor killing" and "headscarves" from the start and used the story to castigate Muslims and challenge the tolerance associated with multiculturalism. Turkish women's rights activists and the German media exploited each other as they seized on Sürücü's murder to campaign against honor crimes, presented themselves as models of enlightened secular modernity, and built their careers.

As the simulacrum "honor killing" became widely understood as a sign of unbridgeable difference between Germans and Turks, it functioned to express both the machismo and cultural authenticity of youths of Turkish origin and Germans' phantasmatic fears of a dangerous parallel society in their midst. The religious other once again became a focal point for concerns about the national future, now as a threat to the democratic principles that are the foundation of the postwar German state. The values of sexual freedom and personal choice become focused on control over women's lives, where Turkish Muslim families are depicted as uniformly oppressive patriarchies and contrasted with a no-less imaginary state of gender equality in contemporary Germany. Rather than feeding such dangerous fantasies, a politics that would advance both human security and women's emancipation would need to acknowledge the complexity of those sites where men and women enact the dance of everyday life.

NOTES

1. Pamela Geller is cofounder, along with Robert Spencer, of the Freedom Defense Initiative and Stop Islamization of America, an organization labeled as a hate group by the Anti-Defamation League.

2. "Ermordet, weil sie ihr Kopftuch wegwarf." *Bild*, February 9, 2005.

3. "Gewalt an deutschen Schulen" *Youtube*. (http://www.youtube.com/watch?v=1kqnBM_tMZk. This is a clip that appears to have been recorded from a German television newscast.) Accessed January 8, 2008, but no longer available.

4. For more detail on controversies surrounding the public statements of these activists, see Ewing 2008:161–166.

5. Though 80 percent of the students at the school were from immigrant families, few of the parents attending the meeting were immigrants.

6. See the website honorenforced.com, maintained by Rhea Wessel and Gunther Kohn for a timeline of events linked to the case of Hatun Sürücü. Wessell and Kohn are coauthoring a forthcoming book about Sürücü—*Honor Enforced*.

7. See, for example, the 2011 public TV documentary, "Verlorene Ehre: Der Irrweg der Familie Sürücü" (Lost Honor: The Folly of the Sürücü Family). Matthias Deiß and Jo Goll, ARD. Films include "Mord im Namen der Ehre? Der Tod von Hatun Sürücü," by Gert Monheim (2005) and David Gould's "Two Sides of the Moon" (2011). For a partial list of media productions, see the German Wikipedia article, "Hatun Sürücü." http://de.wikipedia.org/wiki/ Hatun_S%C3%BCr%C3%BCc%C3%BC.

8. See Ewing 2008:62–70 for discussion of changing representations of Turks in German cinema.

9. Scenes of Istanbul and of the Turkish countryside are dominated by oppressively bleak juxtapositions of desiccated landscapes and incongruous markers of modernity.

REFERENCES

3SAT. 2012. "Verlorene Ehre—Der Irrweg der Familie Sürücü: Deutschlands bekanntester Ehrenmord" (Lost Honor—The Folly of the Sürücü Family: Germany's Most Famous Honor Killing). February. http://www.3sat.de/page/?source=/ard/sendung/160410/index.html

Abu-Lughod, Lila. 2002. "Do Muslim Women Really Need Saving? Anthropological Reflections on Cultural Relativism and Its Others." *American Anthropologist* 104 (3):783–790.

———. 2011. "Seductions of the 'Honor Crime.'" *Differences: A Journal of Feminist Cultural Studies* 22(1):17–63.

Aladağ, Feo, director. 2010. *Die Fremde* (When We Leave). 119 minutes, Germany.

Ateş, Seyran. 2003. *Grosse Reise ins Feuer: die Geschichte einer deutschen Türkin* (Big Journey into Fire: The Story of a German Turkish Woman). Berlin: Rowohlt.

Audouard, Xavier. n.d. "Le Simulacre." *Concept and Form: the Cahiers pour l'Analyse.* Vol. 3, article 3.4. http://cahiers.kingston.ac.uk/vol03/cpa3.4.audouard.html#page57

Bachan, Kyle. 2011. "When We Leave: Translating a Silent Oppression for Worldwide Audiences." *Gender across Borders: A Global Voice for Gender Justice.* January 10. http://www.genderacrossborders.com/2011/01/10/ when-we-leave-translating-a-silent-oppression-for-worldwide-audiences/

Bakirdögen, Ayhan, and Tanja Laninger. 2005. "Lebte Hatun Sürücü zu modern? Kripo vermutet, dass Lebenslust des 23jährigrn Mordopfers Täter provozierte" (Did Hatun Sürücü Live Too Modern? The Criminal Investigation Department Speculates That the Love for Life of the 23-year-old Murder Victim May Have Provoked the Perpetrators). *Die Welt.de* Feb 10. http://www.welt.de/data/2005/02/10/461512. html.

Bauer, Patrick. 2005. "Hinter der Schulfassade" (Behind the School Façade). *Die Tageszeitung*. July 13. http://www.taz.de/pt/2005/03/09/a0272.nf/text.

Beseke, Ulriche. 2006. "Ihr Bruder hat sie sexuell belästigt." Stern TV. April 19.

Biehl, Jody K. 2005. "The Death of a Muslim Woman: 'The Whore Lived Like a German.'" *Spiegel Online International* March 2. http://www.spiegel.de/international/0,1518,344374,00.html.

Bild. 2005. "Ermordet, weil sie ihr Kopftuch wegwarf" (Murdered Because She Threw Away Her Headscarf). February 9.

Bohm, Hark. 1988. *Yasemin*. Hamburg: Hamburger Kino Kompanie.

Burr, Ty. 2011. "Trapped in a Clash of Cultures." *Boston Globe*. April 1. http://www.highbeam.com/doc/1P2-28329567.html.

Çileli, Serap. 2002. *Wir sind eure Töchter, nicht eure Ehre!* (We Are Your Daughters, Not Your Honor). Michelstadt: Neuther.

Dahl, Julia. 2012. "'Honor Killing' under Growing Scrutiny in the U.S." CBS News—Crimesider. April 4. http://www.cbsnews.com/8301-504083_162-57409395-504083/honor-killing-under-growing-scrutiny-in-the-u.s/.

Deiß, Matthias, and Jo Goll, directors. 2011. "Verlorene Ehre: Der Irrweg der Familie Sürücü" (Lost Honor: The Folly of the Sürücü Family). ARD television documentary. July.

Deleuze, Gilles. 1983. "Plato and the Simulacrum." Rosalind Krauss, trans. *October* 27:45–56.

Deutsche Welle. 2006. "German Politicians Outraged by Custody Demands." April 19. http://www.de-world.de/dw/article/0,2144,1974065,00.html.

Doeleke, Karl, and Miriam Schröder. 2006. "Reactions to Honor Killing Sentence: 'Not the Signal We Need.'" Spiegel Online, August 13. http://www.spiegel.de/politik/deutschland/0,1518,411282,00.html.

Ewing, Katherine Pratt. 2008. *Stolen Honor: Stigmatizing Muslim Men in Berlin*. Stanford: Stanford University Press.

Fleishman, Jeffrey. 2005. "'Honor Killings' Show Culture Clash in Berlin: The Latest Slaying of a Muslim Woman in the German Capital Has Sharpened Debate over the Place of Immigrants in Europe." *Los Angeles Times*, March 20, A10.

Frank, Marshall. 2011. "The Rise of Honor Killings in America." *Right Side News* 26 February. http://www.rightsidenews.com/2011022712935/us/islam-in-america/the-rise-of-honor-killings-in-america.html.

Frankfurter Allgemeine Zeitung. 2005. "'Honor Killings' Shock Germans." March 18. http://www.faz.net/s/RubA7251875CDBF4074A4CC29C0D3759240/Doc~E1BE13B9EA1EB48898CA88E128AEA5D64~ATpl~Ecommon!Acontent.html, retrieved March 5, 2006.

Gould, David, director. 2011. "Two Sides of the Moon." MySweetLord Entertainment. http://www.twosidesofthemoon.com/

Kelek, Necla. 2005. *Die Fremde Braut. Ein Bericht aus dem Inneren des türkischen Lebens in Deutschland* (The Foreign Bride: An Inside Account of Turkish Life in Germany). Cologne: Kiepenheuer & Witsch.

Lacan, Jacques. 1997. *The Ethics of Psychoanalysis: The Seminar of Jacques Lacan Book VII.* Jacques Alain-Miller, ed. , Dennis Porter, trans. W. W. Norton.

Laninger, Tanja. 2005. "Mord an Türkin—Brüder verhaftet. Hatun Sürücü soll von ihrer eigenen Familie hingerichtet worden sein—Hintergründe weiter unklar" (Murder of a Turkish Woman—Brothers Arrested. Hatun Sürücü May Have Been Executed by Her Own Family—Details Remain Unclear). *Die Welt,* February 15. Http://www.welt.de/data/2005/02/15/463980.html. Retrieved January 8, 2007.

Lau, Jörg. 2005. "Wie eine Deutsche." (Like a German.) *Die Zeit* 9. http://zeus.de/text/2005/09/Hatin_S_9fr_9fc_9f_09.

Lux Film Prize. 2011. "Die Fremde (When We Leave) Wins Best Film Prize." http://www.luxprize.eu/v1/die-fremde-wins-best-film-prize.html.

Monheim, Gert, director. 2005. "Mord in Namen der Ehre. Der Tod von Hatun Sürücü." (Murder in the Name of Honor: The Death of Hatun Sürücü). Stern TV and RTL. December 7.

Pagel, Christoph, ed. 2011. "Ehrenmorde: Warum Töchter für die Ehre sterben müssen." FOCUS Online. August 2. http://www.focus.de/panorama/welt/ehrenmorde-warum-toechter-fuer-die-ehre-sterben-muessen_aid_651939.html

Phalnikar, Sonia. 2005. "When Freedom Gets the Death Sentence." *Deutsche Welle DW-World.de.* February 24. Http://www.dw-world.de/dw/article/0,1564,1499191_0,00.htm (Accessed 6/5/05).

Spiegel Online. 2004. "Muslim Integration: Germany's Lost Daughters." November 22. http://www.spiegel.de/international/0,1518,329060,00.html.

———. 2007. "Sorgerechts-Gezerre um Hatun Sürücüs Sohn." February 5, 2007.

———. 2009. "German-Turkish Author Seyran Ateş: 'Islam Needs a Sexual Revolution.'" October 13. http://www.spiegel.de/international/europe/0,1518,654704-2,00.html. Retrieved April 27, 2012.

Spiegel Online International. 2007. "Honor Killing Case: Brothers of Slain Turkish Woman to Be Retried." August 29. http://www.spiegel.de/international/germany/0,1518,502651,00.html.

———. 2011. "The Lost Honor of the Sürücü Family." July 28. http://www.spiegel.de/international/germany/murder-in-berlin-the-lost-honor-of-the-sueruecue-family-a-777109.html

Tageszeitung. 2005. "Kopftuch-Mord nicht wegen Kopftuch." Berlin local edition. February 10, p. 6.

Terre des Femmes. http://frauenrechte.de/online/index.php/history-today.html. Accessed January 10, 2012 and February 26, 2013.

Turner, Victor. 1980. "Social Dramas and Stories about Them." Special issue: "On Narrative." *Critical Inquiry* 7(1):141–168.

Vieth-Entus, Susanne, Lars von Törne, and Claudia Keller. 2005. "Support for Honor Killing: Teachers Are Not Surprised." *Tagesspiegel,* February 22. http://archiv.tagesspiegel.de/archiv/22.02.05/1660909.asp.

Volpp, Leti. 2000. "Blaming Culture for Bad Behavior." *Yale Journal of Law and the Humanities* 12:89–116.

Welt Online. 2005. "Türkischer Bund will Tabuthemen in die Diskussion bringen." February 19. http://www.welt.de/print-welt/article471293/Tuerkischer-Bund-will-Tabuthemen-in-die-Diskussion-bringen.html.

Wessel, Rhea. 2009. "Honor Killing/Ehrenmord: Demonstration for Hatun Sürücü, February 7, 2009." Youtube. http://www.youtube.com/watch?v=OrmoK_dnb8g, accessed March 28, 2012.

Williams, Joe. 2011. "Melodrama 'When We Leave' Looks at Turkish Immigrants in Germany." *St. Louis Post-Dispatch*, April 15. http://www.stltoday.com/entertainment/movies/reviews/article_d4423583-5860-526b-baa9-47711a46716f.html.

Zaman. 2005a. "Mutlu Sürücü: 'Kardeşim 5 sene önce başını açtı şimdi niye başörtüsü yüzünden öldürülsün?'" February 11.

———. 2005b. "Dr. Körting: Sürücü olayının Islam dini ile bir ilgisi yok" (Dr. Körting: There Is No Connection between the Sürücü Incident and the Islamic Faith). March 3.

Zizek, Slavoj. 1997. *The Sublime Object of Ideology.* Verso.

PART THREE

Policy Considerations for Reducing Violence
and Increasing Human Security

8

Feminist Collaboration with the State in Response to Sexual Violence

Lessons from the American Experience

KRISTIN BUMILLER

The history of feminist activism against sexual violence in the United States provides an important lesson about counterproductive law reform and unintended consequences. Many of the hallmarks of the American approach to addressing rape and domestic violence, such as mandatory arrest and prosecution, public health surveillance, and shelter-based services, lack efficacy as well as presenting significant threats to women's autonomy. The problems arising from these approaches are closely tied to the way feminists conceived of the problem and to the state's responsibility in addressing it. Examining the challenges facing movements against rape and domestic violence provides lessons for future efforts in the United States and warnings about the application of the American model in other contexts.

An evaluation of the American experience is all the more pressing as its distinctive approach to addressing sexual violence is increasingly being exported abroad and used instrumentally as part of security and human rights policy. The complex development of strategies to combat violence against women in the United States provides an example of the hazards of too much reliance upon the state to address human security issues. A historical analysis of policy responses to sexual violence reveals how state-based action has become more removed from and inconsistent with the initial goals of the feminist movement. While the movement was largely successful in putting into place social, medical, and criminal justice interventions, professionals and bureaucrats unfamiliar with the aspirations of the movement often carry out these interventions. As a result, other priorities guiding state action usually prevail. These unanticipated outcomes in the United States signal the critical importance of designing human security policies in other contexts that account for the dynamic and interlinking effects of powerful states. In this chapter I briefly describe how the relationship between feminist activists and the American state evolved, the consequences of this alliance for criminal justice and social policies, and the implications for future efforts to respond to violence against women nationally and internationally.

Feminist Alliance with the State

The feminist movement's alliance with the state is to a large extent unavoidable. With regard to violent crimes against women, it is difficult to imagine policies that would not ultimately rely upon the carceral capacities of the state. Clearly, there are some instances of grave harm that require the segregation of offenders for the protection of society. Yet in the United States and other national contexts, it is important to be aware of both the potentialities and limitations of using state power to advance the interests of women. The growth of neoliberal politics since the late 1970s has provided even more reason for skepticism as feminists find their innovations incorporated into the regulatory and criminal justice apparatus.[1] In this regard, it is essential to consider how the feminist campaign against sexual violence evolved in alliance with the state, and even more critically, how these campaigns were enabling of countervailing state interests.

Beginning in the late 1960s feminist activists initiated a series of small grassroots campaigns throughout the United States that called attention to the realities of violence in women's lives and particularly to how rape and domestic violence were used as a tool to subordinate women to men. By focusing on law reform, mainstream organizers promoted objectives consistent with the broad agenda of the women's movement. They called on the state to fulfill its obligations to protect all its citizens equally and identified the lack of enforcement of sexual crimes against women as a major obstacle to women's freedom within the public sphere. Most activist groups named the problem as the failure of the state to recognize and protect women; in fact, the often flagrant denial of violence against women was characterized as state-sanctioned violence and was seen to be complicit with other forms of patriarchal control that oppressed women. These reformist objectives have been and remain an important element in the campaign against sexual violence. From this perspective, an alliance with the state is essentially a nonissue, except in terms of compelling the state to follow through on its promises for more aggressive enforcement of the law.

The battered women's movement began from similar ideological roots in terms of its theory of patriarchy, power, and violence. The goal of the movement was to bring into the public realm an everyday event that had been hidden by the ideology of privacy surrounding the patriarchal family. The term *battered woman* had no public significance before the feminist movement politicized the issue by defining it as a form of violence produced by a system of male domination.[2] An essential part of the movement against wife battering was the creation of shelters; these were not institutions, but houses formed through collective action to provide a safe haven from male violence.[3] The shelters were centers of consciousness-raising and staffed by feminist volunteers, some of whom were previously battered women. Part of the core beliefs of the grassroots movement was that the shelter was both a physical and symbolic boundary between women's space and the violence of the male world. Within these homes women could exercise their own strength and autonomy outside relationships of domination.[4] Shelters were built to be homes, albeit temporary, in which women would feel free to come and go as they pleased. It was hoped that battered women's lives would "intersect" with these houses, and that their continued connection with this protected space would vary over time according to their needs and contributions.[5] The core philosophy of the shelter movement was antistate.

This early history was influential; most shelters and rape crisis centers formed as distinctive "feminist organizations" that explicitly recognized the need for less hierarchy, democratic decision making, and women working with women. This meant that women came to understand the violence they experienced as a collectivity, and that there were no rigid boundaries between organizers and women who sought help.[6] Shelters and crisis centers provided a place for women to become whole again after the experience of violence, an experience they learned to see not simply as a series of injurious acts but as a shattering condition that affects many women's lives. Beyond a spiritual component, which stressed the interconnectedness of women's problems, was a practical mission of providing the basic resources needed by the women and their children. The volunteer staff utilized available state services, such as public assistance, food stamps, and Medicare (although not exclusively) in assisting women in their search for housing, jobs, and child care.

As these organizations matured, they encountered numerous challenges in carrying out their purpose and meeting women's needs.[7] The imposition of regulations and the desire for stable funding sources pushed them onto the "terrain of the state."[8] This involved both increased record keeping to assure compliance with state regulations and more reliance upon state agencies to provide services for women. Studies of these organizations show that although state power was actively contested, shelters and rape crisis centers had to make compromises and structural changes to remain in compliance and to take advantage of available resources. Over time, this led to organizations functioning bureaucratically and relying on professionals in order to secure reliable funding.[9] Institutionalization also brought internal conflict and contestation over fundamental questions of theory versus practice.[10]

The consequences of moving onto the terrain of the state are still widely debated: some see these transformations as a betrayal of grassroots sensibilities, while most see them as an inevitable outcome of growth and stability. Overall, the majority of these organizations have been successful at maintaining their feminist identity. The foundational goal of empowering women was not lost; rather new strategies were developed as the conditions for empowerment changed.[11] Yet the internal evolution of these organizations reveals only part of the story. While battered women's shelters and rape crisis centers maintained their quasi-autonomy from the state, other organizations whose primary purposes were not treating rape and domestic battery, and who did not ascribe to feminist ideology, were increasingly called upon by the state to address the problem. The growing recognition of sexual violence as a public health crisis brought legitimacy to the work of feminist organizations, but it also resulted in the broad-scale expansion of the instrumental capacities of the state to address sexual violence. The state's terrain reached far beyond feminist organizations and their agendas.

Growth of Neoliberalism

By the late 1970s, the tenets of neoliberalism began to influence American public policy at home and abroad. Ronald Reagan's first term as president marks the shift to neoliberal principles of governance which are associated with less restraint on free market polices, procorporatism, privatization, and in particular, the transfer of public services to private organizations. This shift significantly affected the already established feminist antiviolence movement in its attempts to reform criminal justice programs and build up victim services. The call for state responsibility for preventing and treating victims was in direct contrast to the new ethics of personal responsibility that was the cornerstone of the neoliberal agenda. This contradiction was resolved, but at the cost of the incorporation of the feminist antiviolence movement into the apparatus of the regulatory state.

For example, the rationale for providing government services was transformed by the neoliberal agenda.[12] Under the new welfare regime, clients were increasingly scrutinized as part of efforts to reduce costs by eliminating waste and discouraging dependence. Prior to the rise of neoliberalism, the organizers of the shelter movement saw the necessity of encouraging women to take advantage of available government benefits as a temporary means to provide for their children. These benefits were seen as entitlements that provided a "safety net" for single women with children. From the perspective of shelter organizers and in the feminist movement more generally, greater reliance on this safety net was the result of the growing insecurity of marriage as an institution. When the new agenda of the state was codified in the 1996 welfare reform (PWORA), there was a shift from viewing welfare as an entitlement to employing it as a means to promote personal responsibility. After this shift, shelter workers still directed their clients to state services, but often women in shelters were *required* to apply for all appropriate state benefits in order to demonstrate that they were taking all necessary steps to gain self-sufficiency. Moreover, specific provisions of PWORA were designed to incentivize marriage and foster responsible motherhood. To achieve these goals, the new welfare system created requirements that entangled women in an increasingly value-laden welfare program tied to the promotion of the traditional nuclear family, fear of dependency, and distrust of women as mothers.[13] These ties, moreover, come with fewer benefits, as the "devolution" of welfare systems has brought about cutbacks in services and rescaling to the local level.[14] At the same time the welfare system has grown more linked to other forms of state involvement, including probate court actions concerning custody, paternity hearings, child protective services, and relationships with school officials.

Another outgrowth of neoliberalism has been the expansion of the regulatory functions of the state. This growing presence of the state is seen within feminist organizations, as discussed above, but it also emerges as more state and quasi-state actors become part of a network of responders to sexual violence. With the growth of the regulatory apparatus, crisis centers and shelters are now a small segment of a service sector for which intimate violence is one of a long list of social problems to which they respond. Some of these organizations are central to the policing function of the state, such as sex crime units in police and prosecutors' offices. Others are more ancillary to the state and even private in form. These include hospital emergency rooms, medical doctors in a range of specialties, mental health professionals, community service, and religious organizations. As the responsibility for recognizing and treating intimate violence has expanded, so has the use of protocols for defining who is eligible for services, client expectations, and treatment methodologies. These systems often function in conjunction with the welfare regulatory apparatus and are obligated to follow protocols and reporting procedures, even though many are private or quasi-state efforts to manage the large numbers of women who experience relationship violence.

While these changes were occurring in the social service sector, there was a dramatic rise in incarceration rates in the United States beginning in the late 1970s. Some see this swell in incarceration as a direct consequence of neoliberalism—a less regulated economy resulted in increased social stratification and a generalized sense of insecurity that then led to more regulation of the poor and minorities. Yet other factors also contributed to the increasingly punitive response of the state. Criminologist David Garland posits that this dramatic upturn is a multifaceted response to both a changing political climate and an evolving logic of penal reform. This brought about a "control of control," which was grounded in conceptions of the essential "otherness" of the criminal and highly dependent on mechanisms of social segregation.[15] In this way, crime control emerged as a new form of social exclusion reinforcing other forms of discrimination against minorities and directed against potentially unruly classes of persons.[16]

Mainstream feminist demands for more certain and severe punishment for crimes against women fed into these reactionary forces. This resulted in a direct alliance between feminist activists and legislators, prosecutors, and other elected officials promoting the crime control business. Although the feminists' "gender war" did not have the same impact on incarceration rates as the "war on drugs," it still contributed to the symbolic message. Sex crimes generated diffuse fears that justified more punitive action by the state. Like other issues on the crime control agenda, the link to an actual rise in the crime rate was less significant than the fact that violence against women shaped a generalized fear of disorder and the image of habitual and recalcitrant criminals.[17] The prominence of sexual violence on the crime control agenda led to the creation of specialized sex crime units in large urban police and prosecutors' offices. These units were responsible for many of the most celebrated cases in the latter part of the century. At the same time, an ostensibly feminist knowledge about sexual violence informed professional practices and spearheaded the surveillance and management of victims. Through these developments, the progressive ideals of this campaign focused on improving women's lives and well-being deferred to crime control prerogatives.

Race and the Culture of Control

On a cultural level, the new feminist consciousness was incorporated within a broader framework of representation;[18] the rallying cry about women in danger mobilized deep-seated fears about sexual terror.

What began as a "gender war" led to more generalized fears about the epidemic of sexual abuse and the pandemic threat of sex criminals. These apocalyptic fears, to some degree, can be attributed to feminist warnings about the pervasive risk of stranger violence and depictions of horrible attacks. Feminists also produced narratives about sadistic violence that took place in the home, often fixated on a primal scene of incest, ripe for appropriation within a larger cultural setting.

Other forces were at work in creating sexual panic, including the mass media, prosecutors, therapists, and law enforcement officials who had a stake in constructing sexual violence as a growing social problem. The last two decades of the twentieth century were also the beginning of a cycle of new fears of societal danger; sex panics were spurred on by fears of AIDS and other sexually transmitted diseases, the war on drugs, increased divorce rates, and shifting gender norms.[19] In this milieu, the feminist concern about rape and domestic abuse merged with a much larger agenda focusing on the sex criminal.[20] This was produced in part by a news media reports about sexual abuse in day care centers (such as the McMartin preschool scandal of 1983) and child abductions.[21] The feminist campaign against rape also fed a new wave of gender-neutral statutory rape law enforcement. In the context of efforts to reinforce middle-class lifestyles and conventional family forms, especially as seen in the new welfare reforms of the 1990s, prohibitions against statutory rape targeted mostly poor minority youth women.[22] These moral panics not only led to selective prosecution, and in the case of child abuse to some spectacular witch hunts, they also served to reinforce a dominant narrative about dangerous elements in society (pedophiles, child predators, and sexual deviants) and to crystallize fears about deviant strangers. The most recent additions to sex crimes codes are Megan Laws, which mandate systems of registration and community notification. Rose Corrigan has argued that these statutes not only reinforce "beliefs that strangers inherently always pose the greatest threat to communities," but ultimately have the effect of fueling racially focused crime control efforts rather than actually improving women's safety "by . . . increasing emphasis on crimes, victims, and offenders who fit more easily with stereotypes about rape held by criminal justice gatekeepers."[23]

This rise of moral panics set the stage for prosecutors to capitalize on these concerns.[24] As the new consciousness about sexual violence assumed its place on the crime control agenda, prosecutors called for punitive action against the most violent offenders. This brought about a series of celebrated sex crime trials, including the New Bedford "Portuguese" Gang Rape case in the 1980s and the Central Park Jogger case in the 1990s, involving celebrity defendants, gang rapes, and interracial crime. The interest in these cases by law enforcement was further stimulated by sensationalized media reports of brutality against women and racial typecasting. Sociologist Lynn Chancer defines these high-profile cases as a distinctive phenomenon of the mid-1980s to mid-1990s that intersected with controversial gender, race, and class issues as they emerged in that time and in their place.[25] In Chancer's terms, these cases and their news coverage "partialized" the stories to arouse and divide public reaction based on identity issues. In this way, these cases reinforced rather than dispelled dominant notions of victims and offenders.

These high-profile cases profoundly influenced the public perception of the causes of sexual violence and raised fears about its potentially cataclysmic effects on society. Prosecutors constructed narratives casting perpetrators as driven by sadistic impulses that led them to target unknown women out of hatred for their gender, ethnicity, or race. For the most part these narratives replayed the themes found in feminist scholarly and popular accounts of sexual trauma about innocent victims, dangerous strangers, and the pervasiveness of sexual violence. Yet in the context of high-profile trials, they authorized racialized images of perpetrators and placed the menace of sexual violence in a backdrop of social disorder. The victim in celebrated cases was subjected not only to public scrutiny, but was cast in a role necessary for the prosecutor's ascription of events and motives. The conventions of the rape trial, which made the victim's story relevant only in terms of its verification of injuries to her body, further disabled a more complete and sympathetic portrayal. In effect, celebrated trials either reinforced iconic representations of victims (as innocent, white, and/or angelic) or sacrificed the actual victim for her failure to live up to this idealization.[26] This production of an iconic image is seen in the intense news reporting of the Central Park Jogger trial, where the victim, a white investment banker in her twenties, was portrayed as attacked by a marauding gang of dark-skinned men, while rapes and murders of black women in New York

City during the same week received little media attention. These characterizations of both perpetrators and victims, however, contributed to the crime control mentality by adding force to the belief that the maintenance of social order depended on ruthlessly castigating violent perpetrators who preyed on innocent victims.

When feminists pointed to these cases to reinforce their message about rape (such as when the National Organization of Women drew attention to the Central Park Jogger trial), they ended up encouraging an all-or-nothing adherence to the women's side in the gender war. This often defeated their purpose, because victims inevitably failed to fit into the stereotyped conceptions of innocence and worthiness. This rigid defense of a feminist position brought about a small, but vocal, voice of dissent among activists. A few radical feminists criticized the movement for selling out to the establishment and following a path inconsistent with the "revolutionary" mission. Even stronger dissent emerged among black feminists who saw rape reform, with its focus on expanding the role of law enforcement, as primarily driven by the interests of white middle-class women. Yet a deeper set of problems emerged, as the threat to women became identified with the risks posed by random criminals. This marking of the rapist was inextricably tied to the history of lynching black men. What had begun as a new feminist sensibility that "any man could be a rapist" was transformed primarily into a campaign driven by fear of dangerous strangers, who were implicitly or explicitly marked as dark-skinned men.

These issues about the racialization of rape were long-standing and did not emerge solely from the capitalization of celebrated rape cases by the law and order forces.[27] In the 1970s, the movement framed the issue of rape without regard to its historical legacy as a tool to control black men. Consequently, there was insufficient attention given to how stricter enforcement of sexual assault and women battering would occur within settings fraught with racism as well as sexism. Subsequently, women of color raised concerns about increasing police involvement in their own communities and the disproportionate impact on black and Hispanic men. They pointed out that in urban minority communities where the population of young black males has been eviscerated by incarceration, the framing of sexual violence as a crime problem and external threat made little sense.

Institutionalizing the Agenda

Rape law reforms were swiftly adopted in jurisdictions across the country spurred on by a "tough on crime" sentiment as well as concerted lobbying by mainstream feminist groups. By the end of the 1980s, the antirape campaign was successful in initiating major law reform and procuring funding for specialized services for rape victims. These efforts culminated in the adoption of the Violence Against Women Act (VAWA) in September 1994, described by some as "perhaps the most significant accomplishment of the anti-rape movement."[28] The legislative proponents of the Act clearly supported it as a continuation of other federal crime control initiatives, but also as an antidiscrimination measure designed to rectify the injustice that occurs when the criminal justice system fails to protect women from violent crime committed by nonstrangers.

Although mainstream feminists were successful in achieving these formal legal victories, they were adopted in the context of the penal-welfare systems of the neoliberal state.[29] Whether or not sexual assault cases are processed by special sex crime units, most cases continue to be diverted. Studies of routine criminal justice processing show that only a small percentage of cases are prosecuted, and the discrediting of victims is a significant factor despite rape law reforms.[30] Prosecutors, motivated by their own presumptions about rape and organizational and political directives for high success rates, selectively bring forth cases involving "good victims," women whose behavior conforms to traditional expectations and whose assaults involve unambiguous circumstances.[31] In order to address the systematic failure of the police to respond to domestic violence, most jurisdictions established mandatory arrest laws and some adopted no-drop prosecution polices by the late 1980s. It is unclear whether changes in arrest and prosecution policies have led either to higher conviction rates or to less violence against women.[32] For many women, particularly those who are poor and racial minorities, mandatory policies have made them worse off.[33] These policies may either lead to dual arrests (of women who likely were defending themselves) or to involvement with officials who put women at greater risk of future violence by perpetrators or unwanted interventions by the state.[34] Donna Coker has summarized this critique of mandatory policies: "Mandatory domestic violence policies increase the risk of [punitive criminal intervention] . . . when women's (unrelated) criminal offending is exposed, when mandatory arrest practices threaten women's probation or parole status, when undocumented women are made more vulnerable to deportation, or when child welfare departments are prompted to investigate neglect or abuse claims based on a domestic violence incident report."[35] The disappointing track record of mandatory polices has produced a cautionary tale for activists about the precariousness of relying on stepped up police enforcement and attempting to control prosecutorial discretion.

These tales of counterproductive law reform and unintended consequences are indicative of the failures of liberal law reform and its misplaced faith in formal legal equality. Many activists in the anti–rape and domestic violence movement, however, view these setbacks as all the more reason to stay on course in efforts to reform mainstream institutions. Yet if these results are viewed in the historical and cultural context, it is clear that they are actually the "productive" and the "intended" consequences of state policies of social control. One of the major factors creating seemingly more punitive actions toward women is that individuals who are not invested in feminist methodologies often carry out the programs. The commitment to eradicating sexual violence, therefore, is not rooted in a collective understanding of this violence or a sense of the interconnectedness of women's problems as expressed by the early grassroots organizers. Even more critically, these programs are implemented according to gender-neutral standards, both formally and in terms of the state's interest in the problem. The most dramatic example of this is dual arrest policies in domestic violence situations that have led to the criminalization of victims. One study summarizes the consequences: "[R]ather than victims of violence being treated the same regardless of gender, female victims are again subject to discrimination. . . . An arrest policy intended to protect battered women as victims is being misapplied and used against them. Battered women have become female offenders."[36] Although the author of this study views these police actions as simply discrimination against women, this treatment occurs as a direct result of the way the sexual violence agenda has been incorporated into state policy. The state's interest in controlling violence is powerfully driven by social control priorities; for example, intimate partnership violence is "of interest" because it unsettles families, harms children, and creates a public health crisis. This mandates intervention for the purposes of containing crises and managing harm, not to address women's systematic oppression.

Moreover, in the context of neoliberalism, the state is primarily invested in limiting its responsibility to provide for dependents, including women, whose experiences with violence have made them homeless or disabled and their children's lives traumatized and disrupted. The retrenchment of the welfare system means the state has little to offer these women and children. Those most reliant on government services are the first to suffer as the social welfare state turns toward increased forms of regulation and coercive government control,[37] such as the restriction of benefits and the implementation of policies that treat single mothers as pathological.[38] As a result, poor, homeless, unemployed, and underemployed women have fewer resources available for general or emergency relief.[39] Specifically, in terms of battered women and rape victims, this has meant that their eligibility and priority for services became increasingly linked to their status as victims and their ability to recognize their problems in medical and psychological terms.

By far the broadest reach of state power is found in its transformation of sexual violence into a social, medical, and legal problem. In addition to programs originated by feminists, a large professional apparatus has developed in response to the problem of rape and family violence. The creation of a professional language to account for, intervene in, and prevent rape and domestic violence is a major part of this apparatus and is regularly used as a means by which violence against women is rationalized as a chronic yet treatable problem.[40] The ascendancy of professional expertise is most clearly seen in the limited options for victims outside the expanding systems of medicalization and criminalization: it has become nearly impossible to understand the causes and consequences of being a victim of violence in terms which do not fit squarely within the purview of medicine or criminal justice. In these frameworks, feminist ideological concepts, like patriarchy or sexual domination, are introduced mainly because of their applicability within the language of surveillance, diagnosis, and social control.

In this highly rationalized form of social control, victims and perpetrators exist in a methodological duality. This duality is at work when perpetrators are turned into a class of dehumanized offenders whose pathologies are beyond treatment.[41] By the same logic, victims become the perfect subject for medical and therapeutic treatments and are rewarded for their adaptability and compliance to treatment protocols. Through these rationalized processes, victims and perpetrators are divided into two categories: those who can be medicalized, controlled, and reformed, and those who must be removed beyond the territory of a civilized society. The routine business of law enforcement also blurs the distinction between victim and criminal, especially when illegal activities are profit-making enterprises within families and supported, sometimes involuntarily, by partners. Moreover, perpetrators are rarely outsiders, and in cases of both rape and battery they are most often spouses, partners, family, and members of one's community. In all situations, prosecutors pursue cases on behalf of the state rather than the victim; but when victims are from criminalized communities (due to poverty, immigrant status, ethnicity, or race) their status as victim may in many cases become the functional equivalent of being a perpetrator in the eyes of the law. The evolving logic of this increased surveillance is most dramatically seen in measures taken against victims of violence themselves, who are now being regularly sanctioned for the "failure to protect" children who view domestic abuse.[42]

As this analysis makes clear, in the United States concerns about rape and domestic violence are rarely addressed in the context of communities and in terms of their links to social disadvantage and impoverishment. But by the turn of the century, the sexual violence agenda had become more universalized rather than integrated into other social movements and community-based activism (with some notable exceptions). This means that sexual violence has become everybody's problem not only culturally but also administratively. Employers, teachers, lawyers, doctors, therapists, and the like are expected to watch for the signs and symptoms of sexual violence and if detected, are often required to take appropriate action to protect victims, treat clients, and report to authorities. Some feminists have challenged this trend, along with sexual harassment regulations, for its effects in desexualizing the workplace, college campuses, and community settings to the point of inhibiting ordinary social expression and interaction.[43] For example, law professor Vicki Schultz has persuasively argued that sexual harassment litigation has created more regulation of sexual behavior by employers without focusing on the root of women's discrimination in the workplace: false stereotypes about women's competency.

In my book, *In an Abusive State,* I further examine how the feminist campaign against sexual violence evolved in the context of neoliberal state policy.[44] I raise concerns about the mainstreaming of the sexual violence movement and provide what some might consider counterintuitive conclusions about the desirability of the widespread incorporation of sexual violence prevention and treatment in the public health and social service sectors. Many activists see problems but remain true to the movement and its underlying logic of social change; in this view, the unintended consequences of the alliance with the state are just collateral damage in a gender war. There is an alternative perspective, however, that raises fundamental concerns about how sexual violence was constructed as a social problem and its evolution into programmatic initiatives, and demonstrates that the feminist alliance with the state has produced something far more significant than unintended consequences—a joining of forces with a neoliberal project of social control.

Beyond Criminalization

An almost exclusively criminalized response to sexual violence contributes to the increasingly punitive response of the state. For example, men who are arrested for battering are most likely to end up in prison if they have a previous or current history of other criminal offenses. And as already noted, battered women often get drawn into the criminal justice system when police follow mandatory arrest policies. The introduction of graduated degrees of sexual assaults and new categories of victims expands the scope of behaviors and age range of persons and activities under criminal surveillance. This means that criminal justice authorities, under the guise of protecting against sexual violence, are able to expand their control over juveniles and those with prior convictions for sexual offenses.

Alternative and potentially more desirable solutions have not been actively pursued in the United States. Such solutions might be neither perpetrator nor "relationship" focused, but directed at addressing the most persistent problems causing and created by sexual violence: the social and economic disadvantage experienced by women and their dependents. The primary goal of such a campaign to prevent sexual violence would be to promote the emotional well-being and economic sustainability of women who suffer repeatedly from sexual violence throughout their life span.[45] This involves providing individual women with the emotional, material, and communal support to empower themselves.

The successful reemergence from situations of domestic violence requires clients of shelters or of welfare bureaucracies to demand the rights to fair treatment that are taken for granted by "ordinary" citizens who are not in dependent relations with the welfare state.[46] Some feminist activists in the United States are working toward reinstating the original impulses of the movement that were focused on grassroots organizing and the founding of shelters and other organizations with a politicized understanding of the problem. This involves drawing connections to other broadly based antiviolence movements both locally and globally, including those that raise concerns about the state as perpetrators of violence in the form of police brutality, discrimination against immigrants, and racism in all aspects of crime enforcement and in foreign wars.

These shifts are deterred, however, by the close links between advocacy and services for victims and the criminal justice apparatus. Under the auspices of the Violence Against Women's Act, the most common funding model is "community coordination" which involves cooperation among a network of community-based organizations and criminal justice personnel. Many in the field see community coordination as the "answer" because it improves the quality and scope of services, and it is urgently needed in rural areas which are lacking in specialized services to treat victims.[47] Since the programs are designed to encourage cooperation among agencies, community coordination allows for more direct influence of feminist-designed rape crisis centers and battered women's shelters on mainstream organizations. Although these programs have opened up new sources of funding for shelters and direct services for women, they also make increased prosecution rates the first priority of community intervention and the measure of program success. These initiatives further entrench local feminist organizations within systems of punitive justice and professionalization of victim support.[48]

There are important differences in perspective, however, about the desirability of community coordination. Some argue that the success of the violence against the women's movement is in fact contingent on improving victims' treatment within mainstream organizations. In her recent book, *Rape Work,* a multidecade analysis of rape crisis organizations and their communities, Patricia Yancey Martin explores why women are revictimized at the hands of agencies designated to process their complaints despite years of reform.[49] Her analysis points to the failure of workers in mainstream organizations like hospitals, police departments, and the courts to "own rape," and their tendency to mistreat victims, not usually out of hostility, but in the process of fulfilling other work objectives. Her conclusions call for a reaffirmation of the feminist vision of rape work and more integration of feminist practices within mainstream institutions. This vision would support continued efforts for community coordination, with the condition that rape crisis centers and other feminist organizations take a more active role. This analysis, however, is instructive regarding the potential pitfalls of this renewed feminist campaign. Even when feminist methodology has been integrated into mainstream professional practice, it does not necessarily yield a system that is supportive and empowering of women. The push for other objectives, often countervailing to feminist purposes, is initiated not only by individual personnel, but also by external pressures on organizations, often derived from a neoliberal political agenda. The historical evidence shows, however, that feminist practices rarely prevail in mainstream institutions without concerted and intrusive interventions designed to transform these institutions.

Extrapolating from the American Experience

In the United States, the movement to address sexual violence against women has not only produced inefficacious policies, but also disempowered women vis-à-vis state actors. Many policies imparted authority to the police, medical professionals, and even specialized service providers to report crimes and pursue criminal action despite the objections of victims. This includes mandatory policies that *de facto* assume that women who experience violence cannot be trusted with decisions regarding their own safety. Moreover, as systems have become institutionalized, expert understanding of the problem have taken precedence over women's self-reports and desired outcomes. In the worst-case scenario, women's choices are treated with suspicion and their failure to cooperate with officials can lead to criminal sanction or removal of their children from their care. These undesirable consequences arise directly from policymakers' failure to fully take into consideration the effects of reforms on women's autonomy and freedom. Considering the impact of antiviolence measures on women's agency is vital for further efforts to promote gender security issues in other national contexts.

However, it is important to consider whether the conditions that brought the movement to its maturity and spawned these unanticipated results are unique to the United States. There are clear similarities between the changing political and economic conditions in the United States and other western democratic countries: the rise of market-centered neoliberal policies, the growth of technocratic bureaucracies, and increasing incarceration rates. However, in the United States these factors have had a more extreme impact, and with regard to incarceration rates, it is a world leader.[50] Yet a generalizable lesson that emerges from this retrospective account is the fallacy of pursuing criminal sanctions as the means to transform the cultural meaning of violence. Criminal justice reforms have increased the power of the state over the most vulnerable citizens, reduced the autonomy of women, and dampened efforts to provide other solutions to endemic gender violence.

Concerns also arise when the American experience is applied in other cultural contexts. International focus on a major new problem, the trafficking of women, renews the energy of feminists and others committed to the cause, but also raises the question—is this human rights campaign simply a vehicle to advance the neoliberal agenda around the globe?[51] Moreover, the political uses of "terrorism" in a post 9/11 context provides additional reason to be concerned about the potential for "sexual terror" to serve as an excuse for the retrenchment of civil liberties or deliberate destabilizing of society.[52] Ironically, the greatest challenge facing movements focused on violence against women today may be forestalling the incorporation of their agendas into the policing function of the state. This certainly requires these movements to draw attention to the structural conditions that enable violence in women's everyday lives rather than the enforcement mechanisms that are designed to punish such violence. Strategies that depend upon policing and punishment are highly likely to accentuate state oppression of marginalized and vulnerable populations. In addition, the American experience makes clear that reforms designed to improve women's security are only successful to the extent that they improve the conditions of individual lives. As efforts continue and new approaches to gender and security are adopted in the United States and internationally, negative consequences can be mitigated by a more conscious consideration of the structural causes of sexual violence and the recognition of the dangers associated with the punitive and regulatory mechanisms of the modern state.

NOTES

1. For an important discussion of the complexities of feminist grassroots organizing and its relation to the state, see Martha Ackelsberg, "Reconceiving Politics? Women's Activism and Democracy in a Time of Retrenchment," *Feminist Studies* 27:2 (Summer 2001):391. For an articulation of the position that feminists should be "wary" in their relations with the state, see Jane Mansbridge, "Anti-Statism and Difference: Feminism in International Social Movements," *International Feminist Journal of Politics* 5 (November 2002):355–360.

2. Linda Gordon, *Heroes of Their Own Lives: The Politics and History of Family Violence: Boston 1880–1960*, 251. New York: Penguin Books, 1988.

3. See, in general, Erin Pizzey, *Scream Quietly or the Neighbors Will Hear*. Short Hills, N.J.: R. Enslow Publishers, 1977; Susan Schechter, *Women and Male Violence: The Visions and Struggles of the Battered Women's Movement*. Boston: South End Press, 1982.

4. This hope for personal liberation through participation in shelter life is described in Micheline Beaudry, *Battered Women*. Montreal: Black Rose Books, 1985.

5. Ibid., 66–70.

6. Ibid., 51–54.

7. See Myra Marx Ferree and Beth B. Hess, *Controversy and Coalition: The New Feminist Movement*. Boston: Twayne Publishers, 1985; Stephanie Riger, "Challenges of Success: Stages of Growth in Feminist Organization," *Feminist Studies* 20 (Summer 1994):275–301; Kathy E. Ferguson, *The Feminist Case against Bureaucracy*. Philadelphia: Temple University Press, 1984.

8. Claire Reinelt, "Moving onto the Terrain of the State: The Battered Women's Movement and the Politics of Engagement," in *Feminist Organizations: Harvest of the New Women's Movement,* edited by Myra Marx Ferree and Patricia Yancey Martin, 84–104. Philadelphia: Temple University Press, 1995.

9. For analysis of this trend and its consequences, see Karen Kendrick, "Producing the Battered Woman," in *Community Action and Feminist Practices*, edited by

Nancy A. Naples, 151–174. New York: Routledge, 1998; Donileen R. Loseke, *The Battered Woman and Shelters: The Social Construction of Wife Abuse*. Albany: State University of New York Press, 1992; Andrea Westlund, "Pre-Modern and Modern Power: Foucault and the Case of Domestic Violence." *Signs: Journal of Women in Culture and Society* 24:4 (Summer 1999):1045–1067.

10. For a discussion of how feminist service organizations responded to this challenge and a generally positive view of these organizations' ability to maintain their integrity, see Diane Kravetz, *Tales from the Trenches: Politics and Practice in Feminist Service Organizations*. Lanham, Md.: University Press of America, 2004.

11. For a comprehensive cross-cultural comparison of the results of this activism and an argument for the autonomy of women's movements, see S. Laurel Weldon, *Protest, Policy, and the Problem of Violence against Women: A Cross-National Comparison*. Pittsburg: University of Pittsburg Press, 2002.

12. For similar analysis, see Nina Laurie and Liz Bondi, *Working in the Spaces of Neoliberalism*. Malden, Mass.: Blackwell Publishing, 2005.

13. See Gwendolyn Mink, "Violating Women: Rights Abuses in the Welfare Police State," in *Lost Ground: Welfare Reform, Poverty, and Beyond*, edited by Randy Albelda and Ann Withorn, 95–112. Cambridge: South End Press, 2002.

14. For an empirical analysis of the consequences of devolution, see Harrell Rodgers, "Evaluating the Devolution Revolution," *Review of Policy Research* 22 (May 2005):275–299.

15. David Garland, *The Culture of Control: Crime and Social Order in Contemporary Society*, 184. Chicago: University of Chicago Press, 2001.

16. Loic Wacquant, "The New 'Peculiar Institution': On Prison as the Surrogate Ghetto," *Theoretical Criminology* 4 (August 2000): 377–390.

17. According to Bureau of Justice statistics, "women are now the most rapidly increasing segment of the population of U.S. prisons." Philip Comey, "Fastest Growing Prison Population," *Corrections Today* 68:1 (February 2006):15. For a discussion of the intersection between women's victimization and offending, see the studies in Karen Heimer and Candace Kruttschnitt, *Gender and Crime: Patterns in Victimization and Offending*. New York: NYU Press, 2006.

18. See, in general, for an illuminating discussion of neoliberalism's cultural project, Lisa Duggan, *The Twilight of Equality? Neoliberalism, Cultural Politics, and the Attack on Democracy*. Boston: Beacon Press, 2003.

19. Philip Jenkins, *Moral Panic: Changing Concepts of the Child Molester in Modern America*, 226–229. New Haven: Yale University Press, 2005.

20. Ibid., 125.

21. Hiroshi Fukurai, Edgar W. Butler, and Richard Krooth, "Sociologists in Action: The McMartin Sexual Abuse Case, Litigation, Justice, and Mass Hysteria," *American Sociologist* 24 (1994):44–71.

22. For an elaboration of this argument, see Carolyn E. Cocca, *Jailbait: The Politics of Statutory Rape Laws in the United States*. Albany: State University of New York Press, 2004; and Carolyn E. Cocca, "From 'Welfare Queen' to 'Exploited Teen':

Welfare Dependency, Statutory Rape, and Moral Panic," *NWSA Journal* 14 (Summer 2002):56–79.

23. Rose Corrigan, "Making Meaning of Megan's Law," *Law & Social Inquiry* 31 (Spring 2006):301, 308.

24. For a discussion of the politicized context of prosecution and its persistence despite reform efforts, see Candace McCoy, "Prosecution," in *The Handbook of Crime and Punishment,* edited by Michael Tonry, 457–473. New York: Oxford University Press, 1998.

25. Lynn Chancer, *High Profile Crimes: When Legal Cases Become Social Causes,* 252. Chicago: University of Chicago Press, 2005.

26. For a general discussion of how this polarization is furthered by media presentation, see Paula Wilcox, "Beauty and the Beast: Gendered and Raced Discourse in the News," *Social and Legal Studies* 14 (2005):515–532.

27. See Sujata Moorti, *The Color of Rape: Gender and Race in Television's Public Spheres.* Albany: State University of New York Press, 2002.

28. Maria Bevacqua, *Rape on the Public Agenda: Feminism and the Politics of Sexual Assault,* 170. Boston: Northeastern University Press, 2000.

29. For a discussion of the growth of penal-welfare systems and its impact on women, see Jael Silliman and Anannya Bhattacharjee, *Policing the National Body: Sex, Race, and Criminalization.* Cambridge: South End Press, 2002.

30. For a study of how prosecutors weed out rape cases by discrediting victim's allegations of sexual assault, see Lisa Frohmann, "Discrediting Victims' Allegations of Sexual Assault: Prosecutorial Accounts of Case Rejections," in *Rape and Society,* edited by Patricia Searles and Ronald J. Berger, 199–214. Boulder: Westview Press, 1995.

31. See Lisa Frohmann, "Convictability and Discordant Locales: Reproducing Race, Class, and Gender Ideologies in Prosecutorial Decisionmaking," *Law & Society Review* 31 (1997):31–556.

32. For an empirical study of the effect of mandatory policies on conviction rates, see Richard R. Peterson and Jo Dixon, "Court Oversight and Conviction under Mandatory and Non-Mandatory Domestic Violence Case Filings," 4:3 *Criminology & Public Policy* (August 2005):535–557. For an interpretation of this study see Joel Garner, "What Does 'Prosecution' of Domestic Violence Mean?" 4:3 *Criminology & Public Policy* (August 2005):567–573. See also Rebecca Emerson Dobash, "Domestic Violence: Arrest, Prosecution, and Reducing Violence," 2:2 *Criminology & Public Policy* (March 2003):313–318.

33. See Eve S. Buzawa and Carl G. Buzama, *Do Arrests and Restraining Orders Work?* Thousand Oaks, Calif.: Sage, 1996.

34. Ruth E. Fleury, "Missing Voices: Patterns of Battered Women's Satisfaction with the Criminal Legal System." *Violence against Women* 8:2 (2002):181–206; Deborah N. Pearlman et al., "Neighborhood Environment, Racial Position, and Risk of Police-Reported Domestic Violence: A Contextual Analysis," *Public Health Reports* 118:1 (2003):44–59; Lois Weis, "Race, Gender and Critique: African-American

Women, White Women, and Domestic Violence in the 1980s and 1990s," *Signs: Journal of Women in Culture and Society* 27:1 (2001):139–169.

35. Donna Coker, "Race, Poverty, and the Crime-Centered Response to Domestic Violence," *Violence Against Women* 10:11 (2004):1332.

36. Susan L Miller, *Victims as Offenders: The Paradox of Women's Violence in Relationships*, 141. New Brunswick: Rutgers University Press, 2005.

37. For a discussion of the growth of coercive government control, see Pat O'Malley, "Social Justice after the 'Death of the Social,'" *Social Justice* 26:2 (1999):92–101; Nikolas S. Rose, *Powers of Freedom: Reframing Political Thought*. Cambridge: Cambridge University Press, 1999.

38. For analysis of the consequences of welfare reform, see Gwendolyn Mink and Rickie Solinger, *Welfare: A Documentary History of U.S. Policy and Politics*. New York: NYU Press, 2003.

39. See Mimi Abramovitz and Ann Withorn, "Playing by the Rules: Welfare Reform and the New Authoritarian State," in *Without Justice for All: The New Liberalism and Our Retreat from Racial Equality*, edited by Adolph Reed, Jr., 151–174. Boulder, Colo.: Westview Press, 1999.

40. This analysis on how political language is used to rationalize chronic social problems is drawn from Murray J. Edelman, *Political Language: Words That Succeed and Policies That Fail*. New York: Academic Press, 1977.

41. Zygmunt Bauman, *Modernity and the Holocaust*, 65. Ithaca: Cornell University Press, 2000.

42. Justine Dunlap, "Sometimes I Feel Like a Motherless Child: The Error of Pursing Battered Mothers for the Failure to Protect," *Loyola Law Review* 50 (Fall 2004):565.

43. For an excellent development of this critique, see Vicki Schultz, "Reconceptualizing Sexual Harrassment," *Yale Law Journal* 107 (1998):1683–1805.

44. Kristin Bumiller, *In an Abusive State*. Durham: Duke University Press, 2008.

45. Judy L. Postmus, "Battered and on Welfare: The Experiences of Women with the Family Violence Option." *Journal of Sociology & Social Welfare* 31:2 (2004):113–123; Geraldine Terry, "Poverty Reduction and Violence against Women: Exploring Links, Assessing Impact." *Development in Practice* 14:4 (2004):469–480.

46. A study finds that poor women who seek help from a legal aid society are satisfied with their treatment, especially if they have minimal expectations. The more pressing question addressed here is whether women in these situations might be inspired to see their problems as situated in a larger context of injustice. See Kimberly D. Richman, "Women, Poverty, and Domestic Violence: Perceptions of Court and Legal Aid Effectiveness." *Sociological Inquiry* 72: 2 (2002):318–344.

47. An example of the successful use of a specialized court is detailed by Rekha Mirchandani, "Battered Women's Movement Ideals and Judge-Led Social Change in Domestic Violence Courts," *The Good Society* 13 (2004):32–37.

48. Holly Bell et al., "Balancing Power through Community Building: Setting the Research Agenda on Violence against Women," *Affilia* 19:4 (2004):404–417; Janine

M. Zweig and Martha R. Burt, "Effects of Interactions among Community Agencies on Legal System Responses to Domestic Violence and Sexual Assault in STOP-Funded Communities," *Criminal Justice Policy Review* 14: 2 (2003):249–253.

49. Patricia Yancey Martin, *Rape Work*, 3. New York: Routledge, 2003; Mimi Abramovitz and Ann Withorn, "Playing by the Rules: Welfare Reform and the New Authoritarian State," in *Without Justice for All: The New Liberalism and Our Retreat from Racial Equality*, edited by Adolph Reed, Jr., 151–174. Boulder, Colo.: Westview Press, 1999.

50. Nicola Lacey, *The Prisoners' Dilemma: Political Economy and Punishment in Contemporary Democracies.* Cambridge University Press, 2008.

51. For a recent article that draws out the connection between domestic policy and security politics, see Inderpal Grewal, "'Security Moms' in the Early Twentieth-Century United States: The Gender of Security in Neoliberalism," in *Women's Studies Quarterly* 34 (Spring/Summer 2006):25–39.

52. See Phil Scraton, *Beyond September 11: An Anthology of Dissent.* London: Pluto Press, 2002. And for an analysis that links together the construction of "terror" and the modern conditions of punitive carcerality, see Dylan Rodriguez, "State Terror and the Reproduction of Imprisoned Dissent," *Social Identities* 9 (2003):183–203.

9

The Vulnerable Protecting the Vulnerable

NGOs and Human Security in the Aftermath of War

LAURA J. HEIDEMAN

War leaves a large footprint. Even after negotiations are concluded and treaties have been signed, war-torn societies do not return to "normal." War leaves long-term legacies: refugees, internally displaced people, homelessness, death, disability, and economic, social, and psychological trauma. There are deeper social problems as well: lingering ethnic and nationalist tensions, threats to and abuse of minorities, demonization of and threats against state critics, and social unrest caused by lingering problems of displacement and economic disruption. Despite these widespread human-scale problems, both the international actors involved in postconflict reconstruction (PCR) and the academics who study PCR focus their attention on reconstructing the state. They concentrate on reforms in government structure and in the structures of the economy, rather than the political and economic lives of citizens. This is surprising, given the shift in security studies in the 1990s from state-level security to human security. While the concept of human security allows both practitioners and researchers to examine security in the lives of individuals, this concept has barely penetrated the study of PCR.

Given this focus on state-level rebuilding, how are vulnerable populations such as refugees, women, and minorities protected in the aftermath of conflict? In my research on postconflict reconstruction in Croatia, I find that human security work was largely relegated to local Croatian nongovernmental organizations (NGOs). These NGOs were funded by western donors, but were not included in larger decision-making bodies that decided the directions postconflict reconstruction should take. Additionally, funding for NGO projects was largely determined by the current interests of donors. NGOs often faced opposition and active hostility from the government both during and after the war. Activists faced media criticism, public harassment, and even death threats for their work on behalf of the vulnerable people in Croatia. This was truly a case of the vulnerable protecting the vulnerable.

Vulnerability can be created through status or through action. For people with status vulnerability, their membership in a particular group makes them vulnerable. Vulnerability is contextual. While women's gender status exposes them to particular types of threats, such as rape, it also protected them in some circumstances: while men and teenage boys were targeted for death during the ethnic cleansing campaigns across former Yugoslavia, women, children, and the elderly were usually sent to safety. Likewise, actions can also create vulnerability. For example, combatants who engage directly in violence are at high risk of PTSD; antiwar activists become targets for violence and ostracization. Vulnerable groups do not lack agency, and indeed advocate on their own behalf through courts, protests, and community activities. However, they face basic limits to agency when their status delegitimizes their voices and limits their ability to access governmental resources or receive public support.

The transnational strategy of funding local NGOs to provide human security fit into the larger agenda of the international actors in two ways. First, they saw these NGOs as representing "civil society," which they believed was crucial for building democracies. By funding NGOs, they believed they were creating civil society and thereby aiding the overall project of democratization. Second, they saw the NGOs as delegates who could engage in the messy, local aspects of postconflict reconstruction, leaving international actors free to focus on the state-level aspects.

Who were these Croatian NGOs? Where did they come from? In my research, I found that most of them were founded by activists who had been encouraged, even pressured, by western donors into forming an NGO. These local NGOs were small and almost exclusively funded by western donors. Donors included both private foundations and bilateral aid agencies; the United States Agency for International Development (USAID) was the largest and most influential. In addition, some international organizations, such as the United Nations High Commissioner for Refugees (UNHCR) and the European Union (EU), also provided considerable funding.

NGOs in Croatia engaged in a large variety of human security-related activities, although they were not explicitly defined in those terms. The United Nations Development Program (UNDP) defines human security as having two elements: "first, safety from such chronic threats as hunger, disease and repression. And second, it means protection from sudden and hurtful disruptions in the patterns of daily life—whether in homes, in jobs or in communities" (UNDP 1994, 23). While the Croatian government and UN troops mostly provided basic physical security, other forms of human security were the province of NGOs. In Croatia, common types of human security provision included advocacy for vulnerable groups such as women, minorities, and refugees; legal aid to assist with housing and citizenship problems; trauma recovery and dealing with war crimes; and activities that directly facilitated interethnic cooperation and peace building.

In this chapter, I use the concept of human security to reframe the issues at stake in postconflict reconstruction. Examining the practices I found in the case of postconflict reconstruction in Croatia, I show how the current system of providing human security works and explore the advantages and flaws of this system. In particular, I examine the intersection of global agendas and local needs as mediated by these NGOs.

My analysis looks at the nature and effects of the power differentials between different pairs of actors: NGOs and donors, NGOs and the Croatian state, and the needs of Croatian citizens and the agenda of the international community. My conclusion points to how understanding these relations could allow the provision of human security to be more effective and sustainable.

Postconflict Reconstruction and Human Security

The concept of human security emerged in the 1990s as an answer to the major problem in security studies identified by Booth (1991) and others: that the concept of security referred to the security of the state, and that actions taken to ensure the security of the state did not necessarily ensure the security of its citizens. The concept was a boon for feminist scholars in particular: it gave them a language to interject concerns about the kinds of interpersonal and structural violence women experience into larger debates on security. Human security gained widespread credence as a concept following the 1994 UNDP Human Development Report. The UNDP's inclusion of chronic threats and protection from disruptions as parts of human security creates a broad definition, capturing many types of threats and disruptions. For instance, both long-term political repression and sudden political riots would be considered forms of insecurity under this definition.

This broad definition of human security is important in postconflict settings, which have varied needs ranging from basic humanitarian aid to more insidious forms of insecurity. Minorities, women, and other groups with vulnerable statuses commonly face both physical and structural violence. Moreover, war and repression go hand in hand. "Enemies of the state" in all forms, from minority groups to human rights advocates to feminists, often face specific repression. The effects of political disruption are more widespread: lack of civil and political rights affects not just targeted groups, but all citizens.

However, the breadth of the concept of human security is also the focus of critique. As Paris (2001) has noted, the concept is so broad that "it is difficult to determine what, if anything, might be excluded" (90). The UNDP report indeed mentions not only protection from torture but also protection from suicide. This makes the concept analytically unwieldy. A number of authors have suggested ways to narrow the definition. For instance, both King and Murray (2001) and Thomas (2001) suggest restricting the definition of human security to economic security, making it essentially a question of development rather than political inclusion and safety.

Paris (2001), alternatively, has suggested splitting security into four categories: national security, intrastate security, redefined security, and human security. National security is the traditional definition in which states are protecting themselves militarily from other states. Intrastate security involves groups within a state protecting themselves militarily from other groups or other states. Redefined security focuses on states protecting themselves from nonmilitary threats, such as environmental or economic dangers (98–99). Paris's fourth category, human security, takes in all "military or non-military threats—or both—to the security of societies, groups, and individuals" (100).

Paris's breakdown of security is troubling because it is antithetical to the reasoning behind the emergence of human security as a concept: recognizing that the actions states take in order to secure themselves from threats, both internal and external, often threaten the security of the state's own citizens. Warfare, whether intrastate or interstate, is not just a political and military matter. War disrupts society at its most basic levels: family life is disturbed, gender roles are altered, communities are broken up, and social hierarchies are rearranged. In other words, war creates social insecurity across all domains, and this insecurity persists after conflict ends. Societies must deal with these issues of human security in the aftermath of conflict. Paris's definition narrows the concept of human security, but in an unacceptable way that divorces war from its social consequences. Paris's new formulation is useful because it illustrates what we must reject: a premise that issues of state security and human security caused by intrastate conflict are separate problems with separate solutions. This formulation sidelines human security as a secondary set of problems; human security is treated as a peripheral rather than a central concern in postconflict reconstruction.

How do we bring together the concepts of postconflict reconstruction and human security? My solution to this is to use the concept of human security to redirect the conversation within postconflict reconstruction, so that the focus moves from state-level security toward individual-level security. Issues of gender, ethnicity, and vulnerability are thus forced back into the center of debates over security.

To do this, we have to start by expanding the study of postconflict reconstruction. In his cross-national study of postconflict reconstruction strategies, Paris (2004) focuses on what he sees as the two central components of international strategy since the end of the Cold War: marketization of the economy and democratization of the government.

At one level, this is a descriptive account of international strategy. However, Paris critiques these strategies while making it clear that he accepts the central tenet of this worldview: namely, that the state is the relevant unit for postconflict reconstruction. He argues that implementation of these policies has been too hasty and that the process should be slowed down in order to allow time for basic institutions such as courts, electoral systems, and a "neutral bureaucracy," to flourish (188). His proposed alternative strategy, which he calls "Institutionalization before Liberalization" (7) continues to focus exclusively on state institutions.

Why do the security concerns of nonstate institutions and actors matter in postconflict settings? Security problems experienced on a human scale in the aftermath of conflict reflect the dynamics of the conflict and interfere with resolving them. The recent literature on conflicts suggests that local dynamics are critical. Kalyvas's (2006) study of the dynamics of violence during the Greek civil war in the 1940s found that local cleavages were far more important than central ones in predicting patterns of violence. More recently, Autesserre's (2010) study of peace building in the Congo found that by focusing on a state-centered strategy, international peacekeepers were blinded to the local dynamics of violence: because they had decided that the state-level problems had been solved, they interpreted ongoing violence as "normal" rather than as pathological, and thus failed to stop it. These studies are highly suggestive for postconflict reconstruction; they suggest that there is tension between the causes and consequences of violence at the state and local levels.

Another reason why we should focus on human-scale problems is that they suggest usable questions about the dynamics of reconstruction. How and by whom are the needs of citizens addressed? Which citizens' needs are prioritized? What kinds of systems are in place to provide human security after conflict? This human security approach puts people at the center of the reconstruction agenda. Too often, the elements of human security are assumed merely to be dividends of peace: if the problems of the government are solved, then citizens will have security. But the mechanisms through which human security is reached are unclear in this model. When human security is instead the central focus of postconflict reconstruction, both researchers and practitioners are asked to evaluate the supposed means of providing human security more carefully. The remainder of this chapter will examine the current system of human security provision, using the case of Croatia to evaluate how it is provided and for whom, and the strengths and weaknesses of this approach.

Methods

This study engages in what Shore and Wright (1997) call "studying through," by following a process across different organizations and sites. This type of ethnography "also offers the potential for a radical reconceptulization of 'the field'; not as a discrete local community or geographical area, but as a social and political space articulated through relations of power and systems of governance" (11). The field is not limited by geography, but rather is composed of a network of individuals and groups involved in an area of work. This approach allows me to examine peace building from the diverse perspectives of politicians, international donors, international NGOs, and local NGOs. I follow the threads of international aid, paying attention at every level to how the aid is distributed, how it is regulated, and how people are held accountable for it.

I began by studying this process in regions around two war-affected cities, Osijek and Zadar, that lay on the border of Serb-occupied territory. In these regions, I examined local projects related to various aspects of human security. I observed activities and interviewed activists, community partners, and leaders of NGOs who supported or ran the projects, as well as local political leaders. I also gathered documents from these organizations on current and previous activities, organizational history, and funding for projects.[1]

I also collected data in the capital, Zagreb. As is typical with projects involving international actors, much of the large-scale activity around human security took place in the capital. In Zagreb, I interviewed individuals at three different types of NGOs: those who had human security projects running in Zagreb, those headquartered in Zagreb but with branches outside the capital, and those based in Zagreb who only ran projects outside the capital. Again, I collected data, both by means of interviews and through documents, on organizational history, previous and current projects, and funding.

The final step was to trace funding and expertise back to its sources. I collected data, both oral and written, from international NGOs involved in Croatia, private and bilateral international donors, and Croatian government officials. These sources allowed me to examine how international money was distributed and how human security projects are regulated at both the national and international levels. In all, I collected hundreds of documents and conducted over 150 interviews.

By "studying through" these levels of human security provision, I gained the valuable insight to which Shore and Wright alluded, namely, the ability to understand the different and often opposing perspectives of individuals situated at different levels of the process. These different perspectives allowed me to triangulate data on projects, but also to understand why the opinions of people at different levels diverged about the role NGOs play in providing human security.

War and Postwar Reconstruction in Croatia

In 1995, the Croatian state had little interest in providing human security for its citizens, especially minorities. The country had just been through a civil war to establish its independence from Yugoslavia and the integrity of its federal borders from the Yugoslav era. The war, which lasted from 1991 to 1995, involved Croatia fighting for its independence from the rest of Yugoslavia and fighting to maintain control over a large section of its territory, approximately one-third of the country, which had been claimed as an independent state by the Serbian minority in Croatia. This quasi-state, called the Republic of Serbian Krajina (RSK), included most of the eastern border with Bosnia, as well as a section in the northeast along the Serbian border.

Ethnic Serbs made up approximately 12 percent of the country's population in 1991, just before the war started (Central Bureau of Statistics, 2006).[2] As the RSK took over Croatian territory in 1991 with the aid of the Yugoslav National Army (JNA), ethnic Croats who lived in Serb-controlled territory were "ethnically cleansed." Ethnic cleansing refers to any actions taken to remove unwanted ethnic groups from a territory, ranging from forcible displacement to displacement under threat to active genocide. In the case of the ethnic cleansing of Croats in

Serb-held territory, the main tactic was forcible displacement, but there were a number of massacres during late 1991.

The UN sent a peacekeeping force in 1992 known as UNPROFOR. They divided the Serb-held territory into four sections and maintained a ceasefire from 1992 through early 1995. In May 1995, the Croatian army forcibly retook UN Sector West. In August 1995, the Croatian army repeated this exercise in UN Sectors North and South. In both operations, ethnic Serbs fled ahead of the Croatian troops, and many who stayed were killed or faced persecution (Silber and Little 1996, 360). In all, approximately 300,000 ethnic Serbs fled the country, about 75 percent of the country's ethnic Serb population (Human Rights Watch 2003). The fourth UN administrative region, Sector East, was returned to Croatia via a negotiated treaty in November 1995. Under the treaty, the UN continued to administer the region, known as UNTAES, until early 1998, in order to stabilize the area.

The war changed the demographics of Croatia. Overall, the population dropped by about 300,000 between the 1991 and 2001 censuses. There were over 580,000 Serbs in Croatia in 1991; by 2001, there were just over 200,000 (Central Bureau of Statistics, 2006). The 2001 number includes some Serbs who had returned from third countries, so the difference between the 1991 and 2001 figures does not reflect the total number displaced. In addition, approximately 220,000 ethnic Croats were internally displaced during the conflict,[3] and at least 200,000 left the country (OSCE 2004). To add to the complications, many ethnic Croats from neighboring Bosnia fled to Croatia between 1992 and 1995. In all, Croatia had over a million refugees and displaced people by 1995. Given that Croatia's total prewar population was only 4.7 million people, this was an enormous disruption of the population. After the war, only the UNTAES region had a sizable Serb population.

The war brought about enormous social and political changes in the country. The political party in charge of the country, the Croatian Democratic Union (Hrvatska Demokratska Zajednica, or HDZ), was a right-wing nationalist party that had widespread public support. Žarkov (2007) writes about the narrowing of gender roles for women during the conflict, as the process of ethnicization included shifting gender narratives that understood women individually as mothers and collectively as reproducers of the nation. Likewise, men's gender repertoire also narrowed as the country militarized. Unsurprisingly in these circumstances, many feminists were vehement state critics. Both during and after the war, the nationalist character of politics made it very difficult for minorities and critics of the government to express their opinions freely. For example, some feminists who were openly critical of the state were accused of being "witches" who were "raping Croatia." Newspapers published details of their ancestry and marriages, as well as their personal information, in order to discredit and threaten them.[4]

This is the basic backdrop for the provision of human security at the end of the conflict. The Croatian state was not a force for advancing human security in the territory it controlled. Through my interviews with Croatian NGO workers, Croatian activists, international NGO workers, and international donors, I found widespread consensus that the still-nationalist Croatian government was actively hostile to efforts to aid minorities and vulnerable groups during the 1990s.

The Croatian government was resistant to the idea of granting citizenship to nonethnic Croats, it made working conditions for NGOs difficult by charging NGOs taxes of over 100 percent on take-home salaries of workers, and created legal difficulties for ethnic Serbs attempting to assert their legal rights to citizenship, property, and pensions. Housing issues were particularly fraught. The war coincided with the end of communist rule and the housing stock was privatized at a time when much of the population was displaced. Refugees and IDPs had a difficult time demonstrating their tenancy rights on properties held before the war. It was especially difficult for ethnic Serbs, as displaced Croats and Bosnian refugees were often housed in Serb properties, and ethnic Serbs could not regain the right to use their properties until alternative housing had been arranged for the current tenants. Moreover, because Serbs' homes were often deliberately destroyed in the conflict, they needed alternate housing arrangements or funding to rebuild their homes. According to the Organization for Security and Cooperation in Europe, UNHCR, and the EU, access to housing is still a major issue for Serb returnees over fifteen years after the conflict has ended.[5]

Because the Croatian state was often the cause of human security problems, particularly for minorities and government critics, the United Nations, which already had a presence in the UNTAES region, began directing state-level policy on issues like refugee return through UNHCR and on redevelopment activities through UNDP. Likewise, the embassies of numerous countries around the world became involved in rebuilding. In the town of Vukovar, which was largely leveled by the conflict, nearly every public building that has been rebuilt bears a plaque indicating which government gave funds to reconstruct it. However, when it came to providing direct legal aid or trauma relief to individuals, or engaging in activities promoting interethnic cooperation at the individual level, these international actors chose not to be directly involved. Instead, they gave funds to local Croatian NGOs to engage in these human security activities on their behalf.

The political situation changed in 2000, when the Croatian Democratic Union or HDZ was defeated by a center-left coalition, which began passing laws that eased the situation for Serbs living in Croatia, such as laws on minority educational rights, and the reconstruction of houses and businesses. This progress toward better treatment of Serbs eased relations with the EU, and Croatia began the process of negotiating for EU accession. Even after the HDZ was voted back into power in the 2003 parliamentary elections in a new center-right coalition, Croatian policy toward the Serbs remained the same. Progress on issues related to human rights and minority rights was relatively slow, leading many NGO activists to complain that the government was not really interested in these issues and was just putting on a show to ease the EU accession process.

Emergence of the NGO Sector

The NGO sector in Croatia played a crucial role in the provision of human security after the end of the war. In this section, I show how this sector emerged from a social movement and was shaped during the 1990s into a formal, professional NGO sector.

Donors saw the NGO sector as having two important functions. First, through its very existence the NGO sector confirmed that Croatia was becoming democratic, since NGOs were conceptualized as a crucial component of a democratic society. In democracy theory, civil society is the intermediate space between the state and the people. Although civil society can include a wide variety of actors—the media, religious organizations, neighborhood associations, sports clubs, advocacy organizations, and labor unions—in newly emerging democracies donors usually emphasize NGOs as civil society.[6] By funding NGOs, donors saw themselves as funding civil society.[7]

The second key role of the NGO sector was implementing projects. Donors gave money to NGOs for specific projects to be carried out in small communities throughout Croatia. These projects were the international community's main effort to directly address threats to human security in various forms, from documenting human rights violations to reversing nationalist incursions against women's rights to providing legal aid for refugees.

While donors actively shaped civil society in Croatia, it would be a mistake to claim that they created it. Bagić (2006), for instance, shows that women's groups were active across Yugoslavia during the 1980s. I also found that the NGOs of the 1990s and 2000s grew out of previous social movements that were active before and during the war.

The strongest of these was the women's movement: feminist activists with strong trans-Yugoslavia relationships had established themselves as early as the 1970s. Others, such as the conscientious objectors movement, designed to help men avoid the mandatory military service required by Yugoslavia, were active in the 1980s as well.

Antiwar activism in Croatia preceded western donors' interventions. During the war, groups of antiwar activists emerged around Croatia. Some, such as the Centre for Women War Victims in Zagreb, arose out of the women's movement (interviews with feminist activists, Feb. 1, 2008, Feb. 9, 2008, and Feb. 27, 2008); others, such as the Anti-War Campaign (ARK, or Antiratna Kampanja Hrvatska) were led by activists from the conscientious objectors' movement. Still others, such as the Centre for Peace, Non-Violence, and Human Rights (CZM) in Osijek, did not have a clear origin in a previous movement, but brought together citizens concerned about the changes war was bringing about in the country (interview with CZM, Feb. 2, 2009). These groups were often fairly nebulous to begin with, but solidified over time. Eventually, the peace groups began to network:

> The Anti-War Campaign started in 1990, in Zagreb, actually. . . . And my friend and myself, we started talking about what could be done for peace

in Osijek in early November or the end of October 1991. And then we read an article about the Anti-War Campaign, and I went to Zagreb. I contacted them, and I asked whether they could help us, that we were also interested in how to stop the war and how to build peace. And it was in maybe December 1991, and then they were very pleased that there were some people in the war zone willing to work on this. (CZM founding member, Feb. 2, 2009)

The Anti-War Campaign was a network of peace organizations across Croatia. By the end of the war in 1995, it had around twenty member organizations from around Croatia, including a number of organizations in war zones.

ARK served a number of purposes for peace activists: it connected groups across Croatia, it communicated with antiwar activists in other former Yugoslav republics, and it served as a conduit for money and expertise once western donors began to get involved: "They [ARK] were really very supportive to us, so they started to send international peace activists to Osijek to visit us and to see whether they could help us" (founding member CZM, Feb. 2, 2009). The process of learning to be a peace organization was long and complicated, as many were not trained activists.

So we started educating [a] group of us people on communication, on analysis, on conflict transformation to understand the dynamics of conflict and where we are now on an individual, emotional, and political level, and also how to advocate in a nonviolent way. So we had five days of training [on] how to advocate for the human rights in our situation with high tensions, wars going on. (CZM founder, Feb. 2, 2009)

The training offered by outsiders was crucial for these organizations, which often had no background in activism. Participants were from a wide variety of backgrounds, including teachers, doctors, former soldiers, housewives, lawyers, writers, and social workers.

The ARK network was critical for the provision of human security in the early years of the war. Member organizations were involved in activities ranging from providing services to refugees, both in refugee camps and in Zagreb, advocating on behalf of ethnic Serbs facing violence and repression, maintaining links with other activists across former Yugoslavia, and demonstrating for peace. In addition to facilitating training, the ARK network also facilitated cooperation on campaigns:

> We would like to stop the violence against Serbs, for instance. We also found out that the situation in Split is similar, and there in Split, there are some people doing the same things as we are doing here. And then people in Zagreb started to do the same protection of people. It was something like—not a movement, but it was a campaign, actually, a spontaneous campaigning in Osijek and Zagreb and Split against these evictions. (CZM founder, Feb. 2, 2009)

Networking by these groups made it easier to coordinate campaigns across the country, even in cities that were on different fronts of the war.

Activism exacted a steep price, however. Early peace activists faced death threats and beatings. Many activists' status was questioned because they were minorities, of mixed ethnicity, or belonged to a now-suspect category such as feminists, socialists, or atheists.[8] Their status in society already made them vulnerable; their work on human security increased this vulnerability. Even in 2010, over a decade after the war had ended, some activists were still receiving threats and being publicly confronted about their work.[9] During the war, working together in a network provided some stability and social support to the organizations and their individual members, so that even if they were isolated in their own communities they were in contact with others who shared their beliefs.

Both private foundations and bilateral donors began to work in Croatia in 1993 and 1994. One of the first requirements they had for groups they worked with was that they formalize their status as NGOs. This was a change in internal structure, rather than a change in government paperwork. To meet western expectations, these organizations were expected to become professionalized in addition to their work with vulnerable populations.

The United States Agency for International Development (USAID) was the largest trainer of NGOs. Among other things, it defined its role in Croatia as creating and professionalizing the NGO sector. From the time of its entry into Croatia in 1992 until 1998, when the UNTAES region was formally returned to Croatia, USAID funded human security projects that leaned toward humanitarian aid. It used an umbrella grant structure for funding, funding international NGOs (INGOs) which in turn trained and funded local Croatian NGOs. The largest of its peace-building grants was to the "Trauma and Humanitarian Assistance for Former Yugoslavia" program. Under this project, eight INGOs worked in Croatia and Bosnia on diverse local projects related to human security: trauma aid in war-torn areas, advocacy for women, legal aid for refugees and internally displaced people (IDPs), and activities in refugee camps (USAID 1996).

To find Croatians to work with, the INGOs sought out active Croatian groups of all kinds, which they developed into NGOs:

> The actual process was competitive for funds in the initial stages, but in order to make sure we had the right people bidding, we beat the bushes to make sure everybody knew that this was an opportunity. So we made sure that everybody had the information to submit the proposals and things like that. We provided training on how to develop proposals and develop budgets so that the organizations were not kind of left to drift on their own to do this. (INGO, May 10, 2009)

In this way, Croatian groups were introduced to the formal processes of receiving international funds. They were told where opportunities existed, told how to apply for them, and trained in the basic skills necessary for creating acceptable proposals. After the proposals were accepted, the organizations continued to receive training on budget management, organizational structure, engaging in advocacy, and writing project reports. This training taught the Croatian organizations how to become professionalized NGOs. These new Croatian NGOs were not particularly large by international standards. Some had only one or two paid staff members, but even the largest had only about thirty people on their staff. A much more typical size was four to eight staff members.

Over time, donor expectations for NGOs increased. In addition to streamlining and formalizing their management, they were told by USAID or USAID-funded international organizations that they needed to have a governing board separate from their in-house leadership, a mission statement, and new division of labor within their organization. They were even given booklets like *A Handbook of NGO Governance*,[10] which told them the proper way to run NGOs (interview, NGO manager, Zagreb, Oct. 10, 2008). The NGOs were even expected to keep up to three sets of records, meeting the criteria for Croatian, U.S., and E.U. accounting practices. As their reporting requirements grew, NGO staff began to complain that they were spending more time on paperwork than on the projects themselves (NGO, April 22, 2009). Some groups designated one or two staff members as grant writers and separated this work from that of actually providing human security.

This emphasis on professionalization also caused NGOs to become separated from their grassroots membership base. One NGO started with about thirty regular volunteers who came to weekly meetings during its formative years.

> About twenty of them were very active—mostly Serbs, or Croats who experienced the war directly. They were displaced, the Serbs had to fight for their rights. It was personal. ... At that stage, we were socially burdened—you had to be mainstream, a Croat to be good, be a "big Croat" in order to love your country. It was a requirement of the government, a part of the whole atmosphere of war. (NGO, April 21, 2010)

She said the organization provided a space for these marginalized individuals and a place for them to become active on the issues that affected them. However, as the international donors came in and the activities switched toward more professional, staff-run projects, the weekly meetings gradually fell away. "Now, we don't have specific things members can participate in" (NGO, April 21, 2010). The activities of the NGO were pushed in a direction that encouraged staff-directed projects rather than grassroots activism, which increased the gap between paid staff and organization members, and caused members to stop being involved in the organization.

The NGO model of human security provision became increasingly problematic once international donors began to withdraw their funds in the 2000s. It became a crisis when the two largest bilateral donors, USAID and SIDA (Swedish International Development Cooperation

Agency), withdrew from Croatia during 2006 and 2007. USAID gave ample warning to the NGOs that they would be withdrawing aid, but they still experienced difficulties, had to reduce staffing, and lost capacity to apply for projects and engage in field projects. SIDA gave little warning; its final report on its work in Croatia notes that several of the organizations it had supported needed to lay off staff and reduce their operating costs, which led to a loss of capacity to run projects (Peck 2007, 20). Doing fieldwork two years after SIDA withdrew, I found that some of the organizations had ceased to exist as professional organizations, and that many had survived by severely reducing their size and impact. Of all Croatian NGOs, only those organizations large enough and bureaucratic enough to successfully apply for EU preaccession grants were able to weather these financial changes intact. The rest disbanded or deprofessionalized.

The lack of a membership base and the negative reputation NGOs had in mainstream society made it very difficult for them to fund-raise successfully. When I raised the question of private donations in interviews, NGO professionals laughed and told stories of failure after failure, all contending that, under current conditions, it was not a feasible solution.

These Croatian organizations were the main source of human security protection for minorities and other vulnerable groups in the 1990s. Both NGO functions—that of providing human security and that of representing "civil society," the participatory base for democracy—were made challenging by the way donors reshaped these organizations. The transition from being community-centered, activist-driven organizations to being professionalized and bureaucratized organizations undermined their ability to respond to the local community and shifted the power to define security needs upward to the donors. The international NGOs and international donors taught them the "right" way to exist as organizations: as professional NGOs who apply for foreign funding to support their work. The withdrawal of much of this international funding exposed a gaping hole in the logic of this model of providing human security, namely, that it is unsustainable without either an international sector willing to fund it indefinitely or a state that is both willing and capable of providing security and supporting democratic participation by all its citizens.

NGOs as Providers of Human Security

Given that these professionalized NGOs are the form that human security provision took in Croatia, how well did they function in this role? The international strategy of using NGOs to provide human security had advantages as well as drawbacks. Being at the nexus of international and local forces, these NGOs had the advantages of a local group, such as local knowledge, authenticity, and passion for the issues based on first-hand experience, and the advantages of international access, such as money and expertise, including knowledge based on other international cases similar to their own, networks of like-minded activists at home and abroad, and high status as professionals in an internationally recognized field of work. However, although these advantages could lead to positive outcomes, the accompanying disadvantages often outweighed them.

One aspect of community-based NGOs that gave them strong credibility was their indigenous nature. They were not outsiders coming into communities. Rather, they were concerned insiders who sought outside assistance. This gave the NGOs two major resources: knowledge of their home communities and local authenticity. Local knowledge was vital for conducting needs assessments, navigating local politics, and creating working relationships in communities, all of which form the foundation for successful peace building. Authenticity is also important for gaining the respect of the local population. Sustaining such credibility and respect became a major problem for many of the NGOs once they began receiving international money. Most of the activists I spoke with had at some point been accused of being an outsider, a foreign spy, or the agent of a foreign government. These accusations came from government officials, media, and private citizens. They were more common in the 1990s, but still occur. In 2009, for example, one NGO had graffiti scrawled on the outside of its building accusing it of being "agents of the Jew Mr. Soros." The message ended with the accusation "Jewish money against Croatia." While this was not a real threat to the organization, it illustrates the persistence of the idea that NGOs working on human security were working against Croatian interests.

The origins of this idea arose during the 1990s. In the postwar period many in the international community considered ethnic Serbs to be a high priority for human security interventions. Some organizations resisted this agenda, but it was difficult.

> When people come to the field, for us they are the same, we never divide them: you are displaced, you are refugees, you are Serb, you are Croat. We had a problem with the big international organizations in the beginning, because they wanted to support only one group of beneficiaries. For us at the Red Cross, that was unacceptable, because at the Red Cross we have our principles and we must support everyone. For us the only principle that is important is the principle of vulnerability. (Croatian Red Cross, June 16, 2009)

The Croatian Red Cross was in a fortunate position because it did not depend on a single powerful donor; but most NGOs in Croatia were under donor pressure to meet the needs of Serbs. The prevailing assumption was that the Croatian government would take care of ethnic Croats. For instance, one organization worked to document war crimes against Serbs, assuming that the government was documenting the crimes against Croats. However, they found out later that this had not been systematically done (interview with Zagreb NGO, Mar. 7, 2008).

This division of labor was problematic for two reasons. First, the Croatian state was not as good at helping ethnic Croats with human security as donors expected it to be. Second, due to ethnic tensions the fact that the NGOs helped Serbs created the impression that they were pro-Serb, and thus anti-Croat. "They have a silly assumption that if you are for the rights of Serbs, you are therefore a pro-Serb organization" (NGO, Apr. 21, 2010). The perception that human security and peace building were "for Serbs" was quite widespread. Most NGOs reported hearing such comments about their work. I encountered them directly when I explained my research to Croatians. The usual response was, "Oh, you're here to study the Serbs."

This framing undermined widespread public support for human security work because it was always seen as aiding some "other." By limiting Croats' realization that these organizations would and could serve ethnic Croats as well, their actions were not seen as serving the common good. This perception changed the understanding of human security interventions from securing universal rights and meeting universal needs to just being a way of helping minorities.

Another framing problem that arose in this system of human security provision was that donors' ideas of what constituted vital issues sometimes differed greatly from those of NGOs. For example, preventing human trafficking was a major goal of international organizations starting in the late 1990s. USAID, SIDA, and OSCE (Organization for Security and Cooperation in Europe) all gave funding to Croatian NGOs to work on these issues (Peck 2007; USAID 2008). Given the amount of international attention given to this one issue, one would suspect that trafficking was widespread. However, local NGO activists told me that at most, Croatia was a transition country through which trafficked women were moved. This view is borne out in the final USAID report, which notes that their funded hotline in Croatia was a success: "[H]otline calls led to 20 cases for police investigation, resulting in the prosecution of at least two human traffickers" (USAID 2008, 48). By comparison, in neighboring Bosnia a single antitrafficking organization serving a remote region assisted around two hundred victims of trafficking by 2009 (Branković 2009, 22). This is not to imply that trafficking is not an important issue but rather that it was not at that time critical in Croatia. To accomplish any project, the NGOs had to depend on donors; in such circumstances donors' focus trumped local concerns. Many of the women's NGOs expressed frustration that trafficking prevention made up such a large proportion of international funding for women's issues. Likewise, human rights NGOs expressed frustration that this was the largest human rights issue receiving funding.

Trafficking appears to be one of a number of transnational fads in funding that reflects more about the nature of global discourse than the realities on the ground. Such fad-driven priorities show the top-down, nonresponsive, noncontextual nature of funding priorities. Even when NGOs attempted to express their assessment of needs to donors, they were rebuffed: "We tried to talk to [the donor], but they just said, 'I know you want us to do that, but we don't want to go that way.' Unfortunately, we were not able to continue with that attitude because projects we think are valuable are not funded—they are left on the road" (NGO, Apr. 21, 2010).

Funded projects respond to international rather than local perceptions of what is needed, which negates the advantage local NGOs have in their ability to assess local needs. In the absence of mechanisms for them to influence international donors, NGOs become implementers of international agendas rather than assets capable of setting a realistic local agenda. Successful implementation of human security projects is especially difficult because of this fundamental power imbalance. International donors and international organizations are by their nature more powerful than small, local NGOs. They have credibility, financial resources, institutional backing, and expertise. Local NGOs are better positioned through their presence in communities to understand the particular human security needs on the ground, but are hamstrung in their ability to address those needs by their dependence on international donors who lack both formal mechanisms and the informal inclination to listen to the NGOs they support. By focusing on international priorities rather than local needs, and by determining who the recipients of aid should be without reference to local conditions, international donors run the risk of making projects ineffective and damaging the local reputation of the NGOs they fund.

Conclusion

Under postconflict reconstruction, this system of human security provision breaks down both in terms of the roles NGOs play as civil society and the roles they play in directly engaging in peace-building activities. There are three main causes of this. First, NGOs and donors fail to exploit the strategic advantage NGOs have in providing local human security: local knowledge and the ability to form lasting community connections. The top-down nature of the donor-NGO relationship allows donors to disregard local knowledge and opinions. Second, the donor-NGO relationships often weaken the democratic base of NGOs by pushing NGOs toward professionalized activities and thus away from a grassroots base, and by pushing them to act in ways that make them appear to be taking a side in a conflict rather than serving as neutral upholders of commonly held values. Finally, this system relegates the provision of human security to those who are in a weak social position by dint of their own social marginality. NGO staff members often have status vulnerability due to their gender or ethnicity; their work, particularly when it is seen as working against Croatian interests, increases their vulnerability. These organizations gain most of their legitimacy from the support of international actors, but at the cost of independence. Indeed, the involvement and agenda of international actors often costs these organizations local legitimacy. Their ability to function as providers of human security is contingent on the support of international actors. Thoughtless actions by international actors further undercut local support for these organizations and increase their vulnerability.

There are several implications of this for human security. First, this indicates the extent to which human security is marginalized in the process of postconflict reconstruction, relegated to some of the most vulnerable actors in the postconflict setting. This ultimately excuses states from meeting their responsibilities for providing human security for their own citizens by furthering the implicit assumptions that international actors will look after these groups. This system is also ultimately unsustainable. The ability of NGOs to perform these roles depends on the financial support of international actors and the legitimacy granted to these organizations by their international connections. One of the inevitabilities in the aftermath of conflict is the end of international involvement. International attention spans are limited; there is a never-ending supply of conflicts for donors to attend to. It is therefore imperative to create a system of human security provision that can withstand donor withdrawal.

Finally, this research shows the inattention to human security prevalent in postconflict reconstruction. This inattention can lead to undesirable outcomes, particularly to the extent that local voices are marginalized in debates around the best course of action. The current PCR system needs more feedback mechanisms that allow those directly involved in human security to make local needs known, set the agenda of human security, and create sustainable, grassroots organizations.

NOTES

1. Most documents and interviews were in English, as NGOs need English-speaking staff members to receive foreign funding. Translations, when applicable, are noted. When necessary, I have edited grammar and repetition for clarity.

2. The Census was completed in April 1991. There were a few skirmishes around this time, but the conflict did not intensify until June 1991, so this predates large-scale displacements.

3. "Croatia: Housing Rights and Employment Still Preventing Durable Solution," Internal Displacement Monitoring Centre, September 1, 2009. http://www.internal-displacement.org/8025708F004CE90B/%28httpCountries%29/7928D486A14C897D80 2570A7004C7215?OpenDocument (retrieved from the internet on February 2, 2011).

4. Globus Investigatory Team, "Croatia's Feminists Rape Croatia," GLOBUS, December 11, 1992.

5. Interviews: March 16, 2009, April 8, 2009, June 8, 2009, April 13, 2010, April 16, 2010, and April 26, 2010.

6. For a detailed discussion of the role of NGOs in new democracies, see Richter 2002; Sperling 1999; and Henderson 2003.

7. See, for example, AED 2007, "CroNGO Program: Legacy for the Future." Zagreb: USAID/AED.

8. Interviews with early activists: February 9, 2008, April 15, 2008, October 10, 2008, and April 21, 2010.

9. Interviews with activists: February 2, 2009, April 9, 2009, and April 15, 2009.

10. Wyatt, Marilyn, *A Handbook of NGO Governance/Priručnik za upravljanje.* Budapest: European Center for Not-for-Profit Law, 2004.

REFERENCES

AED. 2007. "CroNGO Program: Legacy for the Future." Zagreb: USAID/AED.

Autesserre, Severine. 2010. *The Trouble with the Congo: Local Violence and the Failure of International Peacebuilding.* New York: Cambridge University Press.

Bagic, Aida. 2006. "Women's Organizing in Post-Yugoslav Countries: Talking about 'Donors' in Global Feminism." In *Transnational Women's Activism, Organizing, and Human Rights,* edited by Myra Marx Ferree and Aili Mari Tripp, 141–165. New York: NYU Press.

Booth, Ken. 1991. "Security and Emancipation." *Review of International Studies* 17(4): 313.

Branković, Biljana. 2009. *CARE International on Combating Trafficking in Human Beings in the North-West Balkans.* Belgrade: CARE International North-West Balkans.

Central Bureau of Statistics. 2006. *Statistical Yearbook 2006.* Republic of Croatia: Central Bureau of Statistics.

Henderson, Sarah. 2003. *Building Democracy in Contemporary Russia: Western Support for Grassroots Organizations.* Ithaca, N.Y.: Cornell University Press.

Human Rights Watch. 2003. *Broken Promises: Impediments to Refugee Return to Croatia.* New York: Human Rights Watch 15 (6 D).

Kalyvas, Stathis. 2006. *The Logic of Violence in Civil War.* New York: Cambridge University Press.

King, Gary, and Christopher J. L. Murray. 2001. "Rethinking Human Security." *Political Science Quarterly* 16 (4):585–610.

OSCE. 2004. *Croatia's Refugee Challenge*. Zagreb: OSCE Mission to Croatia.

Paris, Roland. 2001. "Human Security: Paradigm Shift or Hot Air?" *International Security* 26 (2):87–102.

———. 2004. *At War's End: Building Peace after Civil Conflict*. New York: Cambridge University Press.

Peck, Lennart. 2007. "SIDA Financed Co-Operation with Civil Society in Croatia: Lessons and Experiences." *Final Report*: SIDA.

Richter, James. 2002. "Evaluating Western Assistance to Russian Women's Organizations." In *The Power and Limits of NGOs: A Critical Look at Building Democracy in Eastern Europe and Eurasia*, edited by Sarah E. Mendelson and John K. Glenn, 54–90. New York: Columbia University Press.

Shore, Cris, and Susan Wright. 1997. "Policy: A New Field of Anthropology." In *Anthropology of Policy: Critical Perspectives on Governance and Power*, edited by Cris Shore and Susan Wright, 3–33. London: Routledge.

Silber, Laura, and Allan Little. 1996. *The Death of Yugoslavia*. New York: Penguin Books.

Sperling, Valerie. 1999. *Organizing Women in Contemporary Russia: Engendering Transition*. New York: Cambridge University Press.

Thomas, Caroline. 2001. "Global Governance, Development and Human Security: Exploring the Links." *Third World Quarterly* 22(2):159–175.

United Nations Development Program (UNDP). 1994. *Human Development Report: New Dimensions of Human Security*. New York: Oxford University Press.

USAID. 1996. "Evaluation of Project 0016 Trauma and Humanitarian Assistance for the Former Yugoslavia." USAID Report PD-ABN-058.

———. 2008. *Celebrating the Croatian-American Partnership: USAID Legacy Publication*. Zagreb: USAID Croatia.

Wyatt, Marilyn. 2004. *A Handbook of NGO Governance/Priručnik za upravljanje*. Budapest: European Center for Not-for-Profit Law.

Žarkov, Dubravka. 2007. *The Body of War: Media, Ethnicity, and Gender in the Break-Up of Yugoslavia*. Durham: Duke University Press.

10

Violence against Women, Human Security, and Human Rights of Women and Girls

Reinforced Obligations in the Context of Structural Vulnerability

RUTH RUBIO-MARÍN AND DOROTHY ESTRADA-TANCK

It has become increasingly clear that women are often the ones most victimized by violence in times of armed conflict: they are the majority of civilian deaths, the majority of refugees, and are often targeted for cruel and degrading practices, such as rape. However, women's basic well-being is also severely threatened in daily life by unequal access to resources, services, and opportunities, not to mention the many forms of violence women experience under "ordinary circumstances." By making the security and basic well-being of persons its main concern, the concept of *human security* is able to capture this broader range of threats and risks. It highlights the need to address violence, whether interpersonal, intergroup, internal, or international, as well as systemic and extreme forms of deprivation and precariousness. It is therefore not surprising that the appearance of the concept was celebrated as offering new lenses through which to understand the difficulties women and girls encounter to live lives free from fear and deprivation (Basch 2004; O'Manique 2006). Recently, there has also been opportunity to celebrate developments in the area of human rights law, which are now also contributing to conceptualizing violence against women and girls as a state problem and a security concern (Von Tigerstrom 2007, 60; Boerefijn and Naezer 2008; Hasselbacher 2010).

This chapter suggests that there are reasons to celebrate both concepts, but that the emerging notion of human security and these recent developments in international human rights law deserve closer and interrelated analysis. More specifically, we argue that fruitful synergies between the concepts of human security and human rights can be identified that will enhance the chances of women and girls to live lives free of violence. Our point of departure is that although there is general understanding that a human security analysis and the human rights framework somehow intersect, the bodies of literature that deal with each have so far failed to spell out more specifically the ways in which the two concepts mutually reinforce each other. They have also fallen short in examining how such synergy may contribute to combating the multiple forms of violence women and girls experience.

More concretely, we argue that the concept of human security should have a stronger gender and human rights component, in particular through adopting women's human rights indicators as well as incorporating the understanding of violence against women that has been gradually gaining ground in human rights law. These changes would make the concept of human security both more precise and gender sensitive, and assist in delineating its content, boundaries, and possible practical applications. At the same time, we seek to flesh out ways in which the notion of human security can contribute to a more comprehensive understanding of women's and girls' human rights and of the set of state obligations that their protection requires, especially in situations where violations of human rights are part of a systematic pattern.

The chapter is organized as follows. The first section reviews the main emerging conceptions of human security and assesses their strengths and weaknesses, especially in view of their potential to capture the threat that violence against women poses to women's and girls' security and to the full realization of their human rights. The second section analyzes two cases resolved by regional human rights courts, *Opuz v. Turkey* (decided by the European Court of Human Rights) and *Cotton Field v. Mexico* (decided by the Inter-American Court of Human Rights), as representing some of the most promising developments in the treatment of violence against women under human rights law, as of October 2011. Drawing from these cases, our third section suggests that human security notions underlie such developments. We show how broader general interpretative synergies between the concepts of human security and human rights can be identified here, and point to important doctrinal implications for the understanding of human rights law in contexts of structural vulnerability. We end with some conclusions on the potential of such synergies to better realize women's and girls' right to live lives secure from violence.

The Quest for a Gendered and Human Rights–Based Approach to Human Security

Traditionally, security was considered a matter of states. States were seen both as the subjects in charge of providing security to the persons under their jurisdiction, as well as the objects worthy of protection and regulation through laws and policies. Security of the state was commonly interpreted as securing its territorial integrity and its sovereign powers, while the security of individual human beings, and in particular women and girls, was largely ignored (MacFarlane and Khong 2006, 19).

The modern concept of human security was initially referenced in 1993 by the United Nations Development Program (UNDP) and then fully articulated through the 1994 UNDP Annual Report on Human Development. The new concept, as coined in the Report, was ambitious. It placed the person at the forefront and sought to express comprehensively the possibility of multiple threats to her basic well-being, departing thereby from prevailing state-centered conceptions of national, military, or territorial security.

Reflecting the new post–Cold War context, the Report contributed to bridging the civil-political versus socioeconomic divide of the old East-West conflict. Reacting against the prioritizing of civil and political rights that had taken place in the West after 1948, the Report recovered the original wording of the 1945 Charter of the United Nations which in its Preamble referred to the Parties' commitment "to promote social progress and better standards of life in larger freedom." The Report also drew strength from the views of the founders of the United Nations (UN) who had interpreted security as covering both *freedom from fear* and *freedom from want* (Benedek 2008, 7; Preamble of the 1948 Universal Declaration of Human Rights), both of which were said to be of equal importance (UNDP 1994, 24). Thus, as defined by the 1994 UNDP Report, threats to human life were supposed to include those related to hunger, disease, and political oppression, and not only those stemming from the violence of international or domestic war or the use of armed force. In grouping the components of human security into seven categories (including economic security, food security, health security, environmental security, personal security, community security, and political security; see UNDP 1994, 23–25), the Report explicitly stressed that "for most people, a feeling of insecurity arises more from worries about daily life than from the dread of a cataclysmic world event" (ibid., 1).

This multifaceted understanding of the notion of threats to human security accounts for its appeal among feminist scholars. Gender researchers had long criticized the traditional notion of state security, with its strong emphasis on domestic and global military security, as not only too narrow but actually even contrary to human security (Reardon and Hans 2010, 3; Pitch 2010, 112–114). The new focus on the daily threats that human beings face opened the door to addressing the security concerns of both women and men, as well as those confronted by children, shedding light on the many forms of severe deprivation and violence that women and girls are more likely to encounter.

Although failing to give a comprehensive account of violence against women and its overall impact in terms of human security, the 1994 UNDP Report explicitly raised the point that women's chances of becoming victims of violence were increased just because of their gender (UNDP 1994, 22 and 31). While the Report recognized that women were making progress in education and employment, it underlined the many shocking practices and customs that still contributed to women's insecurity, including genital cuttings, the norm that women should be the last to eat in the household, and the systematic disregard for health security during childbirth (ibid., 28–31).

Another important step in the shaping of the modern concept of human security came with the creation in 2001 of the UN Commission on Human Security (CHS), cochaired by Amartya Sen, Nobel Laureate in Economics 1998, and Sadako Ogata, former UN High Commissioner for Refugees. In 2003 the CHS issued its report *Human Security Now*. Not unlike the 1994 UNDP report, the CHS Report has tried to capture the original UN spirit of viewing security comprehensively, including protection of both *freedom from fear* and *freedom from want*. According to its definition:

> Human security means to protect the vital core of all human lives in ways that enhance human freedoms and human fulfillment. Human security means protecting fundamental freedoms—freedoms that are the essence of life. It means protecting people from critical (severe) and pervasive (widespread) threats and situations. It means using processes that build on people's strengths and aspirations. It means creating political, social, environmental, economic, military and cultural systems that together give people the building blocks of survival, livelihood and dignity. (CHS 2003, 4)

The CHS Report specifically referred to threats from violence, but also from poverty, ill health, illiteracy, and other maladies, and highlighted that conflict and deprivation are often interconnected (ibid., Outline of the Report, 1). The CHS also pointed to abrupt change as a risk to human security, rather than only absolute levels of deprivation. Thus even in more well-off nations, sudden economic downturns could produce troubling levels of human insecurity (ibid., Box 1.3, 8). The financial crises beginning in 2007, and the austerity politics related to them, have made this point even more evident since then.

The notion of human security used in the 2003 CHS Report gave due recognition to the multiple forms of threat facing women's well-being during violent conflicts and their aftermath. The Report made reference in passing to many forms of gender-based violence, including rape, sexual violence, enforced prostitution, and trafficking, although limited these mentions to the context of war or violent conflict. It raised questions about women's economic security and social protection too, underlining the importance of land security and addressing the problem of gender disparity in education and literacy rates (ibid., 23, 25, 61, 65, 77–79, 81, 107, 114, and 122).

Interestingly, the Report also drew attention to the link between a culture of violence against women in the so-called "private sphere" and violence in the "public domain," and, more broadly, described the inter-relationship between interpersonal violence and interstate or intrastate conflict. It explicitly stated that

> [i]n and immediately following conflict, crime rates soar. So do incidents of gender-based and sexual violence. . . . The increases arise from the trauma of conflict and its impact on interpersonal relations and community networks, and from the broader issues of the breakdown of law and order. . . . But the influence works both ways. High levels of interpersonal violence also appear to affect the likelihood for violent conflict. High rates of communal violence may reflect growing inequalities among communities as well as the manipulation of identity politics. . . . Increases in gender-based and sexual violence may mark a rise in poverty and the collapse of social safety nets. And although by itself interpersonal violence will not lead to conflict, combined with other factors it leads to a widespread sense of insecurity easily manipulated along identity lines. (CHS 2003, 23)

In spite of this, the *Human Security Now* Report fell short of addressing violence against women comprehensively as a human security concern that would include at its center all forms of institutional violence and domestic violence, present also in well-off democratic societies. Issues that predominantly affect women, such as those surrounding women's bodily integrity, reproductive health, and sexual violence, were clearly sidelined (Bunch 2004). Thus, whereas the Report mentions harm to women's physical integrity due to maternal mortality and inadequate systems for reproductive health (CHS 2003, Box 6.2, 100), it fails to relate these issues to violence against women or to analyze in depth the question of women's reproductive autonomy.[1] In other words, the 2003 Report failed to show that the risk factors affecting women and girls' human security frequently are closely linked to broader patterns of gender-based violence and gender-based discrimination.

This is why both the UNDP and CHS definition of human security need to be complemented with a gender and human rights-based approach. This latter line of work offers a more precise picture of the concrete threats that women and girls encounter. In the domain of human security, human rights have generally been used only at a discursive level or treated as a general normative reference point. But a few works have attempted to draw a direct and measurable connection between human security threats and the state's failure to ensure human rights. As we watch human rights law evolve to incorporate more profound understandings of violence against women, gender discrimination, and the connection between the two, we imagine that human security assessments can gain much from incorporating human rights standards and interpretations as indicators in assessing what amounts to a situation of risk or threat in general, and of those affecting women and girls in particular.

Recent Developments Addressing Violence against Women in International Human Rights Law

In recent years international human rights law has evolved in ways that hold promise for women victims of violence. For one thing, it has moved to affirm the positive obligations of the state in this domain. *Positive obligations* are those that refer to the active work of the state in carrying out certain measures for the protection of human rights, as opposed to merely abstaining from violating rights. Also, according to recent developments in international human rights law, the positive obligations of the state to protect the human rights of women and girls include protection from threats or actions of private actors, such as members of the community or family members (Ertürk 2006, para. 29; Hasselbacher 2010, 198–200). Such positive obligations of the state build on *due diligence standards* developed since the late 1980s under human rights law as a general criterion to evaluate state responsibility (Inter-American Court of Human Rights 1988, *Case of Velásquez Rodríguez v. Honduras*). Due diligence standards express the appropriate level of care and prevention measures that a state should take in order to protect and guarantee people's human rights from nonstate actors. These standards include the state's duty to investigate and punish violations by nonstate actors and properly redress the victims.

Due diligence standards have been affirmed by the main global body dealing with the human rights of women: the UN Committee for the Elimination of Discrimination against Women, in charge of monitoring state parties' compliance with the Convention on the Elimination of Discrimination against Women, of 1979 (CEDAW).[2] The UN Special Rapporteur on Violence against Women explicitly reaffirmed the due diligence standard as a legal tool to combat violence against women. Two regional human rights courts, the Inter-American Court of Human Rights and the European Court of Human Rights, have also affirmed due diligence standards in cases of violence against women.

The Inter-American Court of Human Rights (IACHR) reviews the cases of human rights violations presented to it, in light of the Inter-American human rights instruments binding on state parties. The main legal instrument is the 1969 Inter-American Convention on Human Rights, but there is also a specific legal instrument dealing with violence against women, namely, the 1994 Inter-American Convention on the Prevention, Punishment and Eradication of Violence Against Women (called the "Convention Belém do Pará," alluding to the place in which it was adopted). Similarly, the European Court of Human Rights (ECHR) reviews cases of alleged violations of human rights based on the 1950 European Convention for the Protection of Human Rights and Fundamental Freedoms. On May 11, 2011, the Council of Europe adopted the Convention on Preventing and Combating Violence against Women and Domestic Violence (notably under the logo, *safe from fear, safe from violence*). This Convention has not yet entered into force.[3] Both regional courts have concluded that, in terms of international human rights law and based on the *due diligence standards,* states have an obligation to *prevent* violence against women and to *take concrete measures* in order to protect women facing situations of violence.

In applying due diligence standards to cases of violence against women, both courts have taken into account the structural risk factors faced by women and girls. Both have taken into account that specific human rights violations often take place within a social, economic, cultural, and political background of discrimination against women and girls which makes the violations possible and even facilitates them. In both the Americas and Europe, the courts have acknowledged the structural dimensions of the problem and state obligations have been adjusted to reflect the situations of enhanced vulnerability that women and girls encounter. This reveals what we call a human security-sensitive approach to women's and girls' human rights. But before we explore the doctrinal implications of this approach in the next section, it is worth exemplifying it by discussing two recent cases, one from each international court, the first dealing with "domestic" and the second with "societal" violence against women.

Domestic Violence against Women under the European Court of Human Rights: *Opuz v. Turkey*

Opuz v. Turkey was decided by the ECHR in June 2009 and built upon previous similar cases, especially that of *Bevacqua and S. v. Bulgaria.*[4] The Court understood as relevant the general situation of violence against women in Diyarbakir, in southeast Turkey, the area where the applicant, Mrs. Opuz, had lived at the time of the assaults perpetrated against her by her husband. Considering this general situation illustrates what we mean by structural vulnerabilities affecting women.

According to reports and statistics submitted by the applicant, drawn up by two leading nongovernmental organizations, the Diyarbakır Bar Association and Amnesty International, uncontested by the Government of Turkey, the highest number of reported victims of domestic violence in the country was in Diyarbakır. Victims were women, mostly of Kurdish origin, illiterate or with a low level of education, and generally without any independent source of income. Indeed, the reports suggested that domestic violence was generally tolerated by the authorities in the region and that the remedies indicated by the government did not function effectively. When victims reported domestic violence to police stations, police officers did not investigate their complaints but sought to assume the role of mediator and tried to convince them to return home and drop their complaints. Moreover, the perpetrators of domestic violence did not receive dissuasive punishments. Rather, courts mitigated sentences on the grounds of custom, tradition, or honor. Carrying out an uncommon and exemplary path of analysis, the Court took into account these NGO sources of information regarding the general situation of human security for local women, even though they were not strictly legal, to understand the scenario in which the human rights' violations of the plaintiff, Mrs. Opuz, had presumably occurred (ECHR 2009, paras. 185, 193–197).

As to the concrete facts in *Opuz v. Turkey,* the applicant, Nahide Opuz, had been subjected by her husband to different forms of physical and psychological mistreatment, including death threats, over a period of years. Her husband had also directed death threats to her mother, who was eventually shot and killed. For years these actions had been brought to the attention of state officials, but with no significant effect on the protection of Mrs. Opuz or her mother. After the death of the applicant's mother, the husband's actions were not duly prosecuted and punished by the criminal justice system of the state.

In view of this, the ECHR held Turkey responsible for failing to exercise due diligence to adequately protect women from domestic violence. The Court spelled out some of the practical obligations that such protection requires. In particular, the ECHR highlighted the need for enforceable measures of protection and a legislative framework that would enable criminal prosecutions of severe cases of domestic violence. The Court stressed that because these crimes should be prosecuted in the public interest, it should be irrelevant whether the private party, in this case the affected woman, withdrew the charges against the aggressor, in this situation her husband. The worst cases of domestic violence are of such a serious nature and there is such a strong interest for all of society in its eradication, that even if the victim wished the criminal authorities to abandon the investigation or prosecution, they ought to be compelled not to do so.

The Court also saw the events of the case not as isolated incidents but as part of a pattern amounting to a generalized situation of risk. It highlighted both the recurrent events concerning the specific victims and also the impunity around violence against women in the region where the victims lived. The Court asserted that a state's failure to exercise due diligence to protect women against domestic violence, when it "knows or ought to have known of the situation" (ECHR 2009, para. 130), breached its positive obligation to take preventive measures (ibid., para. 148).

The Court viewed the NGO reports as demonstrating that there was a lack of adequate investigation by judicial authorities in Turkey, especially relating to cases of violence against women, which amounted to institutional discrimination against women. This impunity created a climate that was conducive to domestic violence. Bearing that in mind, the violence suffered by Mrs. Opuz and her mother could be regarded as gender-based violence which, the Court affirmed, constitutes a form of discrimination against women because of the differential impact that the state's inaction has on women (ECHR 2009, para. 198).

Although the acts of violence had been carried out by a nonstate actor (the applicant's husband), the Court found that Turkey had violated the right to life of the applicant's mother and the right to physical and moral integrity of the applicant. Tellingly, the decision relied also on the 1979 UN CEDAW, and on the 1994 Inter-American Convention Belém do Pará as interpretive frameworks. This is unusual and innovative, given that these two international treaties fall outside the ordinary realm of jurisdiction of the European Court. Based on its conclusion that the failure to exercise due diligence amounted to gender-based discrimination, the Court also held that the state's inaction amounted to an infringement of women's right to equal protection of the law (art. 14), in this case, in relation to the right to life (art. 2) and to the right to physical and moral integrity, which includes the prohibition of torture (art. 3), of the European Convention (ibid., paras. 200 and 201).

Femicide and the Inter-American Court of Human Rights: The *Cotton Field v. Mexico* Decision

The *Cotton Field v. Mexico* case was resolved in November 2009 by the Inter-American Court of Human Rights. The case is significant not only in affirming women's right to live free from violence but also their right to adequate reparations, as well as the implicit links drawn between these rights and the enjoyment of human security by women (Rubio Marín and Sandoval 2011).

Cotton Field was the first case to reach the Court related to the abductions and killings of more than three hundred women and girls by nonstate actors since 1993 in Ciudad Juárez (Chihuahua, Mexico). These cases have come to be known as the "Ciudad Juárez Feminicidios" because they represent a pattern of criminality targeting women and girls from fifteen to twenty-five years old, usually of disadvantaged socioeconomic background, whereby victims were first disappeared, then usually subjected to sexual violence and torture, and finally mutilated and killed.

The *Cotton Field* decision dealt specifically with the abduction, sexual violence, and killings in 2001 of a young woman, Claudia Ivette

González (20), and two girls, Esmeralda Herrera Monreal (15) and Laura Berenice Ramos Monárrez (17), and the subsequent failure of the state to act with *due diligence* in the investigation, prosecution, and punishment of the perpetrators. The responsible state, Mexico, was found also to have failed to treat in a dignified way the next of kin of the deceased, starting with their mothers. The remains of the three victims were found in a cotton field, hence the name of the case.

The case is revealing because the Court based a significant part of its reasoning on the severe, systemic, and structural threats and conditions of vulnerability experienced by the victims and women in the region. These are precisely the conditions on which the concept of human security particularly and helpfully sheds light. Like the ECHR in *Opuz v. Turkey*, the Inter-American Court relied on reports produced by international bodies and actors such as the UN Committee of CEDAW, the UN Special Rapporteur on Violence against Women, the Inter-American Commission for Human Rights, and even Amnesty International. It also took into account reports produced by Mexico's autonomous human rights supervisory body, the National Human Rights Commission, as well as those issued by different local NGOs.

Basing its decision on the legal parameters offered by the Inter-American Convention of Human Rights (IAC), and parts of the Belém do Pará Convention, the Court considered that the disappearances, killings, and subsequent mistreatment and neglect of the woman and girls' family members violated several rights, including the rights to life, personal integrity, and liberty, the rights of the child, as well as the right to access to justice and judicial protection (articles 4(1), 5(1), 5(2), 7(1), 19, 8(1), and 25(1) of the IAC; and articles 7(b) and 7(c) of the Convention of Belém do Pará). Moreover, the killings and disappearances were considered to be gender based, and thus amounted to gender discrimination (prohibited under article 1(1) of the IAC). The Court pointed to both how such crimes targeted women and girls specifically and that they had taken place in the context of a prevalent culture of discrimination against women (IACHR 2009, para. 144). Indeed, the Court found that the response of the Mexican authorities to these crimes had been plagued with irregularities, gender stereotypes, lack of adequate investigation, and a climate of impunity (ibid., paras. 146, 164, and 273).

In the legal analysis, the IACHR highlighted the obligations of the state derived from the IAC and the Convention Belém do Pará, placing emphasis on the need to take positive measures of prevention as a means to fight against impunity (ibid., para. 163). Literally, the "Tribunal reiterates that the States should not merely abstain from violating rights, but must adopt *positive measures* to be determined based on the specific needs of protection of the subject of law, either because of his or her personal situation or because of the specific circumstances in which he or she finds himself" (ibid., para. 243).

In particular, the Court interpreted article 5 of the Inter-American Convention as entailing the state's duty to prevent and investigate possible acts of torture or other cruel, inhuman, or degrading treatment (ibid., para. 246) and article 7(1) of the same Convention (right to personal liberty and security) as entailing the obligation of the state to prevent the liberty of the individual being violated by the actions of either public officials or private third parties, and to investigate and punish the acts that violate their rights (ibid., para. 247).

In interpreting the duty of due diligence, the Court was guided by article 7(c) of the Belém do Pará Convention, which orders the state to "prevent . . . violence against women." For the Court, the determining factor in triggering the state obligation regarding *prevention* of and attention to gender-based violence as an obligation of the state, including in relation to *third parties,* is the fact that the State *knows or ought to know* of the situation. In this sense the case builds on the line of analysis initiated in 2001 by the Inter-American system of human rights with *Maria da Penha Maia Fernandes v. Brazil.*[5] In the *Cotton Field* case, the Court focused on two separate moments that ought to have prompted the state to attend to its due diligence obligations, First, the general alarm marked by the moment in which the large-scale violations in the region were documented meant that the state authorities were clearly aware of the situation of structural vulnerability that women and girls encountered, and so the Court considered that from that moment Mexico had an obligation to establish an integral policy of prevention capable of adequately responding to the risk factors faced by women in Ciudad Juárez. This would include strengthening the institutions in charge of addressing violence against women and setting up an adequate complaint mechanism (ibid., para. 258). Second, the first hours after the abduction and disappearance of the woman and two girls marked the moment when, based on the previously observed patterns of violence against women, the state *knew* that they could be subjected to sexual violence and then killed. This knowledge gave the state a particularly strong obligation to prevent their deaths (ibid., para. 283).

The decision contains important insights as to how the duty to investigate and the consideration of what amounts to relevant evidence may be affected in a situation which is structurally problematic. In particular, the Court stressed the measures that should be taken in order to collect evidence of sexual violence during the autopsy of a person killed with violence. It pointed out that when systematic human rights violations are taking place, as in this case, not to take the context into account during an investigation could jeopardize the investigation itself (ibid., para. 366). In particular, it considered the rather limited physical traces on the bodies of the victims (found in a state of decomposition), the pattern of criminal conduct in the killings of Ciudad Juárez, and the failure by the Mexican authorities to gather proper evidence by applying the required protocols, and concluded that sexual violence could be presumed even though it had not been duly proven in the case of these specific victims (ibid., para. 220).

In addition to a gender-specified human security-sensitive interpretation of the merits of the *Cotton Field* case, the Inter-American Court made a praiseworthy effort to carry through those sensitivities to the domain of reparations. In particular, the Court explicitly endorsed the need to make sure that reparations were gender sensitive, meaning that they bear in mind the different impact that violence has on men and women (ibid., para. 451). It also indicated that reparations should be duly transformative of the general social situation in which the violations occurred (ibid., para. 450). In other words, the Court held that when violations of human rights are expressions of situations of risk that women systematically encounter, it is those situations of risk that must be addressed and used as the basis on which to grant victims and their families redress in the form of guarantees of nonrepetition.

Consequently, among the concrete reparations measures that the Court ordered, there were not only monetary compensation measures for both material and moral harm, physical and mental rehabilitation measures, and measures of symbolic recognition, but also measures aimed at modifying the structural conditions so as to ensure nonrecurrence (ibid., paras. 446–601). In particular, the Court recognized that impunity generated suffering and hence nonmaterial harm to the families of the victims (ibid., para. 457). Thus, it ordered Mexico to investigate, prosecute, and punish the perpetrators of the abduction, killing, and inhuman treatment of Claudia, Esmeralda, and Laura, not only as a primary obligation under the Inter-American Convention but also as a reparation measure and as a guarantee of nonrepetition. The Court specifically indicated that sexual violence should be investigated taking into account internationally approved guidelines such as those of the Istanbul and Minnesota Protocols (ibid., paras. 497–502).

Other important reparation measures, under the form of guarantees of nonrepetition, included the creation and updating of a national database with information of all missing women and girls and their genetic information (ibid., para. 512), a measure that could be important for the investigations of such abductions and for the identification of any bodies found. The Court also indicated Mexico's positive duty to provide training to personnel directly or indirectly involved in the prevention, investigation, and prosecution of violence against women. The Court held that such training should place emphasis on women's rights, on adopting gender-sensitive measures during different judicial proceedings, and on overcoming social stereotypes.

Unfortunately, the most far-reaching structural remedy asked by the victims was denied by the Court on procedural grounds. Thus, the Inter-American Commission and the victims' representatives requested the Court to order Mexico to design and implement a coordinated and long-term public policy to guarantee that cases of violence against women would be prevented and investigated, the alleged perpetrators prosecuted and punished, and the victims redressed (ibid., para. 475). Mexico argued that it already had such a policy in place, substantiating its claim with evidence of legal and policy measures taken between 2001 and 2009 (ibid., paras. 476–477). The Court abstained from ordering new measures, holding that the Commission and the victims' representatives had not provided the Court with sufficient arguments to prove that the measures adopted by Mexico did not amount to such a policy (ibid., para. 493). Whether this or any Court can expect victims to be able to come up with such evidence is of course questionable (Rubio-Marín and Sandoval 2011, 1090).

As a corollary, it should be noted that after the *Cotton Field* case, the Court resolved two other cases, also against Mexico, the *Inés Fernández Ortega Case* and the *Valentina Rosendo Cantú Case*, both in August 2010.[6] In these sentences, the Court reaffirmed the due diligence standard regarding the protection of women's and girls' human rights. In *Rosendo Cantú*, it explicitly maintained that this standard translated into *reinforced obligations of the state* (paras. 175 and 182). Unfortunately, it failed to draw the logical conclusion of its prior doctrine regarding gender-sensitive and transformative reparations (Rubio-Marín and Sandoval 2011, ibid.).

Human Security and International Human Rights Law: Interpretative Synergies Reinforcing State Obligations

It is worthwhile noticing parallels between these developments in human rights case law and the set of concerns on which the literature around human security has focused. The similarities are so great as to make one wonder whether this can be pure coincidence, or whether the human rights and human security communities are indeed exercising reciprocal influences on each other, with or without explicit acknowledgment.

One certainly finds expressions of the growing awareness about the interconnection between human rights protection and human security goals, with the coining of new rights or the linking of traditional rights to the notion of human security. For instance, the Protocol to the African Charter on Human and Peoples' Rights on the Rights of Women in Africa, of 2003, seems to echo human security concerns when setting forth a new *right to peace for women* (article 10).

The greatest added value of a human security approach to existing human rights law is that it can help to highlight situations in which the violations of rights happen as part of a systematic pattern. Human rights are often abridged against a background of structural discrimination and vulnerability which facilitates the violations in the first place. From this perspective, human security would not be interpreted as a *right* in itself, but rather as a concept addressing the set of collective conditions necessary for the enjoyment of all human rights. Human security is most effectively seen as offering a *guarantee* for the concrete realization of human rights. For courts dealing with specific human rights allegations, keeping in mind the overarching duty of the state to ensure the conditions of human security would be a way to shape decisions about the appropriate contours of state obligations, including those linked to due diligence standards.

In other words, what we see are doors opening for analysis and debate on the *interpretative synergies* that may arise between the concepts of human security and human rights. In light of these particular cases, it seems that the human security approach allows courts to give due emphasis to severe threats and structural vulnerabilities that persons and groups encounter as obstacles to the enjoyment of their most fundamental human rights, and so underscores some of the insufficiencies of the classical doctrine of individual human rights. It also helps to ground theoretically some of the more interesting and expansive recent evolutions in international human rights law (Edwards and Ferstman 2010, 5). Many of these affect women.

In particular, it is our view that interpretive synergies between human rights and human security underscore that the violence from nonstate actors is part of the sphere of primary human rights where states have responsibility. The synergy underlines the need for *positive obligations*, that is, active measures by the state to prevent and guarantee human rights in compliance with *due diligence standards*. These synergies also help to identify structural failures in the protection of human rights in any given society and to flesh out the substantive and procedural implications that such failures have in decisions about concrete allegations of human rights violations. These implications include, substantively, understanding that certain violations of rights with disparate impact on persons facing conditions of vulnerability may also be judged to be a situation of discrimination. The case of gender-based violence as a form of discrimination against women is the model for this. The procedural implications include the need for courts to duly contextualize the cases before them and to rely on nontraditional sources of evidence, such as NGO reports, to understand such contexts.

The human rights–human security synergy also encourages reflection about the collective harm that derives from individual violations, since these can contribute to a systematic pattern of rights violations that generate an insecure environment or vulnerable condition. Once this generative process is recognized legally, some systemic redress through transformative reparations becomes necessary. These are meaningful reparations able not only to help individual victims but also to subvert the previous structures of discrimination creating the prevalent harms (Rubio-Marín 2010).

By Way of Conclusion

Human security adds value to human rights interpretations, as suggested in this chapter, as a framework to reinforce concrete state obligations in contexts of *structural vulnerability*. These are often experienced by women and girls, so the synergy is a way of making both perspectives more gender sensitive and better able to respond appropriately to women's and girls' needs. The synergy allows considering threats to physical integrity by armed force, but also points with equal concern to challenges to human rights that arise from other means of coercion and deprivation which can cause equally serious psychological, moral, and economic harm.

At the same time, a more gender-sensitive concept of human security may contribute to underline the structural inequalities and discrimination that cause general conditions of vulnerabilities for women and girls, conditions that are hard to address when looking at individual violations of human rights as isolated events. Looking at such violations through the lenses of human security instead provides legally usable criteria to assess the adequacy of measures taken by specific states to protect women and girls, either at an individual or community level, in cases when the state *knew or should have known* that they were facing severe threats or risk factors. Altogether, such an approach should encourage a proactive rather than a reactive or defensive attitude on the part of the state.

The identification of situations of risk can then act as a "detonator" activating and reinforcing the human rights obligations of the state, especially with regards to preventive measures. Legal recourse that only becomes available after the fact of harm is crucial but insufficient. Identifying situations of preventable risk should also be used, as these courts did, to strengthen the obligation of the state to address the causes of the human rights violations that have already taken place, granting reparations that redress individuals, families, and communities for the harm they have suffered, while seeking to address the systemic shortcomings that facilitated such violations in the first place.

As we have argued, human security should not be considered a right, at least not in the existing state of the human rights normative framework. Rather, it will be more constructive to define human security as an orienting concept for human rights evaluation and as a background condition for the overall enjoyment of human rights in people's everyday lives. In *Opuz v. Turkey* and *Cotton Field v. Mexico,* both the European and the Inter-American Court of Human Rights have recently reaffirmed that there often is a *causal link* between state negligence and the direct human rights violations of women and girls, individually as victims in concrete cases, and collectively in the society around them. This state inaction violates the due diligence standard that the state must live up to in protecting women against violence, including that perpetrated by nonstate actors.

Our view of the interpretative synergies between the concept of human security and human rights invites a more comprehensive understanding of the human rights of women and girls and may offer more effective guarantees for their protection. If further developed and used in a more self-conscious way, such synergies may enrich interpretations of the content of human rights and state responsibility, including in the domain of reparations. At the same time, recent evolution of the treatment of violence against women under human rights law can give the notion of human security more conceptual precision and indicators for gender sensitivity in this area. This would allow for the framing of some human security policy proposals in terms of human rights, which might make the human security agenda richer, fostering a culture not only based on the "rule of law" but also on a "rule of rights." These could more readily include women's and girls' rights as well. In all these ways, a gendered and human rights-based approach to human security may actually serve as an engine for emancipation and a real challenging force to existing asymmetries in power and resources, deep injustices, and fundamentally serious gender inequalities which involve, allow, and provoke so many of the violations of the human rights of women and girls throughout the world today.

NOTES

1. To illustrate this relationship between violence and women's reproductive health, one may recall the studies revealing "increasing links between violence against women and HIV and AIDS. A survey among 1,366 South African women showed that women who were beaten by their partners were 48 percent more likely to be infected with HIV than those who were not" (UN Women 2011).

2. See para. 9 of UN CEDAW General Recommendation No. 19 on Violence against Women, 1992. Eleventh session. UN Doc. A/47/38. CEDAW also developed the due diligence standard through cases in which the acts affecting human rights were committed by a nonstate actor, for example, the applicant's husband/father, for instance, in *Ms. A.T. v. Hungary,* 2005. See also *Ms. A. S. v. Hungary,* 2006; *Goekce v. Austria,* 2007; *Yildirim v. Austria,* 2007; *Ms. N. S. F. v. United Kingdom,* 2007; *Ms. V. K. v. Bulgaria,* 2008; *Vertido v. Philippines,* 2010.

3. The Convention will enter into force after ratification by ten countries. As of October 2011, sixteen countries had signed the Convention (still pending ratification).

4. See ECHR, *Bevacqua and S. v. Bulgaria* 2008 (Application no. 71127/01, Judgment of June 12, 2008); see also *Kontrova v. Slovakia* 2007 (Application no. 7510/4, Judgment of May 31, 2007); and *Branko Tomasic and Others v. Croatia* 2009 (Application no. 46598/06, Judgment of January 15, 2009), all three cases concerning domestic violence against women and their children, faced by the state's lack of due diligence. The basic doctrine on state responsibility for violence against women by nonstate actors has also been confirmed by later cases of the ECHR, such as *E. S. and Others v. Slovakia* 2009 (Application no. 8227/04, Judgment of September 15, 2009); *Rantsev v. Cyprus and Russia* 2010 (Application no. 25965/04, Judgment of January 7, 2010); *A. v. Croatia* 2010 (Application no. 55164/08, Judgment of October 14, 2010); and *Hajudova v. Slovakia* 2010 (Application no. 2660/03, Judgment of November 13, 2010).

5. This was the first case on gender-based violence and state responsibility dealt with by the Inter-American Commission on Human Rights (Case 12,051, Report No. 54/01, Annual Report, 2000, OEA/Ser. L/V.II.111 Doc.20 rev.). The case referred to a woman beaten by her husband, shot with the intention of killing her, and while in recovery, electrocuted by him while she was bathing. The Commission declared state responsibility of Brazil and issued a series of recommendations including broad remedies related to systematic problems of violence against women.

6. IACHR, *Valentina Rosendo Cantú and Other v. Mexico* (Ser. C) No. 216 (August 31, 2010); *Inés Fernández Ortega and Others v. Mexico* (Ser. C) No. 215 (August 30, 2010).

REFERENCES

Basch, Linda. 2004. "Human Security, Globalization, and Feminist Visions." *Peace Review* 16, 1 (March 2004):5–12.

Benedek, Wolfgang. 2008. "Human Security and Human Rights Interaction." In *Rethinking Human Security*, edited by Moufida Goucha and John Crowley, 7–17. U.K.: Wiley-Blackwell and UNESCO.

Boerefijn, Ineke, and Eva Naezer. 2008. "Emerging Human Rights Obligations for Non-State Actors." In *Due Diligence and Its Application to Protect Women from Violence*, edited by Carin Benninger-Budel, 91–108. The Netherlands: Martinus Nijhoff.

Bunch, Charlotte. 2004. "A Feminist Human Rights Lens." *Peace Review* 16, 1 (March 2004):29–34.

Charter of the United Nations. 1945. Signed on 26 June 1945 in San Francisco. Commission on Human Security. 2003. *Human Security Now*. New York: Commission on Human Security.

Edwards, Alice, and Carla Ferstman, eds. 2010. *Human Security and Non-Citizens: Law, Policy and International Affairs*. Cambridge: Cambridge University Press.

Ertürk, Yakin. 2006. UN Special Rapporteur on Violence against Women, Its Causes and Consequences, *Integration of the Human Rights of Women and the Gender Perspective: Violence against Women. The Due Diligence Standard as a Tool for the Elimination of Violence against Women*. Report prepared according to the UN Commission on Human Rights Resolution 2005/41.

European Court of Human Rights. 2009. *Case of Opuz v. Turkey*, Application no. 33401/02, Judgment of June 9, 2009.

Hasselbacher, Lee. 2010. "State Obligations regarding Domestic Violence: The European Court of Human Rights, Due Diligence, and International Legal Minimums of Protection." *Northwestern University Journal of International Human Rights* 8, 2 (Spring 2010):190–215, http://www.law.northwestern.edu/journals/jihr/v8/n2/3 (last consulted March 2011).

Inter-American Commission of Human Rights. 2001. Case 12,051, Report No. 54/01, *Maria Da Penha Maia Fernandes v. Brazil*, Annual Report, 2000, OEA/Ser.L/V.II.111 Doc.20 rev.

Inter-American Court of Human Rights. 1988. *Case of Velásquez Rodríguez v. Honduras*. (Ser. C) No. 4, 172. Judgment of July 29, 1988.

———. 2009. *Case of González et al. ("Cotton Field") v. Mexico*. Judgment of November 16, 2009 (Preliminary Objection, Merits, Reparations, and Costs).

MacFarlane, Neil S., and Yuen Foong Khong. 2006. *Human Security and the UN: A Critical History*. Bloomington: Indiana University Press, United Nations Intellectual History Project.

O'Manique, Colleen. 2006. "The 'Securitization' of HIV/AIDS in Sub-Saharan Africa: A Critical Feminist Lens." In *A Decade of Human Security: Global Governance and New Multilateralisms*, edited by Sandra J. MacLean, David R. Black, and Timothy M. Shaw, 161–176. U.K./U.S.A.: Ashgate.

Pitch, Tamar. 2010. *Pervasive Prevention: A Feminist Reading of the Rise of the Security Society*. U.K.: Ashgate.

Reardon, Betty A., and Asha Hans, eds. 2010. *The Gender Imperative: Human Security vs. State Security*. New Delhi/U.K.: Routledge.

Rubio-Marín, Ruth. 2010. "Gender and Collective Reparations in the Aftermath of Conflict and Political Repression." In *The Politics of Reconciliation in Multicultural Societies*, edited by Will Kymlicka and Bashir Bashir, 192–214. Oxford: Oxford University Press.

Rubio-Marín, Ruth, and Clara Sandoval. 2011. "Engendering the Reparations Jurisprudence of the Inter-American Court of Human Rights: The Promise of the *Cotton Field* Judgment." *Human Rights Quarterly* 33:1062–1091.

UNDP. 1994. *Human Development Report 1994*, United Nations Development Program. http://hdr.undp.org/en/media/hdr_1994_ (last consulted March 2011).

Universal Declaration of Human Rights. 1948. Proclaimed by the United Nations General Assembly in Paris on 10 December 1948. General Assembly Resolution 217 A (III).

UN Women. 2011. United Nations Entity for Gender Equality and Empowerment of Women http://www.unifem.org/gender_issues/violence_against_women/ (last consulted October 2011).

Von Tigerstrom, Barbara. 2007. *Human Security and International Law. Prospects and Problems.* Oxford/Portland, Oreg.: Hart Publishing.

11

Integrating Gender into Human Security

Peru's Truth and Reconciliation Commission

NARDA HENRÍQUEZ AND CHRISTINA EWIG

Peru's more than decade-long conflict between the government and guerrilla insurgencies in the 1980s and 1990s was emblematic of a human security crisis. This was not a conventional interstate war; it was a civil conflict. A conflict rooted in preexisting human insecurities of poverty and inequality, Peru's war fed on these insecurities, and created even broader and deeper human insecurities. Notable were its gendered dimensions: preexisting gendered insecurities in which poor women were among the most vulnerable to hunger and violence were exacerbated by the conflict, while gendered insecurities such as systematic rape in the context of war were introduced. Perhaps most disturbing were the racial dimensions of the conflict; the women, men, and children most egregiously affected were rural, indigenous Peruvians, while better-off nonindigenous, urban dwellers averted their eyes and ignored the incredible abuses perpetrated by both the military and guerrilla militants in Peru's countryside.[1]

Peru's civil war demonstrates the important links between the everyday violence of poverty and inequality and the direct, physical violence of armed conflict. Recognizing these links, Peru's attempts to heal the wounds of this war through its Truth and Reconciliation Commission is one of the most ambitious examples to date of integrating not only a human security perspective, but a gendered human security perspective into transitional and transformative justice.[2]

The concept of human security was first introduced to an international audience in the 1994 United Nations Human Development Report, which defined human security as "safety from such chronic threats as hunger, disease and repression" and "protection from sudden and hurtful disruptions in the patterns of daily life" (UNDP 1994, 23). Human security seeks to complement, or in some cases challenge, the traditional notion of security as interstate conflict and defense of territory. Instead, human security is focused on people's well-being, which is expressed as "freedom from fear" *and* "freedom from want" (Commission on Human Security 2003, iv). Rather than armaments, development is the key tool advocated for the defense of human security. Human security is broad: it encompasses economic, food, health, environment, personal, community, and political security (UNDP 1994, 24–25). The concept is also explicitly linked with violence, a fact illustrated quite starkly in Peru's civil conflict (Gibson and Reardon 2007, 55; UNDP 1994, 23). However, insecurity and poverty do not explain conflict by themselves; ideology and organization also play important roles (Foran and Goodwin 1993; Selbin 1993; Wieviorka 1991).

The concept of human security has been critiqued on many levels: for being so broad that it becomes meaningless; for reinforcing the central role of the state in providing security when the concept has been applied; and for lacking a clear focus on gender and insecurity (Paris 2001; Hudson 2005; Gibson and Reardon 2007; Hoogensen and Stuvøy 2006).[3] Yet the concept has also opened the way for gender to be included in the conceptualization of security to a greater degree than before (Hudson 2010, 29) and a gender-informed approach to human security can be illuminating; through the feminist practice of making room for the marginalized, nonstate actors may inform our understandings of security in much fuller, more holistic, and ultimately more useful ways (Hoogensen and Stuvøy 2006).

In this chapter we take a gender-informed approach to human security in our analysis of Peru's civil war in order to highlight the multiplicity of insecurities at stake in that conflict, insecurities that especially affected those subordinated by the crosscutting inequalities of gender and race. Further, we describe the work of Peru's Truth and Reconciliation Commission. We argue that Peru's Truth and Reconciliation Commission put into practice not just a human security perspective, but a gendered human security perspective to transitional justice by creating "a discursive space where the structurally excluded actor can speak" (Hoogensen and Stuvøy 2006, 224). The recommendations of the Commission have yet to be carried out; the country remains in a conflicted and complex transition in which wounds are still open, the progression toward making amends is modest, and the fight for memory is fierce. But the Commission was a model in its recognition of the deep connections between the everyday insecurities at the heart of the human security concept and the violence of war. By exposing these insecurities in their multiplicity of dimensions through the voices of the victims themselves, the Commission sought not just to heal the wounds opened by the conflict, but also to address its underlying causes.

We begin by providing a brief background on the Peruvian conflict and its roots in human insecurity. We then focus on Peru's Truth and Reconciliation Commission, highlighting its attention to gender, race, and human security in Peru's conflict and its practice of giving voice to the marginalized. We end with some reflections on the gendered human security challenges Peru still faces, in spite of the efforts and advances made by the Commission.

The Conflict with the Shining Path

Most guerrilla insurgencies have historically risen against authoritarian governments, but Peru's insurgency made itself known at the point of that country's transition to democracy. In 1980, as Peru held elections after over a decade of military rule and the first elections in which illiterates could vote, Shining Path militants burned ballots in the Andean village of Chuschi as an announcement of war against the Peruvian state. The Shining Path was one of two guerrilla groups to challenge Peru's government in the 1980s and 1990s, but compared to its rival revolutionary group, the urban-based Revolutionary Tupac Amaru Movement, the Communist Party of Peru-Shining Path (known simply as the Shining Path) was by far more deadly.

Lack of human security—namely, poverty and inequality that are highly correlated with racial hierarchies in Peru—was a precondition for the growth of the Shining Path.[4] Although led by Abimael Guzmán, a university professor from the provincial University of Huamanga in the highland department of Ayacucho, and a small entourage of elite members from the urban middle class, the Shining Path recruited mainly first-generation college students of poor peasant families attending this university. Many of these recruits were attracted to the message of revolution, especially as they found no opportunities for upward mobility, despite their education, in Peru's hierarchical society in which white and mixed race (*mestizo*) elite residents of coastal cities, and especially the capital, Lima, have traditionally maintained political and economic power (de Wit and Gianotten 1994; Degregori 2012). The relationship between human insecurity and the violence incited by the Shining Path is also evident in the fact that it claimed its strongest footholds in the poorest provinces. In the southern highlands, where the Shining Path was strongest, caloric intake in 1980 was below 70 percent of the United Nations Food and Agriculture Organization minimum requirements, and in some areas of Ayacucho, consumption was less than 420 calories a day. Already poor agricultural productivity rates were seriously challenged by drought in 1983. Illiteracy rates and access to potable water had improved since the 1970s, but they remained high. In Ayacucho, 45 percent of the population was illiterate in 1980 and 85 percent did not have access to potable water (McClintock 2001, 68–69).

While human insecurity lay at the root of Peru's violence, the Shining Path ideology incited a particularly gruesome form. Guzmán, also known as "President Gonzalo," cultivated his cultlike following with a rigid ideology that mixed Maoism, Marxism, Leninism, and the writings of Peruvian Marxist José Carlos Mariateguí. A central characteristic of the Shining Path was dedication to violence, using violence against the "masses" as well as the state in its millenarian quest for power (DeGregori 1994, 2012; Starn 1995). Guzmán glorified violence, viewing it as a strategy by which the process of destroying the old order and building a new one could be accelerated (Portocarrero 1998, 21–22). Adherents had to pledge their willingness to die for the cause. Many of the college students recruited into the Shining Path became teachers in their home communities, bringing not only reading, writing, and math, but also the ideological message of the Shining Path home with them (McClintock 2001, 78; de Wit and Gianotten 1994).

The Shining Path gained a foothold in southern rural villages in part by filling a power vacuum and becoming the new "*patrón*" in communities that had just experienced land reform and the flight of provincial elites (DeGregori 1994; McClintock 2001, 72–73). Traditionally, the *patrón* was the masculine *hacienda* (large estate) owner who exercised economic, social, and even sexual control over the peasants that worked the land. According to testimonies collected by the Truth and Reconciliation Commission, the Shining Path was considered a new *patrón* by local residents. The *patrón*, Neira and Ruiz Bravo argue, is an apt metaphor, in that it signals a "dominant (hegemonic) masculinity," and a "principle of order." The *patrón* not only exploits, but also "governs the people" as a racially superior, elite figure (2001, 216). In their study of rural areas of Peru, Neira and Ruiz Bravo found that the hegemonic masculine figure of the *patrón* continued to have resonance even after the *haciendas* had disappeared (211–231). The Shining Path, as the new, "unjust *patrón*" proposed a new order of violence and submission and inscribed a complex hierarchy based on class, race, and gender distinctions. The new order of the Shining Path challenged not just the state, but local authority structures, and even the family. Some families were required to move with the Shining Path to their revolutionary "retreats" where children were separated from their parents and sent to Shining Path schools and adolescents were forced into "sexual unions." Graduating youth became lookouts and eventually part of the "Fuerza Local" or local Shining Path military forces.[5]

The Shining Path proposed not only a political project, but a "moral" one with respect to sexuality and the family (Henríquez Ayín 2006). Testimonies of young people recruited by the Shining Path refer to the "law of subversion," and a guidebook that contained eight edicts, among them "do not touch the women." Despite these, a significant double discourse was evident. In Maoist philosophy, women are a fundamental pillar of armed revolution, and thus the Shining Path actively recruited women—requiring of them, as with others, their unconditional loyalty (Kirk 1993). Women were thought to compose 40 percent of Shining Path militants and 50 percent of its central command (Barrig 1993). But the Shining Path was far from feminist: for the Shining Path, "Women only can organize themselves correctly through the classist principle of grouping women by their class position."[6] Unlike their male peers, however, the Shining Path also required their bodily as well as mental submission, as mistresses to male leaders. One mother declared, in opposition to militants taking her daughter: "You are making the girls enter so you can have them as your mistresses" (Del Pino 1999, 181). And while the Shining Path recruited women, it also actively reproduced patriarchal hierarchies, for example by using gender stereotypes to characterize its opponents, calling them "fags" (*maricones*) and "little women" (*mujercitas*) (Coral Cordero 1998, 349).

The Peruvian military responded indiscriminately to the growing power of the Shining Path in Peru's countryside, committing murders and abuses irrespective of individuals' true political affiliations. The indigenous Andean peasant became the enemy of the state and at the same time subject to possible annihilation by the Shining Path for noncompliance with its revolutionary project. The history of marginalization of Peru's indigenous population made this abuse easier, as it fed on stereotypes of the indigenous peoples' "uncivilized" nature. After making little headway with military offensives, the government supported and expanded local peasant self-defense militias (*rondas campesinas*) that were initially organized independently in some rural communities as a means of self-defense against the Shining Path (DeGregori et al. 1996; Starn 1999). Thus, three actors became the primary aggressors in this war: Shining Path militants, the state, and the self-defense militias.

Although based in the countryside, throughout the armed conflict the Shining Path also carried out attacks on cities, cutting electricity and calling for armed strikes. Eventually it made its way to Peru's capital, intensifying its presence in Lima from 1986 forward. It infiltrated and terrorized the poor residents of the sprawling shantytowns that surround Lima, inhabited largely by those fleeing war and poverty in the countryside. There, it threatened local grassroots leaders, in particular women leaders who ran communal kitchens and Peru's government-supported "Glass of Milk" program that recruits local mothers to distribute milk rations to poor children. The Shining Path's murder of Maria Elena Moyano, an Afro-Peruvian leftist and feminist neighborhood leader in the poor neighborhood of Villa El Salvador on the outskirts of Lima, was one of the its most publicized violent acts

(Henríquez Ayín 1996; Moyano 2000). Later the Shining Path rocked elite Peruvians by infamously detonating two 1,000 kilogram car bombs in the posh Lima neighborhood of Miraflores in July 1992. In September 1992 the military captured Abimael Guzmán, effectively depriving the organization of leadership and leading to its near-demise. The actions of the Shining Path in Lima forced recognition of a war that had been largely ignored by the urban residents of Peru. However, full recognition of the extent and multidimensionality of the war's violence would not come until a decade later in 2003, with the final report of the Truth and Reconciliation Commission.

Exposing Gendered and Racialized Violence

The Truth and Reconciliation Commission (TRC) was mandated by interim President Valentín Paniagua in 2001 and its final report was delivered in August 2003. Peru's Commission had a number of notable characteristics. First, unlike many other commissions which only seek truth, the mandate of Peru's TRC was to seek truth *and* promote reconciliation. The meaning of "reconciliation" has been a subject of fierce debate and political negotiation, but in practice it has meant giving voice to victims, providing reparations, and preserving memories of the conflict in an effort to both honor the victims and prevent the repetition of violence. The Commission's work brought to light not only the violent acts perpetrated in the war, but also how these were connected to broader issues of human security, such as poverty, inequality, and racism. Peru's Commission shared with the South African and Guatemalan truth commissions an objective of "gender sensitivity," and it was the only one of these commissions to include a chapter on gender in its final report. But more than placing women on the agenda of the Truth Commission, the mode by which it carried out its work integrated a gender perspective by listening to the voices of the most marginalized who prior to this moment had never had a voice in the broader Peruvian society.

While we commend the work of the Commission, we are not uncritical.[7] For example, the inclusion of sexual and gender-based violence was an afterthought; gender experts were invited to serve only after the Commission was formed and initially no budget was allocated for their work (Mantilla Falcon 2008a). Despite these disadvantages, these experts brought to light the gender dimension of the conflict, which may have remained buried had it not been for their persistent research. Their work was also exemplary in bringing to light the way gender and race worked together in the war context. The TRC uncovered gender-based violence at two primary levels: sexual violence and the more quotidian but still highly gendered and life-threatening threats that war presents to mere survival. We draw on the TRC Final Report (CVR 2003) in the sections that follow, to discuss the gendered dimensions of Peru's civil war.

Sexual Violence

Building on advances in international law on the relationship between sexual violence and war, the Peruvian TRC adopted a broad definition of sexual violence that allowed it to include rape, forced marriage, forced abortions, forced nudity, sexual blackmail, and sexual slavery among other abuses in its investigation (Mantilla Falcon 2008b, 225). Sexual violence, especially in a war context, is not about individual victims and perpetrators, instead it is part of a process of subjugation—feminizing and racializing the opponent to provoke submission and to legitimize further violence by creating a dehumanized, feminine, and racialized "other." Women often become sexual targets because they are seen as the "wombs" of the nation, making their violation powerfully symbolic (Enloe 1989, 42–64). At other times women are viewed as mere sexual objects, an opportunity for the pleasure and sexual relief of the combatants (Enloe 2000). When men are targeted with sexual violence, it is a means to "feminize," as well as dehumanize them.

Sexual violence was a generalized, widespread practice in Peru's civil war. The TRC found that sexual violence took place in at least fifteen of Peru's twenty-four departments, in distant villages, and in urban state detention centers, perpetrated by all three participating actors (agents from the Shining Path, the state, and the self-defense militias). State agents were responsible primarily for rape (83 percent of all rapes), of which the overwhelming majority of victims were women (CVR 2003, 1.5, 273, 277). With respect to the Shining Path, testimonies to the Truth Commission pointed principally to the sexual mutilation of men and women, forced sexual unions, and forced abortion—but rape as well, to some extent. The cases of documented sexual violence underrepresent the reality; victims felt shame in coming forward with testimonies of sexual violence.[8] Moreover, such violence often occurred in the context of other human rights violations—such as massacres and torture—making victims of sexual violence feel as though their experience was negligible by comparison (Mantilla Falcon 2008b, 226; CVR 2003, 1.5, 275).

In Peru's war, as in other wars, sexual violence became a form of torture and rape a tactic endorsed by military superiors. In rural villages, military officers used sexual violence as part of public demonstrations to instill fear and forcible collaboration from community members. They used it on individuals to get information and to provoke admissions of terrorist collaboration. Rape and other forms of sexual violence were also common in the state prisons where suspected terrorists were detained; of 118 testimonies gathered by the Commission in the Chorillos Women's Prison, 30 testified that they had suffered rape, while another 66 had been victims of other forms of sexual violence. Altogether they made up 81 percent of those interviewed (CVR 2003, 1.5, 275).

Sexual violence in Peru's war actively created race and gender hierarchies; hierarchies which appear with palpable harshness in the testimonies of sexual violence perpetrated by the military. The experience of Georgina Gamboa is illustrative of rural village women who confronted the army, and her story reached national prominence. At the age of sixteen, she was raped by members of the military, first in her house and then in a police station in Vilcashuaman, Ayacucho. In her testimony to the TRC she recounted her experience:

> [T]hey hit me and then started to abuse me, rape me, they raped me all night. I screamed for help, they put a handkerchief in my mouth and when I would scream and ask for help they beat me. I was totally mistreated that night. That night seven raped me, seven military men—seven *sinchis* entered to rape me. One left, one came in, one left, one came in. (CVR 2003, 1.5, 308)

A former army member testified to witnessing the rape of a twenty-seven-year-old woman detainee, raped by "six or eight" officers who afterwards commented on the act saying, "[S]he was good, the *chola* was a *puta madre* [mother whore]" (CVR 2003, 1.5, 305). In another testimony, a soldier described the rape of a dead woman before her decapitation and disposal in a river: "[T]all, *gringa*, nice. But she was already bad, she no longer satisfied any use. The troops were raping her."

The rapes and their associated commentary reveal a process in which gender and race are invoked; the act of raping a woman suspected of being a terrorist served to solidify the masculine superiority of the army and police members. In gang rapes, it was also a mechanism of creating a hypermasculine and hierarchal group unity among the officers and conscripts (Theidon 2007). At the same time, rape feminized and dehumanized the victim as well as the more generalized opponent. The comments of the military officers, noted above, also demonstrate the process of racialization involved. "*Chola*" is a pejorative term referring to indigenous peasant women who migrate to urban centers. For the detainee described as "*chola*," the officers created a racialized caricature that "deserved" sexual abuse. The white, "*gringa*" woman, by contrast, is described as "nice," but because she was a suspected terrorist she was "bad," and deserving of rape even after her death. Despite some variation, the victims of sexual violence (and of the violence of the war more generally) were overwhelmingly indigenous. The TRC final report notes that the "great majority" of victims of sexual violence were illiterate or had only finished primary school and 75 percent were Quechua speakers; the profile of indigenous women in Peru (CVR 2003, 1.5, 275–276). By the same token, the great majority of military troops could be considered "*cholos*" as well, with rural indigenous roots.

Sexual violence was also bargained in Peru's war. Often victims were given the option of trading one form of human security, their sexual autonomy and dignity, for other forms of human security, like life or family. In the prisons, some of these victims were promised freedom or visits with family members if they "agreed" to being raped (CVR 2003, 1.5, 341–342). In the rural villages, women would consent to rape in exchange for the protection of a relative from death, or to obtain information about missing loved ones. In the account of one woman from Hualla, "They raped me because I wouldn't let them rape my daughter. That's why my daughter says 'To save me, they raped you,' and that's why I suffer alone" (Theidon 2007, 468). Because single women and widows were those most often targeted, some women married, unwillingly, as a source of protection (Theidon 2007, 465).

While the Shining Path declared that sexual violence was unacceptable, the reality was different. Although the numbers of rapes committed by the Shining Path were far fewer than those committed by the state, they did occur. As one former member of the Shining Path testified to the TR: "They allowed us to rape a woman three times, but the fourth time there was no pardon, they buried you" (CVR 2003, 1.5, 281). But the types of sexual violence committed by the Shining Path was generally different, for example, keeping persons in positions of sexual slavery in Shining Path encampments or forcing "sexual unions" between Shining Path militants. Women and girls held by the Shining Path against their will were forced to cook and serve, and often were the objects of sexual abuse (CVR 2003, chapter 2, 45). Those held were young, usually under twenty years old (CVR 2003, chapter 2, 49). Whereas the army would rape prior to killing villagers, the Shining Path would mutilate genitals and other body parts of men and women prior to a massacre (CVR 2003, chapter 2, 60).

Whether perpetrated by the state, the Shining Path, or the peasant militias, the violence of rape extended far beyond the act itself. Some women were abandoned by their husbands when they discovered they had been raped, as happened to the woman from Hualla who was quoted above. Other women committed suicide upon the realization that they were pregnant with the child of a soldier or terrorist. Some, alternatively, maintained that the rapist was their partner, clinging to some legitimacy for themselves and the child. Many women were unable to register the children upon their birth, because the father's name was unknown, a situation which perpetuated a cycle of marginalization by effectively denying citizenship to these children.

Quotidian Gendered Violence of War

The TRC did not limit its investigation of "gender" to sexual violence. It also investigated the differential ways in which women and men were affected by the civil conflict beyond sexual violence due to the different roles that each played in the conflict and in Peruvian society, highlighting the gendered nature of human security in the war and its aftermath.

Men, for example, were 77 percent of those killed in the conflict, a number much greater than women (CVR 2003, chapter 2, 58). Among the women who were killed were those found in indiscriminate massacres as well as selective murders. The selective murders targeted those accused of aiding subversives or those who themselves were rebel leaders. In turn, as mentioned above, the Shining Path targeted the women in provincial capitals and in Lima who had organized forms of self-help. These women provided an alternative, peaceful means of dealing with the country's human security crisis and directly confronted the Shining Path in marches "for peace" in 1988 in Ayacucho and "against hunger and terror" in 1991 in Lima (CVR 2003, chapter 2, 52–53). They therefore posed a real threat to the Shining Path, which assassinated many of their leaders.

The fact that so many men were killed or disappeared left many women in the position of caring for family (and often farm or small business) alone. Many lamented not just the horrific loss of a partner, but also the quality of life that they could have had had their partner survived. Women had to take full responsibility for farming, for caring for livestock, and ultimately for ensuring that their families were fed. And the actions of the military officers sometimes targeted those very tasks, stealing livestock from villagers or raiding and destroying their stocks of grain. Of course these episodes hurt men and women alike, but women who had lost their partners struggled particularly hard. As one woman related in a testimony:

> In my community we suffered a lot, I was left alone when the Shining Path entered into my community and my husband escaped to Lima because he was a local leader, they burned my house, and I stayed in my community to work like a man, alone, and now I don't feel well, I can't work for all the worries that I have.[9]

As the survivors, women were also those who searched for justice for their missing or killed loved ones. The search for justice itself often put these women in greater danger of human rights abuse, including sexual abuse (CVR 2003, chapter 2, 46). Because so many of these women were indigenous, monolingual Quechua speakers, their efforts were made all the more difficult by language barriers with state officials. Some of them joined together in Ayacucho in 1983 to create the National Association of Relatives of the Kidnapped, Detained and Disappeared of Peru (Asociacion Nacional de Familiares de Secuestrados, Detenidos y Desaparecidos del Perú, ANFASEP) in which they pooled their efforts in the search for their loved ones and offered each other material and emotional support.

Gendering Human Security: Bringing Voice to the Voiceless

The Truth and Reconciliation Commission had great symbolic value in providing voice, visibility, and legitimacy to Quechua-, Ashaninka-, and Aymara-speaking indigenous Peruvian women who are located at the very bottom of Peru's social hierarchy. At the same time, literate and urban Peruvians found themselves having to confront this community of oral tradition, which vividly depicted Peru's tragic war to the nation. Wars and armed conflicts are usually presented as epic narratives about aggressive confrontations, even in Peru, where the conflict was unconventional. The Truth and Reconciliation Commission, for all its challenges, worked against this narrative by including the claims for justice of those usually omitted from these histories. This, in and of itself, was a process that Hoogensen and Stuvøy (2006) call a gender-integrated approach to human security.

Of the 18,123 testimonies gathered by Peru's Truth and Reconciliation Commission, 54 percent were from women and 46 percent from men. The reasons for this gender imbalance are diverse; women survived the war in greater numbers, but in addition gender norms in Peru allow women greater public expression of grief than men (CVR 2003, chapter 2, 51). Among those who testified in public hearings, 75 percent were Quechua-speaking victims. Hearing from indigenous women also went against all the preexisting cultural codes: in Peru, the voices of indigenous people, and indigenous women especially, are usually ignored. They are also regularly the target of scorn and ridicule as a result of racist stereotypes. Even in their home villages, indigenous women rarely are granted a public voice as men almost exclusively dominate village governance. Thus, providing voice to indigenous women on a national level was truly a break from past social practices. Many of the testimonies were nationally televised as well as reported on in the press and in the Commission's own reports. By giving voice to the most marginalized of Peru's society, some have argued that the TRC has begun a process of deepening Peru's democracy (LaPlante 2007). Many of those who testified, moreover, have become advocates for their communities vis-á-vis state authorities in the ongoing struggle to see the recommendations of the Truth and Reconciliation Commission become reality.

Continuing Challenges

Despite the accomplishments of the TRC, the Commission and Peruvian society still face tremendous challenges in overcoming the legacy of Peru's civil conflict and the inequalities at its root. Among these challenges we can point to a militarist culture, the very slow pace of achieving justice and awarding reparations, and societal polarization with regard to memory of the war. These challenges have been made more difficult because the promotion and protection of human rights have not been a priority of either the national or regional governments; while interim President Paniagua created the Commission, its work was carried out under subsequent presidents Alejandro Toledo and Alan García, both of whom were less supportive of the Commission's work. Yet, there are also positive signs in Peru's civil society of individuals and organizations working toward greater justice.

The conflict in Peru resulted in a process of militarization of Peruvian society, with important gendered effects. The war increased the importance of the military as an institution, and consequently its political influence as well. The military was a key political player behind the scenes, especially under the government of Alberto Fujimori. But the impact of the military went beyond its military might and political power to influence society. As with many societies that experience war, Peru's conflict led to a "militarization" of society, in which military values became societal values. The process of societal militarization manipulates masculinities and femininities, creating gendered archetypes such as the woeful mother and the valiant soldier. Militarist constructions of gender create and reinforce rigid gender roles and can also serve as justification for rape or prostitution (Enloe 2000; Ruddick 1995; Tickner 1992). These gendered constructions were reinforced during Peru's years of war and can be observed in the gendered violence that we described in previous sections.[10] The continuing militarization of Peruvian society is evident in direct and discursive ways. Directly, in areas of Peru where the Shining Path is still active (but now is mainly interested in drug trafficking), old practices continue, for example the abduction of young people by Shining Path militants to sustain their ranks. In turn, Shining Path activity has resulted in a continued presence of the military in these communities. On a more discursive level, the state has used fear of a return of terrorism as an instrument of control and as a way to gain legitimacy for authoritarian actions (Burt 2006). This discourse of fear had some ironic gendered aspects in the 2011 election campaign when the female candidate Keiko Fujimori used both the fear of a return to terrorism and the more peaceful trope of motherhood to advance her (ultimately failed) campaign (Ewig 2012).

The pace of implementation of the TRC's recommendations has been exceedingly slow. The TRC was mandated to collaborate with Peru's justice system in order to identify victims and perpetrators. Based on the findings of the TRC, prosecutions were then to have been carried out by the Peruvian justice system. There have been some very significant trials, such as the trial of former President Alberto Fujimori, who was convicted for his role in two massacres carried out by special military forces under his command. But the TRC itself has had challenges, like most truth commissions, in unearthing the kind of evidence necessary for convictions. It thus chose to pursue specific, high-profile cases which both fit the broader patterns of violence that it found, and for which it felt there was sufficient evidence (Ciurlizza and González 2006, 11–12). However, often when it handed over these cases to the Ministry of Public Prosecution, the ministry showed little willingness to prioritize TRC cases, and it has been extremely slow to act, resulting in a backlog that exists to this day (Ciurlizza and González 2006, 13). The slow pace of punishment has led to disappointment among those affected by the violence, many of whom mistakenly assumed the TRC itself had the power of a court to bring perpetrators to justice (Cano and Ninaquispe 2006, 43). Of the forty-seven cases handed over to the Ministry of Public Prosecution by the TRC, two were cases of sexual violence. These, like the other cases, have been acted on only slowly. They face difficulties of both finding evidence for the crimes due to the years that have passed, and of fear and resistance by the women themselves, who in some cases prefer not to prove that soldiers fathered their children, for fear of losing parental rights (Salazar Luzula 2006).

An important aspect of the TRC was to recommend reparations, something not all truth commissions have done. The TRC argued that the state had a responsibility to provide reparations for not having respected human rights and for not carrying out its responsibility to protect its citizens. Moreover, the Commission felt reparations were important for restoring trust in the state (CVR 2003, Vol. IX, 149). Reparations were conceived of broadly, including both symbolic and economic measures. In 2004, the government of Alejandro Toledo created a Commission (*La Comisión Multisectoral de Alto Nivel*) to distribute reparations; but this Commission was woefully understaffed and underfinanced, resulting in very little progress. The process of reparations was helped somewhat in 2005, when Congress passed Law 28592, which codified the reparations process into law, and which specified six types of reparations: restitution of citizen rights, housing assistance, and reparations relating to education and health as well as symbolic and collective reparations. But the law also had important flaws, such as specifically defining subversives as not "victims" (even if they had been victims of abuse), thus contradicting United Nations definitions of who constitutes a victim (Guillerot 2008, 12, 26). Under Alan Garcia, the process improved only slightly. Municipalities established special health and education services directed at victims of violence, and the national Commission did deliver some collective reparations for communities or groups that were affected by violence, although in some cases this distribution was tarnished by clientelism. At other times, general government social services were called "reparations," when in fact they were not specifically reparations (Guillerot 2008, 25). In particular, the distribution of individual economic reparations has been painfully slow. It only began in late 2011, under the new government of President Ollanta Humala, nearly twenty years after the capture of the Shining Path leader, Abimael Guzmán, which led to the end of the war.

Yet another challenge has been growing social polarization in Peru around the issue of human rights. The years from 2008 to 2010 saw intensifying aggression against national human rights organizations. Peruvians themselves were divided over the final report of the Truth Commission, some feeling that it was fair whereas others felt that the report's indictment of the military was unfair. Some likened Commission members to "terrorists" themselves. These tensions eventually came to a head in relation to two main issues: the construction of a Museum of Memory, and the international award garnered by a film about Peru's civil conflict, *La Teta Asustada* (The Milk of Sorrow). The German government had offered Peru two million US dollars in aid to build a national Museum of Memory, dedicated to honoring the memory of the victims of Peru's civil conflict. But in 2009, prominent members of the government, in particular the Minister of Defense Antero Flores Aráoz, criticized the museum project, saying the money would be better spent on aid to the poor. A polemical public debate ensued, in which supporters of the military expressed the fear that the museum would lack objectivity, would honor the subversives, and would tarnish the image of the military. Others, like the daughter of former President Fujimori, argued for a museum of "victory" honoring the military and not the victims. The project was only saved when renowned Peruvian novelist Mario Vargas Llosa persuaded President García of its importance. The president approved the project and named Vargas Llosa president of the commission, with the mission of maintaining its objectivity. But Vargas Llosa resigned soon after in protest over a proposed law that would have allowed amnesty for officials prosecuted for violations of human rights. Although the law was not passed, Vargas Llosa refused to return to the post. The museum has now been built, but the debate highlighted the deep fissures among Peruvians left by the war.

At almost the same time, in 2009 Claudia Llosa, a young filmmaker, received the Berlin Golden Bear award and in 2010 an Oscar nomination for the film *La Teta Asustada*. This is the first movie to place an Andean subject at the center of attention; its protagonist is a young girl who experiences the pain of her mother, a Quechua speaker who had been raped during Peru's internal war. "Milk of Sorrow" refers to a rare disease contracted by women who suffered violence in Peru's war, and transmit the disease to their children through their breast milk. The disease is an allegory for the lingering effects of the war on subsequent generations. In one of her first interviews Claudia Llosa pointed out that in the film, she did not speak of blame, rather she tried to capture the pain of the women who suffered the barbarity of war and sexual violence and how this pain passes from generation to generation without due analysis. Furthermore, she said that everyone should find a way to heal without leaving their memory behind. It was the first Peruvian film nominated for an academy award for best foreign language film.

Despite these important challenges, there is a growing consciousness of rights among new generations of Peruvians in both the countryside and the cities, and there are growing numbers of organizations of those affected. These organizations are mobilizing and serving as interlocutors between the government and the population, and they are making proposals for change. For example, ANFASAP, the organization of women from Ayacucho mentioned previously, continues to press on, providing support to its members. In the postviolence era, between 2006 and 2007 various regional and local organizations founded the national Coordinating Committee of Populations Affected by Political Violence (Coordinadora Nacional de Poblaciones Afectadas por la Violencia Política, CONAVIP). CONAVIP was formed by families organized in the regions of Peru most affected by violence, and was led primarily by young people. The organization of CONVIP has facilitated greater communication with the state during the reparations process. In addition to these organizations of families of victims, the Human Rights Coordinating Committee (Coordinadora de Derechos Humanos) and Citizens Movement for No Repetition (Movimiento Ciudadano "Para que no se Repita") are networks that coordinate NGOs, human rights activists, and other interested civil society organizations. More recently, artists and university students have added to these efforts new strategies—such as street protests and internet campaigns, protesting, for example, the candidacy of former president Alberto Fujimori's daughter, Keiko Fujimori, for president in 2011.

Conclusion

Peru's internal war with the Shining Path opened the door to violations of human rights, terror, and militarization. The war was sparked by a fanatical ideologue who successfully organized an armed uprising. But the conditions of human insecurity that had existed in Peru prior to the conflict in many ways made this organizing possible and this ideology stick. Incredible poverty and high degrees of inequality and racism enabled this ideology to take hold, as young people saw no way out except through violence. The war in the countryside continued unabated for so long in part because the white and *mestizo* residents of urban areas saw the conflict as a war among indigenous peoples, something apart from their own reality, which could be conveniently ignored. Ultimately, the fear and terror wielded by the Shining Path brought no opportunities for the excluded and marginalized those whom the movement purported to represent. If anything, it opened the way for President Alberto Fujimori and his followers to deploy new forms of coercion and intimidation in the countryside.

Today, while thousands of families still live in precarious conditions—conditions that are arguably more precarious psychologically and economically as a result of the conflict—sections of Peru's political elite continue to resist and defy the recommendations of the Final Report of the TRC. Human rights are not a priority, and the gravity of the conflict is still not fully recognized. This lack of recognition can be attributed in part to the fact that there never was a formal deposing of arms to mark the end of the conflict. But the larger reason is that the lives of those most affected by the violence, those of the communities in the highlands of Peru, continue to be looked at as distant and different by most Peruvians in the cities. This reality demands that Peruvians grapple with racism, which manifests itself in distinct forms against indigenous peoples of the Amazon, the Andes, and the indigenous and Afro-Peruvian residents of the cities.

While huge challenges remain, we can also point to some remarkably positive outcomes as a result of the work of the TRC, outcomes that we think can be attributed to its gendered approach to human security. Perhaps most importantly, the final report of the TRC integrated sexual violence and the gendered experience of violence, aspects that have been largely ignored by other truth commissions, bringing to light the gendered nature of Peru's war and atrocities like sexual violence that may not otherwise have been documented. In addition, perhaps inspired by the TRC's emphasis on the importance of symbolism and memory, local memorial initiatives have sprung up; municipalities, especially in Ayacucho and Huancavelica have erected monuments and places of remembrance. The women of ANFASAP even created a museum dedicated to memory in 2005. We have also seen the consolidation of human rights activist networks at local and regional levels and the growth of a new generation of leaders among the populations affected by violence. The work of the TRC in bringing voice to the voiceless, while not perfect, has helped to foster a sense of empowerment among those affected by violence. It is also one small step in what must be a much larger project, that of overcoming the deep gendered, racial, and economic inequalities that exist in Peru today.

NOTES

1. While "ethnicity" is often the term used in Peru to differentiate among indigenous, mixed race (*mestizo*), and whites, we prefer the term race because race refers to dynamics of power based upon negative stereotypes, and thus more accurately describes these relations in Peru, whereas ethnicity refers only to cultural differences. See discussion in Ewig 2010, 13–16.

2. "Transformative" justice refers to processes of justice that not only transition a state and society out of conflict, but also seek to change preconflict structures so that they are more inclusive and fair, and takes into account broader issues such as state fragility (Lambourne 2009).

3. See also the September 2004 issue of *Security Dialogue* for a range of views on the concept.

4. On the significant correlation between social and economic inequality and race/ethnicity in Peru, see chapter 3 of Thorp and Paredes 2010.

5. For an insightful account of the early years of the Shining Path, see Gorriti 1999.

6. Shining Path document, cited in Henríquez Ayín 2006, 21.

7. One of the authors, Narda Henríquez, worked for the Commission.

8. The Council on Reparations, which is in charge of registering individual victims of violence for the purpose of reparations, has found triple the number of sexual violence cases than the number found by the TRC.

9. Testimony quoted in Henríquez Ayín 2006, 39.

10. In some instances war also brought a break with traditional gender roles, for example, a few women joined the mainly male self-defense militias formed to protect communities from the Shining Path. Following the conflict, however, many of these women were unable to maintain their newly gained authority.

REFERENCES

Barrig, Marruja. 1993. "Liderazgo Femenino y Violencia Política en el Perú de los 90." *Debates en Sociología* 18:96–97.

Burt, Jo-Marie. 2006. "'QUIEN HABLA ES TERRORISTA': The Political Use of Fear in Fujimori's Peru." *Latin American Research Review* 41(3):32–62.

Cano, Gloria, and Karim Ninaquispe. 2006. "The Role of Civil Society in Demanding and Promoting Justice." In *The Legacy of Truth: Criminal Justice in the Peruvian Transition,* edited by Lisa Magarrell and Leonardo Filippini, 39–48. New York: International Center for Transitional Justice.

CDHDF. 1999. "La violación de mujeres en las guerras: delito grave contra los derecho humanos." Basada en no existe justicia sin género, Ximena Bedregal, Doble Jornada No. 79, agosto de 1993 y Thais Aguilar/CIMAC, 10 diciembre de 1988. En http://www.jornada.unam.mx/1999/ene99/990105/violacion-en-guerra.htm. Accessed on March 4, 2002.

Ciurlizza, Javier, and Eduardo González. 2006. "Truth and Justice from the Perspective of the Truth and Reconciliation Commission." In *The Legacy of Truth: Criminal Justice in the Peruvian Transition,* edited by Lisa Magarrell and Leonardo Filippini, 5–28. New York: International Center for Transitional Justice.

Comisión de la Verdad y Reconciliación (CVR). 2003. Informe Final. Lima: CVR.

Commission on Human Security. 2003. *Human Security Now.* New York: Commission on Human Security/United Nations Office for Project Services.

Coral Cordero, Isabel. 1998. "Women in War: Impact and Responses." In *Shining and Other Paths: War and Society in Peru: 1980–1995,* edited by Steve J. Stern, 345–374. Durham: Duke University Press.

Degregori, Carlos Iván. 1994. "Return to the Past." In *The Shining Path of Peru,* edited by David Scott Palmer, 51–62. New York: St. Martin's Press.

———. 2012. *How Difficult It Is to Be God: Shining Path's Politics of War in Peru, 1980–1999.* Madison: University of Wisconsin Press.

Degregori, Carlos Iván, José Coronel, Ponciano del Pino, and Orin Starn. 1996. *Las Rondas Campesinas y la Derrota de Sendero Luminoso.* Lima: Instituto de Estudios Peruanos.

Del Pino, Ponciano. 1999. "Familia, Cultura y 'Revolución.' Vida Cotidiana en Sendero Luminoso." In *Los Senderos Insólitos del Perú,* edited by Steve Stern, 161–191. Lima: Instituto de Estudios Peruanos and Universidad San Cristóbal de Huamanga.

de Wit, Ton, and Vera Gianotten. 1994. "The Center's Multiple Failures." In *The Shining Path of Peru,* edited by David Scott Palmer, 63–75. New York: St. Martin's Press.

Enloe, Cynthia H. 1989. *Bananas, Beaches and Bases.* Berkeley: University of California Press.

———. 2000. *Maneuvers: The International Politics of Militarizing Women's Lives.* Berkeley: University of California Press.

Ewig, Christina. 2010. *Second-Wave Neoliberalism: Gender, Race and Health Sector Reform in Peru.* University Park: Pennsylvania State University Press.

———. 2012. "The Strategic Use of Gender and Race in Peru's 2011 Presidential Campaign." *Politics & Gender* 8(2):267–274.

Foran, John, and Jeff Goodwin. 1993. "Revolutionary Outcomes in Iran and Nicaragua: Coalition Fragmentation, War, and the Limits of Social Transformation." *Theory and Society* 22(2):209–247.

Gibson, Ian R., and Betty A. Reardon. 2007. "Human Security: Toward Gender Inclusion." In *Protecting Human Security in a Post 9/11 World: Critical and Global Insights*, edited by Giorgio Shani, Makoto Sato, and Mustapha Kamal Pasha, 50–63. New York: Palgrave.

Gorriti, Gustavo. 1999. *The Shining Path: A History of the Millenarian War in Peru*. Chapel Hill: University of North Carolina Press.

Guillerot, Julie. 2008. *Reparaciones en la Transición Peruana: ¿Dónde estamos y hacía donde vamos?* New York: International Center for Transitional Justice.

Henríquez Ayín, Narda Z. 1996. "Las señoras dirigentes, experiencias de ciudadanía en barrios Populares." In *Detrás de la Puerta*, edited by Patricia Ruiz Bravo, 143–162. Lima: PUCP.

———. 2006. *Cuestiones de Género y Poder en el Conflicto Armado en el Perú*. Lima: Consejo Nacional de Ciencia, Tecnología e Innovación.

Hoogensen, Gunhild, and Kirsti Stuvøy. 2006. "Gender, Resistance and Human Security." *Security Dialogue* 37:207–228.

Hudson, Heidi. 2005. "'Doing' Security as Though Humans Matter: A Feminist Perspective on Gender and the Politics of Human Security." *Security Dialogue* 36:155–174.

Hudson, Natalie Florea. 2010. *Gender, Human Security and the United Nations*. New York: Routledge.

Kirk, Robin. 1993. *Grabado en Piedra: Las Mujeres de Sendero Luminoso*. Lima: Instituto de Estudios Peruanos.

Lambourne, Wendy. 2009. "Transitional Justice and Peace-Building after Mass Violence." *International Journal of Transitional Justice* 3(1):28–48.

LaPlante, Lisa. 2007. "The Peruvian Truth Commission's Historical Memory Project: Empowering Truth-Tellers to Confront Truth Deniers." *Journal of Human Rights* 6:433–452.

Mantilla Falcon, Julissa. 2008a. "Gender and Truth Commissions: The Peruvian Case." Presentation for the TARGET Research Circle and the Global Legal Studies Center, University of Wisconsin-Madison, March 25.

———. 2008b. "Sexual Violence against Women and the Experience of Truth Commissions." In *Global Empowerment of Women: Responses to Globalization and Politicized Religions*, edited by Carolyn M. Elliott, 215–232. New York: Routledge.

McClintock, Cynthia. 2001 [1989]. "Peru's Sendero Luminoso Rebellion: Origins and Trajectory." In *Power and Popular Protest: Latin American Social Movements*, edited by Susan Eckstein, 61–101. Berkeley: University of California Press.

Moyano, María Elena. 2000. *The Autobiography of María Elena Moyano: The Life and Death of a Peruvian Activist*. Gainesville: University Press of Florida.

Neira, Eloy, and Patricia Ruiz Bravo. 2001. "Enfrentados al patrón: una aproximación al estudio de la masculinidad en el Perú." In *Estudios Culturales en Ciencias Sociales*, edited by Santiago López Maguiña, 215–232. Lima: Red para el Desarrollo de las Ciencias Sociales, PUCP.

Paris, Roland. 2001. "Human Security: Paradigm Shift or Hot Air?" *International Security* 26(2):87–102.

Portocarrero, Gonzalo. 1998. *Razones de Sangre: Aproximaciones a la Violencia Política.* Lima: Fondo Editorial de la Universidad Católica del Perú.

Ruddick, Sara. 1995. *Material Thinking: Toward a Politics of Peace.* Boston, Mass.: Beacon Press.

Salazar Luzula, Katya. 2006. "Gender, Sexual Violence and Criminal Law in Post-Conflict Peru." In *The Legacy of Truth: Criminal Justice in the Peruvian Transition*, edited by Lisa Magarrell and Leonardo Filippini, 56–69. New York: International Center for Transitional Justice.

Selbin, Eric. 1993. *Modern Latin American Revolutions.* Boulder, Colo.: Westview Press.

Starn, Orin. 1995. "Maoism in the Andes: The Communist Party of Peru—Shining Path and the Refusal of History." *Journal of Latin American Studies* 27(2):399–421.

———. 1999. *Nightwatch: The Politics of Protest in the Andes.* Durham: Duke University Press.

Theidon, Kimberly. 2007. "Gender in Transition: Common Sense, Women and War." *Journal of Human Rights* 6:453–478.

Thorp, Rosemary, and Maritza Paredes. 2010. *Ethnicity and the Persistence of Inequality: The Case of Peru.* New York: Palgrave.

Tickner, J. Ann.1992. *Gender in International Relations: Feminist Perspectives on Achieving Global Security.* New York: Columbia University Press.

United Nations Development Program (UNDP). 1994. *Human Development Report 1994.* New York: Oxford University Press.

Wieviorka, Michel. 1991. *El Terrorismo, La Violencia Política en el Mundo.* España: Plaza de Janés.

PART FOUR

Conclusion

12

The Discursive Politics of Gendering Human Security

Beyond the Binaries

MYRA MARX FERREE

This book has shown the concept of human security to be a catch-all term. Sometimes it stresses freedom from fear of violence, both interpersonal and militarized, and sometimes freedom from want in the sense of combatting the starvation and disease that kill more people worldwide than guns do. Sometimes it is used to legitimate and encourage police actions, both within local communities and by powerful states across national borders, as in U.S. interventions in Iraq and Afghanistan. But at other times it is used to hold states accountable for their militarized drug and sex politics, ethnic repressions, and clashes over resources, arguing that violence in the name of ending violence is also a source of pervasive insecurity for those caught in the crosshairs.

So why try to "gender" such an amorphous and polysemic concept? By means of gendering human security, this book has offered a frame for all types of violence that reveals how they are embedded in gender relations, and used this frame as a means of advancing a more clearly feminist discourse of human security. Thinking of gender, violence, and human security together is sometimes done in essentialist and stereotyped ways, but the feminist approach offered in this volume instead presents these relationships as complex, contested, and intersectional. This approach is fundamentally a political one, in that it keeps the issue of power in the foreground. Feminist thinking about gender differs in this critical regard from using gender to mean thinking just about women or just about sex differences. A feminist gendering of human security discourse is a means of reconfiguring the idea of what human security should be and imagining new approaches to applying it for the good of both women and men, not the old "add women and stir" type of inclusion.

The chapters of this volume offer a variety of ways for feminist scholars to engage constructively with the concept of human security, but perhaps just as importantly, the chapters offer significant practical reasons why it is essential not to ignore the development and impact of this human security discourse on national and international policymaking. Whether by pointing to a problem in the way the concept is applied, or finding promising uses for it in specific cases, each chapter provides an example of the practical importance of a critically informed, feminist understanding for ongoing political work, not only in peace building but in advancing social inclusion and economic justice.

In this chapter, I first review some key theoretical claims about the notions of human security and of gender that animate this volume. I particularly emphasize the ways that gendering human security is a way of doing politics with discourse. The study of discursive politics is an outgrowth of analyses of the work that social movements, political parties, and transnational advocacy networks do to name problems, set agendas, and motivate normative change across multiple potential issues (Keck and Sikkink 1998; Stone 2001; Lombardo, Meier, and Verloo 2009). I specifically highlight the ways that feminists have choices in how to gender human security discourse, define the approach called intersectionality, and argue for the importance of an intersectional feminist perspective. I emphasize that even with gender included, human security can be defined in terms that hide power and injustice, that emphasize only violent conflicts, and that become as top-down and authoritarian as the state security models the discourse was supposed to correct. The implication for feminist discursive politics is that the concrete implications of gender for human security and human security for gender should be reciprocally intersectional; both together can add breadth to the scope of what needs are considered political and particularity to the complexity of voices heard in particular struggles, but especially so when each concept is allowed to deuniversalize the other.

After developing this argument, this chapter reprises the practical implications of gendering human security that these various chapters suggest and concludes by pointing out policy directions sensitive to these concerns. Although the authors stress different aspects of the application of gender to human security struggles, they are complementary in the way they bring a wider understanding of politics to bear, join the micro and macro aspects of human insecurity, and challenge the intersectional processes of constructing and subordinating others. Taken as a whole, their analyses reveal that mainstreaming gender into human security discussions will demand more than just bringing in attention to women but that, nonetheless, justice can only be done if particular attention is given to women. Making human security a more feminist framework is thus a discursive challenge, one that demands incorporating all women's voices in a framework which values both inclusion and diversity.

Gendering Human Security as Intersectional Feminist Politics

Human security has been defined as safeguarding "the vital core of all human lives from critical pervasive threats, in a way that is consistent with long-term human fulfillment" (Alkire 2003). In addition to being an unrealized goal of actual global politics, human security is a discourse with claims to configuring power, a way of thinking about the world and its material social relations that both reflects existing power relations and is used to reinforce and to challenge them. In the discursive work around human security, we suggest that separating the concept of security from justice is particularly problematic, and not only for women. The very idea of peace without justice implies a politics of silencing and disempowering groups whose needs are being systematically ignored and excluded. Such exclusions connect as well as divide the interests of particular women and men in crosscutting ways; this is what has come to be called intersectionality, a concept that this chapter will unpack in several dimensions.

As Tripp's first chapter amply documented, the current discourse of human security has contradictory elements; it has not been stabilized into any one hegemonic form, and although there are efforts by various actors (from the UN to defense intellectuals) to do so, it has not gained the invisibility, naturalness, and "taken-for-granted" status that characterizes hegemonic ideas. The ambiguity of what human security will be thought to mean in specific situations also leaves the way that human security can be "gendered" still open for debate. Gender itself is a discourse with configuring power on social relations but one that is also subject to various political interpretations, including some claims that are determinist (fixity ordained by God or nature), essentialist (in binary opposition), or social constructionist (separating sexed bodies from gender performance). Since invoking gender relations as relevant can suggest a number of quite different political projects, even feminists vary in their understanding of gender.

For the feminist view of gender advanced in this book, the crucial intervention into the framing of gender has been the development of intersectionality as a specific approach, one that is particularly critical of binary views of men and women and committed to a broadly inclusive understanding of social justice. Intersectional theories of gender stress its macrosocial grounding in relationships of power. Among other theorists, initially mostly women of color in the United States, Patricia Hill Collins (1986) is notable for highlighting the crisscrossing relations of injustice formed by gender, race, and class oppressions and emphasizing that the downtrodden in one relationship can still be oppressors in another relationship. Kimberlé Crenshaw (1991) devised the specific and now widely used term intersectionality to describe the multidimensionality and non-additivity of such social relations of injustice. Both Hancock (2007) and McCall (2005) point out that intersectionality has since become a broad term, covering a variety of specific analytic strategies, but that such an approach also offers some generally important considerations for gender politics. These apply strongly in the case of human security discourses.

First, from an intersectional feminist perspective, gender is not the only relationship that matters, but it does matter. Seeking justice implies acknowledging gender as a process relevant to the individual and collective security of both women and men, but it also demands responding to women's particular interests in resisting patriarchal power and ending gendered inequalities, recognizing how these are also embedded within and shaped by other power relations (Choo and Ferree 2010; Lutz, Vivar, and Supik 2011). Second, the intersectional perspective also connects the macrolevel and microlevel by highlighting the ways that structure and agency are both involved in oppression. Last, but certainly not least, intersectional approaches problematize any essentialist view of women and men as binary groups in eternal opposition. By relying on the intersectional version of gendering human security, this book sets out to bring the positions and perspectives of both women and men into view and to prioritize the value of social justice for all.

This is not always what is meant by gendering human security: some nonintersectional versions of feminist human security discourse bring attention only to women, as the chapter by Ní Aoláin has pointed out; some may ignore the other power relationships in which women are embedded, presenting the women of more nationally powerful groups as rescuers and women in the global South as victims, as Ewing's chapter suggests; some assume all women are innocent of the oppression of others and fail to recognize their own involvement in systems that perpetuate injustice, as Peterson notes. Internationally, feminists struggle among themselves and with other social justice movements to bring particular understandings of gendered security politics to bear, some of which are more intersectional than others (Lakkimsetti 2013; Liu 2006; Lombardo, Meier, and Verloo 2009; Thayer 2010).

It is important to emphasize that patriarchal versions of gendering human security are also commonplace. Such discourses frame women as vulnerable victims, safety as home and hearth, peace as weakness, and all people as served by reaffirming relations of natural subordination. For example, Buss and Herman (2003) outline how an international coalition of religious fundamentalists draws on patriarchal versions of gender expressed within specific Christian, Jewish, and Islamic traditions to frame conventional gender arrangements as "family values" and fight feminist initiatives for gender equality as endangering women and their families. As the chapter by Brush points out, other conservative and some feminist discourses in the United States converge in defining women themselves as responsible for their own human security by means of the market. In the context of human security discourses, the hegemonic framing of gender as permanent and immutable can be a symbolic anchor to essentialize men and women into two diametrically opposed groups and to channel desires for peace and stability into a reactionary politics of restoring "traditions" of gender and family relations, a discourse that was common in Eastern Europe after the dissolution of communist state control (Gal and Kligman 2000). Talking about gender as a way of mobilizing the association of women with family and reproduction can be a way of using women's need for physical or economic security to drum up support for religious or state interests in population growth or limitation (Yuval-Davis 1997); naming women as vulnerable may be a way of creating or directing anger against other socially marginalized groups (Korteweg and Yurdakul 2009).

Because diverse feminist and antifeminist discourses struggle to represent the most "correct" form of advocacy for human security that names gender as a significant relationship, this chapter tries to clarify just what a feminist intersectional framing of gendered human security offers as well as to critique ways of bringing gender into human security discourse that fail to be either intersectional or feminist. For feminists, naming patriarchal power relations is critical to the analysis of gender, but believing that more justice is possible and being committed to making such change is no less important (Scott 1986; Connell 2009). Gendering human security in intersectional feminist terms, as this book presents it, is importantly a discursive political project that also resists the imposition of gendered binaries: whether of men and women, masculinity and femininity, agents and victims, weakness and strength, or peace and war.

Beyond Binaries to Realizing Intersectionality

Human security as a political discourse offers a range of opportunities and resources to both feminists and nonfeminists because it is still such a complex and amorphous term. In the present struggle to give meaning to the concept of human security, intersectional feminists have a stake in ensuring that this frame is able to recognize and respond to injustice in more than binary terms. The human security framework, as its feminist critics have pointed out, initially only saw "people" rather than acknowledging the gendered distributions of risks that women and men face. But for it to shift to see gender only as "women," a single special interest or especially vulnerable category, is to leave men to be the "people" who remain central to any general view of the human. Such a binary approach to gendering human security also understates the intersectionality of the material insecurities violence imposes and ignores the way gender meanings are actively mobilized to empower, humiliate, incite and deter, legitimate, and exacerbate individual and institutional violence.

Human security discourse, although a relatively new framing of the problems of violence and inequality, has demonstrated in various settings that it has real configuring power on gender relations. The feedback effect of human security framing is manifested in shifting political relationships at the global level, such as the UN's articulation of the policy of "Right to Protect" (R2P) as a justification for actual international interventions to prevent states from engaging in or permitting widespread abuse. Moreover, in 2002 the UN Convention on the Status of Refugees was revised to grant women who were facing gender-based violence (rape, battering, trafficking, etc.) carried out by civil actors with political impunity in their home countries the right to claim asylum as refugees facing group-based persecution on the grounds of gender. Women refugees were themselves central actors in the Canadian feminist network that led this successful struggle to gender international asylum law; they were by no means passive victims (Alfredson 2009).

This volume has also drawn out a number of positive elements in the discourse of human security that particularly overlap with intersectional feminist approaches. Most centrally, human security discourse is more collective and less legalistic than human rights claims, offering a proactive strategy for making group claims on power holders. As Rubio-Marín and Estrada-Tanck argue, human security discourse is not a good alternative to making human rights claims, but can be a way to enrich the interpretation of what rights include beyond those exercised in existing power relations. This encourages women's collective agency, offering a discourse that appeals to those who are socially located in positions of vulnerability and in ongoing conflicts by adding moral force to their demands for change in the status quo. It is also a tool that women can deploy in postconflict situations to resist returning to the *status quo ante* as if "traditional families" offered a state of safety rather than being a situation of real and abiding insecurity for many women and for all nonconformists to its gender binary values. By empowering resistance to gender "traditional" versions, feminist framings of human security encourage human agency (by both men and women) in defining their needs in the future-oriented, aspirational terms of gender justice.

The concept of human security also widens the scope of security politics to encompass more pervasive, slow, and not obviously violent threats to human survival such as disease and hunger. This also is a move toward an understanding of politics that fits well with intersectional feminist understandings of gender relations. Just as feminists of the 1970s had to draw attention to the issues of violence and redistribution within households by mobilizing around battering and housework, feminists today need discursive tools for drawing attention to the linkages between macro- and microlevels of intersectional insecurities for women and men. Using the discourse of gender relations helps analyze human insecurities such as those that Stites identifies in her chapter on Uganda's Karimojong communities wracked by increasing male violence. By connecting the gender-specific interactions among economic insecurity and the local physical environment, generational power relations and community reproduction, interpersonal conflict and the international trade in small arms, she situates the politics of masculinity simultaneously at the macro- and microlevels. While such problems in family formation and generational succession are not likely to be resolved just by addressing the gender assumptions embedded in them, understanding how they operate for men and women might also empower women in these communities to begin to articulate their own interests in human and social reproduction and resolve them in ways that do not naturalize gender domination.

As Tripp argues in the Introduction, "Human security is, in principle, an attractive normative frame for feminists because it looks at the impact of insecurities on people, not just the consequences of conflict for the state. It focuses on societal activities, not just on state action. It highlights the agency of those affected by insecurity, and focuses on positive action to expand human capabilities, not just defenses of rights" (xx). But as she also notes, to advance a gendered view of human security without awareness of the crosscutting power relations of national interests that situate some women as well as men in positions of global privilege risks depicting less privileged women primarily in terms of victimization and in need of being saved. Moreover, if analysts look only to those groups that explicitly call themselves feminist movements, many of the diverse forms of women's organizing and collective agency in the struggle to expand human security may be overlooked (Ewig and Ferree 2013).

Indeed, even as human security enters into the discourse of international organizations and governments dealing with the violence and misery resulting from famine, migration, economic crisis, environmental degradation, and religious or ethnic animosities, thinking about gender in terms other than a binary recognition of women as victims in need of special protection or rescue remains rare, as Ní Aoláin has shown. Rather than looking to alliances with the state for top-down change, movements that offer analyses of human security from positions of crosscutting oppression are more likely to bring in an intersectional feminism from below, as women's voices in many different justice movements introduce greater gender awareness along with other demands for justice into the human security agenda (Alfredson 2009; Thayer 2010).

Intersectional feminist versions of gendering human security expand the idea of human security to draw connections between political voice and protection from victimization, emphasizing political inclusion in decision making not only for women but for all endangered people. This approach means not only breaking down the binary between freedom from fear and freedom from want, but also undermining the conventional binary understanding of negative (freedom from) and positive (freedom to) liberty. Freedom to develop human capabilities is also freedom to acquire future aspirations and articulate present interests; it demands such freedom from the oppressions of the past that unraveling the matrix of domination becomes imaginable and safe to attempt. Political agency and positive inclusion, from all levels from family decision making through local community councils to national parliaments and international tribunals is essential to formulating a vision of security for all. A stunted, defensive image of human security is inconsistent both with the intersectional analysis of social justice and the feminist struggle to allow all women's interests and aspirations to be voiced.

Human security understood as necessarily inclusive of democratic participation is therefore a politics inconsistent with the militarized discourse employed in such state-led politics as the war on poverty, war on drugs, or war on trafficking. Although some feminists may be drawn to such discourses as presenting opportunities for engaging states in addressing the situation of vulnerable and exploited groups, the chapters of this book have repeatedly shown how militarized discourses criminalize neediness and convert these same groups into potential enemies of the state. Too often, feminist alliances with lawmakers in specific contexts have increased penalties for rape, trafficking, and other forms of gender-based violence in ways that have failed to be aware of the intersectional injustices that ensue: the chapter by Bumiller points to racially biased incarceration in the United States, and Kinney to the ethnicized definition of trafficking in Thailand as processes that feminist antiviolence campaigners need to address more adequately than they have to date. States themselves articulate concern about human security in ways that justify the combined mobilization of their military power and criminal laws, enhancing their uses of coercive force in the name of protecting "domestic" populations. Such securitization of national and international politics to fight human trafficking or carry out a war on drugs may heighten collective and individual insecurities, depending on where the boundaries of state concern are drawn, as Peterson has shown. Human security discourse justifies building walls when it is framed in binary rather than intersectional terms, even by feminists; it becomes a matter of defending "us" from them, whether the walls are at the edges of nation-states, gated communities, or prisons.

Human security as a feminist discourse also has to be intersectional to reach beyond the familiar gendered binaries of peace and war, to critique rather than reproduce the historical association of peacemaking with women (and thus as weak and "wimpy") and war with men (and thus with power and protection of the "homefront"). As modern technologies of conflict and rules of war have changed, any distinction between soldiers and civilians has become difficult to draw, and binary gender norms about fighting are increasingly counterproductive. As Hoganson (2000) shows, the gendered discourse of peace as weak can be used by some men to bully others toward war. The gendered discourse of war as "men's business" also gives women little say when civic discourse is directed toward decisions about going to war (Christensen and Ferree 2008). The practical impacts of wars on women and men can empower women to lead efforts to redirect popular mobilizations toward peace building; but rather than stirring some binary and intrinsic female inclination to peace, violent conflicts may just disrupt men's usual political alliances enough that previously marginalized women can find space to emerge as political leaders (Tripp 2009).

Since human security is not only a discourse about overtly violent conflicts, its multidimensionality also offers nonbinary ways of thinking about what "ending" a conflict means. Unlike talking peace, one cannot proclaim human security to be achieved simply because treaties are signed or militaries are withdrawn to their homeland barracks. Seeking to create human security does not imply that violence ever will vanish, even if there are clear instances where insecurity greatly increases or declines. For both better and worse, human security offers the conceptual space to think in terms of a continuum of possibilities for human development, including the development of capabilities for resilience and resistance, rather than a binary state of presence or absence of violence, harm, and danger.

Moving away from imagining "womenandchildren" (Enloe 1993) as innocent, powerless, and only victimized in relation to violence is therefore a critical first step toward gendering human security as a feminist concept that does not lead to what Kinney decries in her chapter as the "strategic securitization" of social problems. Challenging the binary of gender, no less than undoing the binary of war and peace, is thus essential to creating a usable concept of human security. Human security is not something women desire more than men do, nor are either women or men a monolithic group, all members of which have common interests that are served by violence or its suppression. Women may be complicit in violence (including drawing benefits from racial-ethnic intolerance and the insecurity it generates), and women may be perpetrators of violence aimed at upsetting the status quo of power. An essentialized view of women as nurturing and loving, peaceful and passive denies the reality of some women's participation in combat and some women's fierce encouragement of men to fight on their behalf. For example, women were recruited to be nearly half of the horrifically brutal Shining Path guerilla movement in Peru, as Henríquez and Ewig note in their chapter. Men, too, have diverse reasons for embracing violence, and stereotypes of warriors as essentially violent are just as misleading as images of women as peaceful (Dudink, Hagemann, and Tosh 2004).

If gender is misunderstood as a polarity of such opposites, insisting upon its importance will lead back to the classic "protection racket" that Judith Stiehm (1981) exposed, where women are most victimized by these same "men of their group" who claim to protect them, and men's violence terrorizes the women to whom they are closest. Fearful women then accept such unreliable male guards against other men portrayed as even more dangerous. There is considerable evidence, including Ewing's chapter in this book, of such dynamics. As Ewing's analysis of stigmatizing discourses about Muslim men and boys in Germany shows, some feminists fall victim to the assumption that ending violence against women means mobilizing against men of other nations, religions, or racial-ethnic groups rather than dealing with the complex dynamics of gender inequality with "their own" men.

Even the importance of gender in specific human security discourses can be better understood if not approached in binary terms. Not only has the discourse of individual gender oppositeness rendered the concept of peace thin and passive, but it has also devalued the women who remain active in this uphill struggle by making their struggle seem a "natural" outgrowth of their femininity rather than a political commitment. Reaching to binary concepts of gender, even to explain women's agency rather than their victimization, oversimplifies the contextual significance gender has in relation to many other forms of injustice, endangerment, and activism. When gender is allowed to recede into the background, it leaves just "people" to be seen. Such low salience can be a good thing, as when attention to gender would be otherwise used to draw invidious distinctions and attribute differential value, but it can also be a form of ignorance, as when the material situations of women and men are already differentiated but not recognized and responded to as such. Gendering human security discourses intersectionally demands attention to the variability of both the discursive salience and material significance of gender in particular relationships, and even more to the mismatch between discourses and the relationships they claim to represent.

Willed ignorance of gender relations often serves gendered interests, but it may also reflect a failure of imagination that information—especially when personalized and situationally relevant—can address (Ridgeway and Correll 2006). The political work of gendering human security often takes such a consciousness-raising tack, drawing attention of transnational elites to the gendered dimensions of social relations. Yet even awareness of gender as a process can be distorted, particularly when it involves binary rather than intersectional notions of progress. Because gender is neither an individual trait nor a single social role, there is no "traditional" meaning it carries across contexts that can or should be "defended," "restored," or "overcome." There are cultural similarities in the way female gender and subordinate status are linked, and there have long been struggles to contest and change this association, but there is no "modern" society that is free of gender inequality, nor any one style of "traditional" gender relations to be found in "the past." Framing assaults on women's self-determination from one side as a "war on women" and on the other side as a "war on the family" pits women's desires for both autonomy and connection against each other, and allows a dehumanizing binary discourse of "enemies" and "traitors" to displace more inclusive concerns for reproductive justice and social care.

In sum, gendering human security will be most useful if it is consciously critical of binary views of gender that are popularly available and being mobilized politically to defend "traditional" values of men and women. Moreover, the gendered ascription of political agency to men and victimization to women overlooks and even undermines the actual efforts of women and men in particular groups to participate in democratic processes of articulating their concerns. Freedom to mobilize collectively and to act autonomously are political liberties essential to achieving freedom from economic want and from fear of violence, just as health, safety, and hope are vital to achieving inclusive democratic participation.

Finally, human security as a political discourse has potential to move beyond conventional binaries of war and peace, but its ability to do so will be stunted if the gender connotations of these binaries are not challenged as well. Women are not in need of "special" protection that reifies difference in them and universalizes the masculine as a norm of human; women in general and feminists in particular should be cautious about politics that name women in order to instrumentalize their needs in service of something defined as "more general" and "bigger" than they are. Rather than some fixed set of "gender roles," institutionally specific roles are gendered and in complex, sometimes contradictory, ways that are more or less salient and significant in particular situations. Being a soldier and being a victim are culturally gendered roles, but these are roles that both women and men assume. War remains a familiar, polarizing, and often dehumanizing metaphor for power struggles, and continues to privilege masculinized forms of authority and violent means of control. Our intersectional feminist approach to gendering human security has tried to bring this complex and continually contested view of gender to bear.

Reprising Specific Themes of This Book

Although the chapters offer only small and selective glimpses of the full continuum of structural and institutional issues in the global struggle to increase human security, they provide a shared frame of reference for considering gender in an intersectional matrix of domination. Most especially, they show how "human" is always specific, not abstract: human relations are those of class, gender, race, nation, sexuality, generation and can only be seen from the specific standpoints of those affected in particular ways. As Glenn (1999) argued, the strength of such intersectional analysis is especially clear when it shows how positions of privilege are also sites of oppression and when it highlights the power relations at the periphery, that is, among groups that are themselves marginalized.

The cases we have chosen stress particular ways that intersectionality becomes more visible in human security discourse. The chapters by Brush, Bumiller, and Ewing bring a human security framework to the rich countries of the global North and make connections, theoretically and empirically, among social exclusion, physical violence, and economic need in the United States and Europe, challenging the conventional us-them binary of empowered rescuers and needy victims. Not only do they bring the analysis of human insecurities "home," but they also point to feminist participation in framing the recurrent dynamic of threat and rescue in us-them terms that erect rather than undermine social barriers. They highlight the problems in the framing of human security from the standpoint of those (be they feminists, social scientists, or journalists) in these richer countries who have the ear of authorities and are complicit with the state defining the needs of others in terms that stress the dangers to themselves. Although U.S. feminists' responses to sexual assault, German media accounts of Muslim threats to gender equality, and U.S. social science arguments about using paid employment as a way out of domestic violence for poor women are certainly discourses that are quite different in many regards, they share a common theme of misrecognition of the human security needs in the populations they purport to describe.

Another theme that runs through many chapters but is especially evident in chapters by Ní Aoláin, Henríquez and Ewig, and Heideman is the emphasis on bottom-up participation by marginalized women and men in the active processes of articulating issues, making political claims, and resolving conflicts. Although the duration and focus of ethnicized political violence in Peru, Thailand, and Croatia are very different, the way that peace building works in each country highlights the need for a grassroots mobilization of the people affected in creating the new structures of accountability that emerge after the conflict. When the discourse of political conflict identifies the parties involved as if they were homogeneous and clearly bounded entities, the lines of violence that run into and across families and local communities are harder to address. Transnational one-size-fits-all formulas need to be remade to change local conditions of postconflict insecurity, including endemic relations of gender and ethnic subordination. Insecure people need to identify sources of insecurity in their own voices in order to help create fit between the problem definition and solutions that they can recognize as helpful.

Recognition of women's gender-specific insecurities (collective as well as individual) provide a mandate for insuring that women are included in the arduous work of building more just and lasting peace, whether in Croatia or Peru. The global spread of peace and reconciliation processes highlight the need for the postconflict process to be democratic, deliberative, participatory, but as Ní Aoláin points out, this proactive, long term, and explicitly political work must include critical analysis of local patriarchal relations, which will not happen unless the complementary patriarchal relations built into powerful transnational organizations are also equally subject to critique and change. Gender mainstreaming into peace-building work—not as a cover for backing off from concern with women but in order to approach women's insecurities without essentializing, instrumentalizing, or infantilizing women—demands active attention to empowerment at a global level, too, including whatever training, accountability, and budgeting the organization needs.

A third theme that has come to the fore through our intersectional feminist gendering of human security is how gender works as a macro process with micro implications. The social organization of gender plays a crucial role in the macrolevel human insecurities to which Stites, Brush, Peterson, and Kinney all draw attention. Yet while they emphasize the significance of gender they do so by showing how making a living is a deeply gendered process for individuals too. As Stites and Brush emphasize, the day-to-day experiences of violence emerge from and affect work relationships, both in Karamoja and in Pittsburgh, and both men and women need economic security in order to have a stable and emotionally supportive family life, even sometimes to have a family at all. As Kinney and Peterson stress, conflict economies draw women and men into different kinds of work, and channel profits in different ways up and out of the local situation to men (and a few women) with greater power. All four authors offer unmistakable evidence that gender security and economic survival are inseparable needs. While women's particular relationships to biological and social reproduction situate them differently than men to the work involved in caring for, participating in, and protecting their families, their day-to-day reproductive labors are intertwined with the macro structure of the economy in ways that produce different vulnerabilities. Women survive, cope creatively, and as Brush shows, dream of a different future as more than mere victims, but their gender specific insecurities in the global economy demand more than gender-neutral concern with economic growth and (re)distribution.

One common pitfall in trying to bring gender analysis into any political framework that was initially understood without gender is to define gender as meaning "bringing *women* in" to a still conventionally gendered framework, as Ní Aoláin argues in her chapter. Not only does this equation of gender with women ignore how gendered processes affect men (itself a major problem), but it also sweeps away the actual relationality, even among women, in gender relations. In addition to her chapter, those by Ewing, Stites, and Kinney make clear that gendering human security only goes halfway at best if it fails to notice how women are situated in a variety of institutional roles with human security interests that vary depending on these particular situations. Even as mothers and wives (for example), they may have different positions and perspectives: mothers who are not wives and wives who are not mothers face different sorts of economic insecurities and risks from societal violence. Kinney shows how those sex workers in Thailand who are immigrants or native-born face different insecurities and levels of awareness. But Ní Aoláin also argues that bringing all women in still would not go far enough, since it would fail also to recognize men's gendered human security needs, which both Ewing and Stites highlight.

Another important theme highlighted across chapters by our intersectional feminist approach is the joint significance of the material and cultural aspects of gender relations. These connections take quite different forms. Peterson's chapter stresses the material side, showing how the global restructuring called neoliberalism has had effects on both women and men. But she also notes the cultural significance of understanding these trends as "feminizing" or bringing more men into the lower valued, unstable, and economically precarious work relations associated with women and more often found to be acceptable for women workers. She notes how gender operates as a thread that connects the political and the economic dimensions of restructuring and produces different kinds of informalization for women and for men, while situating them differently in combat economies. Ewing's chapter conversely stresses the cultural aspects of insecurity by looking at the media construction of a Muslim menace in Germany, but ties this to the very material circumstances of migration and marginalization that Turkish families face in Berlin. She also stresses the agency involved, showing how some Turkish-German women's rights activists and some macho Turkish-German young men play starring roles in constructing the story. Not just this one Berlin story, but many atrocity stories around the globe share the process by which very material violence against women—rapes in the former Yugoslavia or post–World War II Berlin, ripping fetuses out of pregnant women in El Salvador, female genital cutting in Somalia, honor killing in Nigeria—is converted into tropes about the monstrosity of men of the "other" group (e.g., Bos 2006; Viterna 2012).

These types of moral panics are intersectional, placing women and men of different religions or ethnic groups into very different relationships with gendered violence. Bumiller's chapter shows the implications of such gendered moral panics in the development of U.S. policies on battering and rape, connecting a materialist argument about neoliberal restructuring that is also Peterson's concern with a cultural account of how media and activist mobilization against violence against women turns into stereotyped attacks on minority communities similar to that in Ewing's chapter. By telling a complex story of how U.S. feminist mobilizations against battering and rape allied with the state to protect women and were coopted into becoming advocates or at least apologists for punitive policy, Bumiller uses the U.S. experience to warn feminists about the potential harm done to minority women and men by allowing experts and media to define "violence against women" as a social problem that intensified state control can solve.

The people-centered view of human security that Tripp praises as its distinctive improvement over classic state-centered security studies and security politics brings in a microdimension that might otherwise be overlooked. Analyses of agency and awareness of the work of grassroots groups are most visible in studies that examine individual women and men and their framing work, such as Ewing offers. But even in relation to the macrolevel material structures of the global political economy that Peterson identifies as critical, attention to the daily struggles of women and men to survive informs the analysis. The connections of gender relations and human security concerns across levels are especially evident in the chapter by Henríquez and Ewig. They highlight the "ordinary" insecurities that individual men and women face "at home" before, during, and after a conflict. Their richly intersectional account of the Shining Path in Peru and the Truth and Reconciliation Commission (TRC) established after its war with the Peruvian state offers insights into how material (gendered insecurities) and cultural (gendered discourses) aspects of this struggle relate. Working across levels, Henríquez and Ewig connect the provider-protector tropes of masculinity locally attributed to the prewar *patrón* and to Shining Path guerrillas, the special targeting of indigenous women for abuse, the types of sexual assault practiced by both sides in the rural Andean communities where the war raged, the gendered challenges to economic survival that also accompanied torture and exile. Like Brush, they find hope in the end in the way that the voices of the most marginalized—in this case, the largely illiterate poor women of the rural Andes—can sometimes be heard, even if the odds of the state actually providing adequate reparations to the victims and justice to the perpetrators still seem low.

In sum, the intersectional feminist approach taken across the chapters we selected offers both critical and constructive insights into gendering human security as a discursive process in particular situations. It brings in countries of the global North, transnational organizations, and men in ways that show not only their complicity in creating insecurities but also the ways that they are vulnerable to them. It highlights the political value of empowering actors at the grassroots to name the insecurities that shape their lives and imagine alternatives to them, but also the risks of such communities focusing on the surveillance, control, or exclusion of those they define as "others." It emphasizes the variability in the material significance and cultural salience gender has across situations, but also connects the material and cultural aspects of gender relations with each other, across levels, and among apparently dissimilar countries and particular issues.

Conclusion

What then can a feminist intersectional gendering of human security offer as specific pragmatic suggestions for using this perspective more effectively and appropriately in the future? Three particular policy directions stand out. First, the many applications of rights discourse to gender relations have been very successful in reframing women's rights as human rights, but that success has limited use as an analogy for gendering human security. Human rights discourse is, as has been noted earlier, individualizing, legalistic, and retroactive. In all these respects, it can be applied to "women" as legally identifiable units with specific claims about something that has already happened. Human security discourses seem more appealing to some precisely because they are not the same in these regards. But this also means that human security as a discourse has to be proactively concerned with the complexity of relationships in which human beings are embedded, which are permeated by inequalities of gender, race/ethnicity, class, generation, and nation. Across all the chapters, the specific workings of (trans)national law (and legal change), civil society (and the organizations that instantiate it), the global/local economy (in both formal and informal sectors), and kinship institutions (with and without state recognition) are recognized as sites for the working out of a gendered politics of human security.

Arguing that gender relations are thus always and everywhere intersectional and that all other social relations are gendered, an intersectional feminist gendering of human security discourse in policy work demands attention to the way relationships of power operate in specific cases. "Women" can be framed as subjects and agents of human rights struggles, but human security is about power relationships as such, and demands attention to power in both cultural and material forms. To try to create "women's human security" is a problematic effort regardless of what groups try to advance such a goal, including feminist organizations and activists, since as we have seen such feminist politics can lead too often to racist, nationalist, and imperialist collaborations. Feminists who would like to see a gendered human security discourse replace a nongendered one should be particularly attentive to such risks in their advocacy, and work affirmatively to construct more intersectional, nonbinary security goals.

Second, the intersectional feminist perspective advanced on human security offers a case for seeing the need for making security policy more open, transparent, and inclusive of multiple voices. Creating space for individual testimonies and even, as in Brush's chapter, the ability to articulate a vision of the future, should not be so rare or apparently difficult in the various venues where human insecurities are addressed, be they truth and reconciliation commissions or welfare offices. The specific policy consequences of this inclusivity are various, but especially important to making the process more able to capture the needs of the socially marginalized. Abused women who have the extraordinary courage to raise their voices to testify to what has been done to them are agents of social change who should not be ignored, and their visions of what a society that could offer real human security to both men and women should not be ignored either. As Henríquez and Ewig's chapter argues, the desire to pursue justice in horrific cases, such as systematic rape or genocide, should also not silence voices telling less hair-raising stories about displacement, destruction of livelihood, sexual and domestic servitude in guerilla camps, and militarization of social relations. They praise the Peruvian truth and reconciliation process for at least trying to achieve this goal.

As Rubio-Marín and Estrada-Tanck show in their discussion of supranational court decisions by the European Court of Human Rights and the Inter-American Court of Human Rights, even highly placed authorities can adopt human security concerns that include the "ordinary" violence of daily life. Even when such a "perspective from above" is more intersectional, the failure to bring in participation from below can lead to perverse results. Heideman's chapter makes clear the unintended consequences of the well-meaning way that reparations were done, since the Croats not participating in the decisions and allocation process constructed a notion of the Serbian minority being the special favorites of the international community and became more rather than less antagonistic to them. The chapters point to the fact that policy processes working toward human security are improved by local involvement and openness to imagining a future that is truly different, but warn of the desires by some participants at every level to turn the process to their own advantage. Adding transparency and accountability across levels to the process is a policy direction that these chapters suggest will increase access to the voices and visions of women, among others.

Finally, the chapters also suggest a cautious attitude to the feminist alliances with the state and its various agendas. Instrumental use of security discourses, even a feminist gendered human security discourse, can be turned in problematically militarized directions by more powerful global actors, as Kinney shows in her account of the strategic use of "security" as discourse in confronting problems of trafficking in Thailand. For some activists, adopting security language was viewed as opening opportunities to mobilize the state, gain resources, and direct global attention to the sexual victimization of women and young girls, while others pointed to the perverse effects of "protecting women" rather than protecting women's rights. Bumiller critiques U.S. feminists for uncritically taking state support to combat violence against women, and as Brush further notes, even feminists who are trying to help women escape violent partners may accept a framing of employment as escape that serves to undercut the critique of state cuts in welfare for women in need of support. Peterson shows how criminal and coping economies intersect, so that economically vulnerable women are pressured into illegal activities by armies or gangs or even intimate partners, and are prosecuted by the state for succumbing to these threats rather than being offered safer alternatives. As the welfare states of the global North decrease social and economic support for poor people in their own populations, they channel more of their investments into surveillance technologies and militarized control, whether of their own citizens or those in other countries. Responsibility to protect seems often to slide into prying into what should be the private decisions of mothers, pregnant women, and poor people in general as well as protecting the state from protestors. A gendered human security discourse that is intersectional and feminist will be suspicious of policy directions that privilege control over caring.

Rubio-Marín and Estrada-Tanck argue for combining the best features of both human rights and human security approaches rather than choosing between them. This strategy may mitigate the risks to individual rights that overreliance on collective versions of human security poses, whether coming from the state or from transnational NGOs with their own agendas. The specific cases collected in this volume support this conclusion. Gendering human security should not be attempted as a sequel to and replacement of the feminist discursive struggle that redefined women's rights as human rights, nor as an excuse to ignore calls to develop all people's human capabilities more fully and fairly as a matter of justice. But as an intersectional addition to the repertoire of concerns that human rights discourse has raised, a feminist human security discourse can widen policy attention to more issues, bring in more marginalized voices, and add accountability to the way states and other actors deploy claims to protect and aid women. While the path to achieving such goals remains rocky, the chapters of this volume do much to illuminate the way forward.

REFERENCES

Alfredson, Lisa. 2009. *Creating Human Rights: How Noncitizens Made Sex Persecution Matter to the World.* Philadelphia: University of Pennsylvania Press.

Alkire, Sabina. 2003. "A Conceptual Framework for Human Security." In CRISE Working Paper. Queen Elizabeth House, University of Oxford: Centre for Research on Inequality, Human Security and Ethnicity.

Bos, Pasquale R. 2006. "Feminists Interpreting the Politics of Wartime Rape: Berlin, 1945; Yugoslavia, 1992–1993." *Signs: Journal of Women in Culture and Society* 31 (4):995–1025.

Buss, Doris, and Didi Herman. 2003. *Globalizing Family Values: The Christian Right in International Politics.* Minneapolis: University of Minnesota Press.

Choo, Hae Yeon, and Myra Marx Ferree. 2010. "Practicing Intersectionality in Sociological Research: A Critical Analysis of Inclusions, Interactions and Institutions in the Study of Inequalities." *Sociological Theory* 28 (2):29–49.

Christensen, Wendy, and Myra Marx Ferree. 2008. "Cowboy of the World? Gendered Discourse in the Iraq War Debate." *Qualitative Sociology* 31 (3):287–306.

Collins, Patricia Hill. 1986. *Black Feminist Thought.* New York: Routledge.

Connell, Raewyn. 2009. *Gender: A Short Introduction.* 2nd edition. Malden, Mass.: Polity Press.

Crenshaw, Kimberlé. 1991. "Mapping the Margins: Intersectionality, Identity Politics, and Violence against Women of Color." *Stanford Law Review* 43 (6):1241–1299.

Dudink, Stefan, Karen Hagemann, and John Tosh, eds. 2004. *Masculinities in Politics and War: Gendering Modern History.* Manchester, U.K.: Manchester University Press.

Enloe, Cynthia. 1993. *The Morning After: Sexual Politics at the End of the Cold War.* Berkeley: University of California Press.

Ewig, Christine, and Myra Marx Ferree. 2013. "Feminist Organizing: What's Old, What's New? History, Trends and Issues." Chapter 17 in *Oxford Handbook of Gender and Politics*, edited by Georgina Waylen, Karen Celis, Johanna Kantola, and S. Laurel Weldon. New York: Oxford University Press.

Ferree, Myra Marx. 2009. "Inequality, Intersectionality and the Politics of Discourse: Framing Feminist Alliances." Chapter 6 in *The Discursive Politics of Gender Equality: Stretching, Bending and Policy-Making*, edited by Emanuela Lombardo, Petra Meier, and Mieke Verloo. New York: Routledge.

———. 2012. *Varieties of Feminism: German Gender Politics in Global Perspective.* Palo Alto, Calif.: Stanford University Press.

Gal, Susan, and Gail Kligman. 2000. *The Politics of Gender after Socialism.* Princeton: Princeton University Press.

Glenn, Evelyn Nakano. 1999. "The Social Construction and Institutionalization of Gender and Race: An Integrative Framework." In *Revisioning Gender*, edited by Myra Marx Ferree, Judith Lorber, and Beth B. Hess, 3–43. New York: Sage.

Hancock, Ange-Marie. 2007. "When Multiplication Doesn't Equal Quick Addition: Examining Intersectionality as a Research Paradigm." *Perspectives on Politics* 5(1):63–79.

Hoganson, Kristen L. 2000. *Fighting for American Manhood: How Gender Politics Provoked the Spanish-American and Philippine-American Wars*. New Haven, Conn.: Yale University Press.

Keck, Margaret E., and Kathryn Sikkink. 1998. *Activists beyond Borders: Advocacy Networks in International Politics*. Ithaca: Cornell University Press.

Korteweg, Anna, and Gökçe Yurdakul. 2009. "Gender, Islam and Immigrant Integration: Boundary Drawing on Honour Killing in the Netherlands and Germany." *Ethnic and Racial Studies* 32(2):218–238.

Lakkimsetti, Chaitanya. 2013. "'HIV Is Our Friend': Prostitution, Power and State in Postcolonial India." *Signs: Journal of Women in Culture and Society* (forthcoming).

Liu, Dongxiao. 2006. "When Do National Movements Adopt or Reject International Agendas? A Comparative Analysis of the Chinese and Indian Women's Movements." *American Sociological Review* 71(6):921–942.

Lombardo, Emanuela, Petra Meier, and Mieke Verloo, eds. 2009. *The Discursive Politics of Gender Equality: Stretching, Bending and Policy-Making*. New York: Routledge.

Lutz, Helma, Maria Theresa Vivar, and Linda Supik, eds. 2011. *Framing Intersectionality. Debates on a Multi-Faceted Concept in Gender Studies*. Abingdon: Ashgate.

McCall, Leslie. 2005. "The Complexity of Intersectionality." *Signs: Journal of Women in Culture and Society* 30(3):1771–1800.

Ridgeway, Cecilia, and Shelley J. Correll. 2006. "Unpacking the Gender System—A Theoretical Perspective on Gender Beliefs and Social Relations." *Gender & Society* 18 (4):510–531.

Scott, Joan Wallach. 1999. *Gender and the Politics of History*. 2nd edition. New York: Columbia University Press.

Stiehm, Judith. 1981. *Bring Me Men and Women: Mandated Change at the US Air Force Academy*. Berkeley: University of California Press.

Stone, Deborah. 2001. *Policy Paradox: The Art of Political Decision-Making*. 3rd edition. New York: Norton.

Thayer, Millie. 2010. *Making Transnational Feminism: Rural Women, NGO Activists, and Northern Donors in Brazil*. New York: Routledge.

Tripp, Aili Mari. 2009. *African Women's Movements: Transforming Political Landscapes*. Cambridge; New York: Cambridge University Press.

Viterna, Jocelyn. 2012. "Radical or Righteous? Using Gender to Shape Public Perceptions of Political Violence." Presentation at Sawyer Seminar, Department of Gender and Women's Studies, University of Wisconsin. March 30.

Yuval Davis, Nira. 1997. *Gender and Nation*. Thousand Oaks, Calif.: Sage.

Lisa D. Brush is Associate Professor of Sociology at the University of Pittsburgh, where she teaches graduate and undergraduate students about theory, gender and work, class, and the social aspects of sexuality. Her articles on work, welfare, and violence against women have appeared in numerous disciplinary and interdisciplinary journals. Her books are *Gender and Governance* (AltaMira Press/Rowman & Littlefield, 2003) and *Poverty, Battered Women, and Work in U.S. Public Policy* (Oxford University Press, 2011). Lisa is an award-winning editor and photographer and an advanced beginner on the French horn, which she plays in the East Liberty Community Engagement Orchestra.

Kristin Bumiller is Professor of Political Science at Amherst College and the author of the award-winning book, *In an Abusive State* (Victoria Schuck Book Prize, American Political Science Association, 2009). Her works on employment discrimination, the Civil Rights Society, and "Victims in the Shadow of the Law" have been widely recognized. Her articles, which span a broad range of interests in antidiscrimination policy, feminist theory, gender and punishment, and disability rights, have been published in major journals in her field. She has had a long-term affiliation with the Feminism and Legal Theory Project at Emory University, served on the Board of Trustees for the Law & Society Association, and is currently on the National Steering Committee for the Inside-Out Program.

Dorothy Estrada-Tanck received her Ph.D. in Law from the European University Institute, Florence. Her thesis was on human rights and human security in International Law. She holds an M.Sc. in Political Theory from LSE and a law degree from Escuela Libre de Derecho (Mexico). She has worked in the Mexican Ministry of Foreign Affairs, the UN Office of the High Commissioner for Human Rights, and the

Mexico City Human Rights Commission. She has taught in different universities and published on international human rights law, including a book on the International Legal Regime for Transnational Corporations in the Sphere of Human Rights.

Christina Ewig is Associate Professor in the Departments of Gender & Women's Studies and Political Science at the University of Wisconsin–Madison. Her research centers on gender, race, and the politics of inequality in Latin America. Her book, *Second-Wave Neoliberalism: Gender, Race and Neoliberal Health Sector Reform in Peru* (Penn State Press, 2010), was the 2012 winner of the Flora Tristán book award for best book on Peru from the Peru Section of the Latin American Studies Association. Her articles have appeared in numerous disciplinary and interdisciplinary journals. She edits the book series *Crossing Boundaries of Gender and Politics in the Global South* for Palgrave Macmillan.

Katherine Pratt Ewing is Professor of Religion at Columbia University and Professor Emerita of Cultural Anthropology at Duke University. She received her Ph.D. in Anthropology from the University of Chicago and postdoctoral training at the Chicago Institute for Psychoanalysis. She has done ethnographic fieldwork in Pakistan, Turkey, India, and Germany and has had residential fellowships at the American Academy in Berlin and the Russell Sage Foundation. Publications include *Arguing Sainthood: Modernity, Psychoanalysis and Islam* (1997), *Stolen Honor: Stigmatizing Muslim Men in Berlin* (2008), and *Being and Belonging: Muslim Communities in the US since 9/11* (2008, editor).

Myra Marx Ferree is the Alice H. Cook Professor of Sociology and Director of the European Union Center of Excellence at the University of Wisconsin–Madison. Her research focuses on gender, social movements, and political discourse. Much of her work has been done on gender politics in Germany and Europe, including her most recent book, *Varieties of Feminism: German Gender Politics in Global Perspective* (2012). As part of an ongoing collaboration, she and Aili Mari Tripp coedited *Global Feminism: Women's Transnational Activism, Organizations and Human Rights* (2006), and they, with Christina Ewig, organized a year-long symposium in 2011-12 on gender, globalization, and human rights, with the generous support of the Mellon Foundation's Sawyer Seminar Program.

Laura J. Heideman is an assistant professor in Sociology and the Center for NGO Leadership and Development at Northern Illinois University. Her research examines the ways in which transnational flows of money, expertise, and legitimacy affected local peace-building projects in Croatia. This research was funded by a Fulbright fellowship, a National Science Foundation Graduate Research Fellowship, and the European Union Center of Excellence at the University of Wisconsin-Madison. Heideman has long-term interests in postconflict studies, development studies, and political sociology. She has done previous research on the long-term reintegration of guerrilla ex-combatants in South Africa.

Narda Henríquez is a Peruvian sociologist with a long trajectory in the areas of social change, poverty studies, and gender studies. Dr. Henríquez is a professor at the Catholic University of Peru (PUCP), Peru's leading university and one of the 500 best universities in the world according to European ranking systems (*Higher Education Chronicle of The Times*, 2003). Dr. Henríquez was one of the founders of the first women's studies programs at PUCP and has produced several books on issues of social and political change. She was a major gender consultant to Peru's Commission on Truth and Reconciliation. Dr. Henríquez is a former president of the Peruvian Association of Sociologists and is currently Director of Postgraduate Studies in Sociology (Masters and Ph.D.) at PUCP.

Edith Kinney received a J.D. from Berkeley Law, and completed her Ph.D. in Jurisprudence & Social Policy at the University of California, Berkeley. She is currently a Visiting Assistant Professor in the Social Sciences Division at Mills College in Oakland, California. Her research interests are in the intersections between law and society, particularly the role feminist activists and social movement organizations play in criminal justice reform. Her work has appeared in the *Berkeley Journal of Gender, Law & Justice*, and her current research project explores the sexual politics of security in local and transnational arenas.

Fionnuala Ní Aoláin is concurrently the Dorsey and Whitney Chair in Law at the University of Minnesota Law School and Professor of Law at the University of Ulster's Transitional Justice Institute in Belfast, Northern Ireland. She has published extensively in the fields of emergency powers, conflict regulation, transitional justice, and sex based violence in times of war. Her book *Law in Times of Crisis* (Cambridge University Press, 2006) was awarded the American Society of International Law's preeminent prize in 2007—the Certificate of Merit for creative scholarship. Her book *On the Frontlines: Gender, War and the Post Conflict Process* has recently been published by Oxford University Press (2011).

V. Spike Peterson is Professor of International Relations in the School of Government and Public Policy at the University of Arizona, with courtesy appointments in the Department of Gender and Women's Studies and Institute for LGBT Studies. She is the author of *A Critical Rewriting of Global Political Economy: Integrating Reproductive, Productive, and Virtual Economies* (Routledge, 2003) and coauthor of *Global Gender Issues in the New Millennium* (with Anne S. Runyan, Westview Press 2010). Her research interests include feminist/queer approaches to informalization, global householding, nation-state politics, and attendant insecurities.

Ruth Rubio-Marín holds a Chair in Comparative Public Law at the European University Institute in Florence, Italy. Formerly she was Professor of Constitutional Law at the University of Seville, Spain, and a member of the Faculty of the Hauser Global Law School Program at New York University. Her interests include comparative constitutional law, transitional justice, human rights, migration, minority rights, and feminist theory. She is the author and editor of several books, including *Immigration as a Democratic Challenge* (2000); *What Happened to the Women? Gender and Reparations for Human Rights Violations* (editor, 2006), and *The Gender of Reparations: Subverting Sexual Hierarchies while Redressing Human Rights Violations* (editor, 2009). She has extensive in-country experience with reparations in postconflict societies including in Morocco, Nepal, and Colombia. She assisted UN Special Rapporteur, Rashida Manjoo, on Violence against Women on Reparations for Women Subjected to Violence.

Elizabeth Stites, Ph.D., is a Senior Researcher in Conflict and Liveli-hoods at the Feinstein International Center, Tufts University. Her work focuses on the effects of conflict on civilian livelihoods, and ways in which communities, households, and individuals adapt or change their livelihood strategies in conflict environments and the repercussions of these changes. She is particularly interested in the shifts that occur within households or communities in conflict, and how these changes are made and experienced by people of different genders and genera-tions. At the policy level, Dr. Stites is interested in the effects of inter-national and national humanitarian and development policies on com-munity-based livelihood and coping strategies.

Aili Mari Tripp is Professor of Political Science and Gender & Wom-en's Studies at the University of Wisconsin–Madison and Director of the university's Center for Research on Gender and Women. Tripp has published numerous books and articles on global feminism, gen-der, and politics in Africa and globally, and on women in postconflict African countries. She is completing a book entitled *Gender, Power and Peacemaking in Africa*. She has published *Museveni's Uganda: Para-doxes of Power* (2010), coauthored, with Isabel Casimiro, Joy Kwesiga, and Alice Mungwa, *African Women's Movements: Transforming Politi-cal Landscapes* (2009), and is author of *Women and Politics in Uganda* (2000), and *Changing the Rules: The Politics of Liberalization and the Urban Informal Economy in Tanzania* (1997).